THE WAR ON DISA

About the author

ELLEN CLIFFORD is a disabled activist who has worked within the disability sector for over 20 years. She currently serves on the National Steering Group for Disabled People Against Cuts (DPAC).

THE WAR ON DISABLED PEOPLE

Capitalism, Welfare and the Making of a Human Catastrophe

ELLEN CLIFFORD

BLOOMSBURY ACADEMIC
LONDON • NEW YORK • OXFORD • NEW DELHI • SYDNEY

Bloomsbury Academic
Bloomsbury Publishing Plc
50 Bedford Square, London, WC1B 3DP, UK
1385 Broadway, New York, NY 10018, USA
29 Earlsfort Terrace, Dublin 2, Ireland

BLOOMSBURY, BLOOMSBURY ACADEMIC and the Diana logo are
trademarks of Bloomsbury Publishing Plc

First published in Great Britain in 2020 by Zed Books
Reprinted 2021
Reprinted by Bloomsbury Academic in 2022

Cover design by Alice Marwick
Cover photo © Vandervelden/Getty Images

A catalogue record for this book is available from the British Library.

A catalog record for this book is available from the Library of Congress.

ISBN: HB: 978-1-7869-9890-3
PB: 978-1-3503-4816-5
ePDF: 978-1-7869-9665-7
eBook: 978-1-7869-9666-4

Typeset in Bulmer by Swales and Willis Ltd, Exeter, Devon
Printed and bound in Great Britain

To find out more about our authors and books visit www.bloomsbury.com
and sign up for our newsletters.

For Debbie and Linda

Contents

Acknowledgements

This book would not have existed had Ken Barlow, then at Zed Books, not first approached me in 2018 to kick-start the project. The biggest thanks must go to him. Thanks also to editor Kim Walker from Zed, who has been remarkably patient and reassuring, and to editors Sue Lascelles and Judith Forshaw for their assiduous efforts.

A special acknowledgement is needed for my co-thinker, Mark Dunk, for all the debates, discussions and political analysis that helped with the formation of a number of arguments in this book, and to him and Karen Grayson as well as Camilla Royle, Andy Greene, Bob Ellard and Linda Burnip for looking over my drafts. The impact of my impairment has meant that, on my best days, getting each word out required an effort that felt like pushing through a fog of self-doubt – the worst days felt more like having to punch them through a wall. This could not have been done without your belief and encouragement. The book has also benefited from valuable discussions with Eileen Short, Nicola Field, Rebecca Yeo, Roger Lewis and Rosa Morris, and input from Roddy Slorach. All errors are my responsibility.

A huge debt of thanks to my family, including all six parents, for the support necessary for doing this. I am extremely lucky to have had the opportunity. Also: Polly, Benny, Mark B., Justin, Una, Myla, Avril, Ethan, Anne, Nick, Jacob, Sam, Harry, Jane and, of course, Smudge.

Thanks for all the help, insights, inspiration and comradeship from within the Disabled People Against Cuts (DPAC) activist network. There are too many inspirational fighters to name – and in the current climate of surveillance it is dangerous to do so – but personal thanks in particular to Andy M., Annie, Arjun, Catherine, Cathy, Denise, Ellen M., Jen, John K., Keith, Linda, Mark H., Mary-Ellen, Miriam, Nathan, Nicky, Paula, Peter, Rob, Sarah and Sean. Thanks also to comrades in South East London and South London SWP districts, and friends from Ruskin House in Croydon. Together we are stronger!

John Pring of *Disability News Service* requires a special mention for his tireless and invaluable work since 2010. Thanks to Frances Ryan for the great peer support as someone with personal experience of the barriers to writing as a disabled working-class woman; also to Liz Carr for first introducing me to the social model of disability in a training room in Coventry many moons ago!

Thanks for the amazing help with accessing articles and support from Daniel Edmiston and Michael Orton.

The book was written from my home on the Downham Estate in south-east London. Throughout the process I benefited from the public library, swimming pool and community parks. We must keep up the fight for our public services.

This book is dedicated to Debbie Jolly and Linda Burnip as co-founders of DPAC but also to all the disabled activists and friends who have been taken from us too soon since 2010 – including Debbie herself, but also Katherine Araniello, Stephen Aselford, Nick Danagher, Robert Dellar, Debbie Domb, Eleanor Firman, Patrick Lynch, Juliet Marlow, Sophie Partridge and Christian Wilcox. Each of them has left an unfillable hole but their memories encourage us to go on.

Acronyms and abbreviations

ATU	Assessment and Treatment Unit
AtW	Access to Work
BPS	biopsychosocial
BSL	British Sign Language
CBT	cognitive behaviour therapy
CCG	Clinical Commissioning Group
CFS	chronic fatigue syndrome
CHC	Continuing Healthcare
CIA	cumulative impact assessment
CIL	Centre for Independent Living
CTB	Council Tax Benefit
CTR	Council Tax Reduction
DANDLA	Disability Living Allowance
DNS	*Disability News Service*
DPAC	Disabled People Against Cuts
DPM	Disabled People's Movement
DRUK	Disability Rights UK
DSA	Disabled Students Allowance
DWP	Department for Work and Pensions
EDP	Enhanced Disability Premium
EHCP	Education, Health and Care Plan
EHRC	Equality and Human Rights Commission
ESA	Employment and Support Allowance

EU	European Union
GLAD	Greater London Action on Disability
HB	Housing Benefit
HMRC	Her Majesty's Revenue and Customs
HWC	Health and Work Conversation
IAPT	Increasing Access to Psychological Therapies
IB	Incapacity Benefit
ICT	information and communications technology
ILF	Independent Living Fund
ILSG	Independent Living Strategy Group
JSA	Jobseeker's Allowance
LASPO	Legal Aid, Sentencing and Punishment of Offenders Act 2012
LCW	Limited Capability for Work
LCWRA	Limited Capability for Work-Related Activity
LHA	Local Housing Allowance
LiMA	Logic Integrated Medical Assessment
LNPD	Liberation Network of People with Disabilities
ME	myalgic encephalomyelitis
MHRN	Mental Health Resistance Network
MR	Mandatory Reconsideration
MWC	Mental Welfare Commission for Scotland
NAO	National Audit Office
NSUN	National Survivor User Network
NUWM	National Unemployed Workers' Movement
OBR	Office for Budget Responsibility
OECD	Organisation for Economic Co-operation and Development
ONS	Office for National Statistics
PIP	Personal Independence Payment
RITB	Recovery in the Bin
RNIB	Royal National Institute of Blind People

ROFA	Reclaiming Our Futures Alliance
SDP	Severe Disability Premium
SEN	Special Educational Needs
SEND	Special Educational Needs and Disability
SG	Support Group
SNP	Scottish National Party
TANF	Temporary Assistance for Needy Families
UC	Universal Credit
UN	United Nations
UN CRPD	United Nations Convention on the Rights of Persons with Disabilities
UPIAS	Union of the Physically Impaired Against Segregation
WCA	Work Capability Assessment
WHO	World Health Organization
WILG	Welsh Independent Living Grant
WPC	Work and Pensions Committee
WRAG	Work-Related Activity Group

Introduction

> Men make their own history, but they do not make it as they
> please; they do not make it under self-selected circumstances,
> but under circumstances existing already, given and transmitted
> from the past.
>
> Karl Marx[1]

In the years before his death, the widely esteemed disabled academic Mike Oliver warned disabled campaigners that we need to record our own history, 'or it will be rewritten to serve the purposes of others'.[2] This book is an attempt to do exactly that. It records a pivotal moment in disability history from an activist perspective. This is the period from 2010 onwards when the British government went to war on disabled people.

Prior to 2010, the UK government was known as a world leader in disability. A decision was made under the Coalition government and carried forward by successive Conservative administrations elected in 2015, 2017 and 2019 that progress had gone too far. The implementation of a fast reverse turn was of international significance, marking the first time in the history of modern social policy that things had gone backwards for disabled people.[3] The fact that this was to make disabled people pay for a financial crisis we did not cause is abhorrent. It needed to be concealed from the public. The way in which right-wing politicians and media achieved this – by creating a narrative that blamed disabled people themselves, purposefully stoking fires of division and hatred – makes it even worse.

What the government did is one half of the story. On the other is the resistance mounted by disabled people. With the Disabled People's Movement (DPM) in decline from the mid-1990s, resistance from 2010 onwards can be characterised as a return to grassroots activism. In a conscious departure from the identity politics era of disability campaigning, new groups such as Disabled People Against Cuts (DPAC) were set up with the explicit aim of building alliances and joining the wider anti-capitalist movement.

Disabled activists are now regarded as having been at the forefront of the anti-austerity movement. We succeeded in pushing disability issues onto the mainstream agenda. These are no small achievements. At the same time, despite discrete wins along the way, material conditions are growing ever worse and more desperate for disabled people. After more than 10 years of tireless campaigning, there is so much more to do. This book presents an opportunity for reflection – not for its own sake, but with a view to learning lessons, reconsolidating and getting back out there to fight for 'a society fit for all'.[4]

Although this book is written by a disabled activist, one of its central arguments is that the events under inquiry should not just be of interest to disabled people. Disability issues are hidden and misunderstood within mainstream society precisely because of the relationship between disability and capitalism. Interrogating that relationship is a powerful way to expose the inequalities and cruelty of the system of exploitation under which we live. That system needs to be shrouded in myths and misconceptions in order to protect its continuation. What has happened since 2010 is a sharp reflection of the fundamentally important role that disability plays within capitalist political economy. It therefore has a relevance to anyone seriously interested in what is wrong with capitalism and how we fight it.

While it will take more than this book alone to penetrate the near invisibility of disability as a political rather than a personal issue, I hope that it takes some small steps in bringing 'disability from the margins to the centre of historical inquiry'.[5]

The book is also written from a historical materialist perspective – one that sees history as the result of material conditions rather than ideas – and argues that this is the only way to make sense of disability policy since 2010. As disabled researcher Rosa Morris comments in her dissertation on the Work Capability Assessment, one of the most notoriously cruel measures rolled out under Conservative rule: '[I]t is impossible to fully understand the current position of disabled people who are unable to engage in waged labour without considering their role and position in the capitalist mode of production.'[6] In this way, the book joins up with the ideas of the pioneers of the British DPM, who also came from this position.

The book follows the social model of disability, a tool developed by disabled people as a guide for social action. It draws a distinction between impairment and disability. Disability consists of the barriers that a person with impairment experiences as a result of the way in which society is organised that excludes or devalues them. According to this analysis, preferred terminology in Britain is to describe people as disabled – because they are disabled by society – not people *with disabilities*, which makes no sense from a social model perspective.

One of the ways in which the British government was able to get away with making war on disabled people was by the sheer volume and complexity of the measures they unleashed. Where disabled people and their allies succeeded in holding them back was through intense and varied activity operating on many fronts and involving many people, each making an invaluable contribution in their own way. Resistance has used every tool at its disposal – from research to lobbying to protests to endless legal challenges to awareness raising to direct action to triggering an unprecedented United Nations inquiry. It is impossible to record it all in one place.

With regard to naming all those involved in the resistance, it is an indictment of the current climate of fear and surveillance that individual names have had to be omitted deliberately in places in this book – the risk is too great that disabled people's benefits will be stopped on the basis that if they are well enough to protest, they are not entitled to state-funded support.

The content of this book reflects areas of policy and campaigning that have been most central to activity by DPAC and its allies. Inevitably, there are important disability-related issues that have been missed. This is not meant in any way as a devaluation of the importance of those issues or of the contributions that have been made in resisting them; rather, it is a reflection of space and time constraints.

In terms of approach, the final thing to say is in defence of history written by a protagonist – even an extremely minor one – with no claim to objectivity. I, along with many disabled people in Britain since 2010, have been politicised by my experiences. Working within the disability sector, my colleagues and I have witnessed the individual suffering caused by the removal of the social safety net from those who need it most. Considerable numbers of people have been left without the support they need to cope in life and with nowhere to turn for help. As a person who lives with mental distress, I have experienced growing barriers to employment linked to the intensification of labour. At the same time, accessing unemployment social security has become out of the question and the services that help me to function have been cut.

Personal involvement in the struggle that this book details provides added insights and information from inside disabled people's resistance. As a former student of ancient history, I cannot help but add that ideas pertaining to the desirability of objectivity in historical accounts are fairly modern. Graeco-Roman historiography blurred boundaries between what we would now think of as a number of different disciplines, including biography, geography, ethnography and history. It was also explicitly didactic in nature, aiming to have a real-world use. That is absolutely my intention here.

Part I begins by setting out the context for the war on disabled people, the origins of which have a long history bound up with the rise of capitalism. The Conservatives were able to get away with such brutal attacks on disabled people because we live with the realities of our existence unseen by wider society. This is the result of socio-economic structures that segregate and divide, and, flowing from these, prevailing attitudes towards disability of pity, paternalism, aversion and disinterest.

As examined in this section, significant progress had been achieved for disabled people since the days of asylums, eugenics and long-stay hospitals. These were hard won through resistance from disabled people and our allies. Nevertheless, alongside these advances, significant inequalities persisted or even worsened. The idea of disabled people's exclusion from society as both natural and inevitable is so ingrained as to be still widely held to be common sense. Without an understanding of the history and politics of disability, it is impossible to make sense of events since 2010.

Part II provides an overview of legislation, policy and practice in key areas affecting disabled people's lives since 2010. It is through these voluminous and complex measures that any advances in disabled people's living standards have been so dramatically reversed. At the same time, decisions were made to benefit the rich and to help households with the highest incomes.

Comparisons between public spending in England and in the devolved nations (Scotland, Wales and Northern Ireland) show that cuts in England were not an inevitable result of the financial crash. Austerity and welfare reform were not necessities but deliberate political choices.

The section is divided into chapters covering measures related to welfare reform and those that pertain to independent living. The definition for independent living used within this book is in keeping with independent living philosophy and refers to disabled people's ability to live in the community with equal chances to participate, make choices and exercise control over our everyday lives.[7]

Part III assesses the brutal impacts and fallout of the measures examined in the previous section, described by the chair of the United Nations Disability Committee as 'a human catastrophe for disabled people'.[8] At an individual level, there has been a dramatic escalation in misery and distress, with rising poverty, homelessness and hunger. Benefit changes have been consistently linked to deaths and suicides but the government still denies a causal link – and refuses to investigate. On a societal level, austerity and welfare reform measures are essentially producing a re-segregation of disabled people. The hard-won gains of decades of resistance and progress are in the process of being wiped away.

The last chapter in this section considers the political fallout arising from the government's war on disabled people, arguing that it has played a significant but overlooked role in the political upheaval of the current climate. Attacks of such range and magnitude by a government on its own citizens could not have been carried out without consequence, but the marginalisation of disability issues and the abundance of misconceptions that still exist led to a vast underestimation of the political importance of the impacts of welfare reform and austerity.

Part IV argues that a historical materialist perspective is needed in order to understand the war on disabled people. It is only from the vantage points of the relationship between disability and capitalism and of how disability policy fits within the wider political-economic moment that the treatment of disabled people by the British government since 2010 can be made sense of and effective strategies for resistance developed.

This section assesses the ideological priorities of the neoliberal era. It presents the view that the core aim behind welfare reform is not to get rid of the welfare state altogether but to reshape it through cuts and privatisation and by entrenching punitive approaches; welfare reform is being used as a weapon against benefit claimants while serving to discipline the workforce in the interests of business. The section argues that, although we must take heart from the fact that successive Conservative governments have not been able to achieve as much of their agenda as they had hoped, they are unlikely to change direction and will keep coming for us. More and better coordinated resistance is required if worse is not to come.

Part V, the final section of the book, focuses on the proud tradition of disabled people's resistance. Prevailing myths and misconceptions that see disabled people as passive victims mean that protest by even just a few visibly disabled people can make an impact. Disability is also an issue with the potential to cause significant social unrest as it affects a much larger number of people than its profile suggests – and it can happen to anyone. Governments are nervous of disability issues. At the same time, disability is an effective way of exposing the cruelty of the system we live under and of building resistance against it. The section argues that disabled people have a key role to play in the fightback.

The penultimate chapter attempts to provide an overview of disabled people's resistance in Britain during the age of austerity.

It examines points of continuation and departure from the DPM and argues that disability now has an unprecedented public and political profile. This is an important, tangible outcome achieved by hard-fought resistance since 2010. The backdrop to this increased profile is a continuing regression of disabled people's material living standards, which is making it more difficult for disabled people to mobilise and organise. It ends with a warning that, if this continues, we will end up once again spoken *for* and *about*, with our own voices silenced within society.

Part V ends with concluding thoughts on the way forward. It argues that disabled people need to fight for material improvements in the here and now while developing our wider political analysis. This includes the understanding that the oppression of disabled people will be fully transcended only once capitalism is transcended.[9] In terms of organising, we need to build on what has been most effective about the return to grassroots activism that took place after 2010, with regard in particular to more inclusive campaigning, but we also need to build greater capacity for communication and the political development of our members. This must not be to replace activity with talking and navel-gazing, but to enhance our activism and ensure greater unity between practice and theory.

The final thoughts concern the need for a reinvigoration of the social model of disability. The social model has proven itself to be an incredibly powerful tool for effecting social change, but it was undermined by criticism and co-option by government. The social model can act as a guide for action rather than as a subject of endless debate. A collaborative grassroots effort to reinvigorate it could provide the cornerstone for an expanded collective identity focused on activity and social change.

PART I
'HIDDEN IN PLAIN SIGHT'

The social context for the war on disabled people

> Disability is everywhere in history once you begin looking for it,
> but conspicuously absent in the histories we write. When historians
> do take note of disability, they usually treat it merely as personal
> tragedy or an insult to be deplored and a label to be denied, rather
> than as a cultural construct to be questioned and explored.
>
> Douglas Baynton[1]

Prior to 2010, significant progress had been achieved for disabled people since the days of asylums, eugenics and long-stay hospitals, won through resistance from disabled people and our allies. Most notably, disabled people had obtained the right to live in the community instead of being forcibly detained for life, segregated from the rest of society. Legislation against disability discrimination was passed in the 1990s and the New Labour government promised full disability equality by 2025.

Alongside these advances, significant inequalities persisted or even worsened, while the idea that disabled people are of lesser human worth never fully went away. Research commissioned by Leonard Cheshire in 2008 revealed that disabled people were twice more likely to suffer economic hardship than others and more likely to live in poverty than 10 years previously.[2] The employment gap between disabled and non-disabled people was at 30 percentage points in 2010. Investigations started by the charity Mencap in 2007 exposed institutional discrimination within the NHS against people with learning difficulties, leading to 1,200 avoidable deaths in England every year.[3]

One of the cases publicised by Mencap was of Martin, a 43-year-old man with learning difficulties and no speech. Martin had a stroke and was sent to hospital. While there, he contracted pneumonia. He had trouble swallowing after the stroke and could not take food or water orally. He was put on a drip but this failed to provide him with adequate nutrition.

By the third week, his veins collapsed. By the time the doctors decided that they needed to insert a feeding tube into his stomach, his condition was too poor to withstand surgery. Five days later, Martin died.

This is a manifestation of the same underlying belief about the relative value of disabled people's lives that underpins hostility towards disabled people.

An inquiry by the Equality and Human Rights Commission into disability hate crime concluded that disability harassment was widespread. The inquiry report *Hidden in Plain Sight* detailed 10 murders of disabled people, including the case of Brent Martin, a man with learning difficulties attacked for a bet by three people he considered his friends. One of the murderers is reported to have told friends, 'I am not going down for a muppet,' a clear reference to Brent's impairment. In late 2010, Kathryn Stone, CEO of Voice UK, warned of 'real increases in the most horrendous murders and very, very serious sexual assaults'.[4] A poll that same year revealed that one-quarter of the public believed that disabled people should be in institutions.[5]

Meanwhile, the Disabled People's Movement, which had gained advances since its inception in the 1970s, went into decline.

The history of disabled people's oppression and the immediate background to the situation in 2010 are important for understanding why the Tories targeted disabled people, the full effects of how their policies impacted on disabled people, and how they have been getting away with it. Chapter 1 begins by looking at who disabled people are, a question that any account of disability must start with due to the complexity of disabled people's oppression. Chapter 2 examines attitudes towards disability and the 'othering' of disabled people, which have facilitated the government in pursual of its agenda to make the poorest and most disadvantaged members of society pay for a financial crisis we did not cause. Chapter 3 then provides an overview of the history of disability and of the enduring struggle between oppression and resistance in the years leading up to the election of the Coalition government in 2010.

ONE | Who are disabled people?

The complexity of disabled people's oppression is evident in how any discussion of it must necessarily begin with an explanation of who disabled people are. As Roddy Slorach, Senior Disability Advisor at Imperial College London, writes: 'Disability in contemporary society is a complex and widely misunderstood issue.'[1] We are a significant proportion of the population and rising – recorded numbers of disabled people are growing both for demographic reasons and as people increasingly seek protection against discrimination and impoverishment by identifying under the legal definition of disability. Yet our issues are marginalised within wider society and beset with misconceptions.

The diversity of impairments and the distribution of people with them across the population present a barrier to organising against shared injustice. The complexity is compounded by the fact that many people with impairments do not identify as disabled. The social model, where properly understood and applied, is an immensely useful tool for overcoming impairment differences and for uniting those with unmet needs within collective resistance. It is a far stronger basis for resistance than can be formed with an approach that focuses on the differing experiences of impairment that divide us.

A not insignificant group of people
Disabled people are the world's largest minority group. Disability under the Equality Act 2010 is defined as: 'a physical or mental

impairment which has a substantial and long-term adverse effect on your ability to carry out normal day-to-day activities'. The World Health Organization (WHO) recorded over 1 billion disabled people worldwide in 2011, making up 15 per cent of the global population. Latest figures put the number of disabled people in the UK at 13.9 million people; 24 per cent of the population reported 'a disability' in 2016–17, an increase of 6 per cent since 2007–08.[2] Despite popular concern with an ageing population, the change came from increases in the percentages of working-age adults and children, while the period saw a decrease in adults of State Pension age reporting a disability.

The number of those affected by disability issues are even greater when we take into consideration the 6.5 million providing informal support for disabled relatives and friends in the UK today. The charity Carers UK reports that every day another 6,000 people become carers and anticipate that by 2037 the figure will have risen to 9 million. As Professor Colin Barnes told Disabled People Against Cuts in 2013, 'More disabled people are around today than ever before so to suggest that impairment is a minority issue is nonsense'.[3]

The number of disabled people is rising. The fact that people are living longer and acquiring impairments in older age is just one aspect of this: according to the charity Alzheimer's Society, there are 850,000 people with dementia in the UK in 2020, with numbers set to rise to 1.6 million by 2040. Other factors include longer life expectancies for babies born with complex needs, increasing numbers of working-age disabled people and skyrocketing levels of mental distress. A response by London Councils in 2017 pointed to a 'far greater than average growth of adults with learning and physical disabilities, and those with mental health problems'.[4]

Dramatic increases in children and young people experiencing mental distress is a cause for concern. Mental distress (or psychological distress) describes a range of symptoms and experiences of a person's internal life that are commonly held to be troubling, confusing or out of the ordinary; these can range from anxiety and stress to hearing voices and intrusive thoughts.

A study by researchers from University College London, Imperial College London, Exeter University and the Nuffield Trust, published in 2018, showed a six-fold increase over 20 years in children and young people stating that they have a mental health condition.[5] Although this can be attributed in part to greater mental health awareness, incidences of self-harm are unquestionably escalating: hospital admissions for self-injury among young women doubled over the two decades to 2018 (NHS data show that girls were admitted to hospital 7,327 times in 1997 compared with 13,463 times in 2017), while a study of over 40,000 self-poisonings among 10- to 24-year-olds found that those involving the five most common substances all increased steadily between 1998 and 2014 in both sexes.[6]

The drop in the ages of children experiencing mental distress is significant, with teachers reporting that children as young as three are self-harming. As the UK Coalition of Deaf and Disabled People's Organisations wrote in its 2018 United Nations report, 'inadequate responses to dramatically rising incidences of mental distress experienced by children and young people will have serious consequences both for those individuals and society as a whole'.[7]

Incidences of certain impairments are rising but increasing numbers of people identifying as disabled can also be attributed both to proliferation of diagnoses and to greater disability awareness. The first edition of the *Diagnostic and Statistical Manual of Mental Disorders*, published in 1952, listed 106 disorders; the most recent version, DSM-5, has over 300.

This growth has been critically linked to the relationship between psychiatry and 'Big Pharma', with the latter profiting from an expanding market.[8] As a tool for directly progressing the rights of disabled people, the value of the Disability Discrimination Act 1995, now replaced by the Equality Act 2010, has been questioned.[9] However, the legal definition of disability it set out has extended awareness of the potential to identify as disabled to people with impairments outside popular ideas of 'disability'.

Misconceptions about disability abound, not helped by the fact that the international symbol for disability is a wheelchair. Less than 8 per cent of disabled people require the use of a wheelchair yet over 50 per cent of people think of disability as a physical impairment. Of those who reported a disability in 2017–18, 25 per cent reported a 'mental health impairment'. Substantial numbers of people have 'invisible' impairments: for example, there are approximately 1.5 million people in the UK who have a learning difficulty; 700,000, more than one in 100, are autistic; and an estimated 250,000 adults and children in the UK are affected by myalgic encephalomyelitis (ME).

Mistaken impressions extend to the issues that impact on disabled people's lives. This became evident from the outcry against the Tories' 'dementia tax', as critics labelled it, in the 2017 General Election campaign. The proposal was to raise the upper capital limit for eligibility for social care support from its current value of £23,250 to £100,000. The public response revealed a considerable number of people to be under the misapprehension that social care support is currently free at the point of delivery, as with the NHS – considerable enough that the issue dominated the debate and forced the Tories to perform a U-turn on their manifesto commitment before the election had even happened.

The irony of this, given the onslaught of regressive policymaking by the Tories since 2010, was that these particular proposals represented what can be described as an improvement on the current system in that there would have been a number of 'winners'. Under the existing system, anyone with savings above the upper limit must fund their own social care. Below that, local authorities still have the power to charge for social care support, with most taking income from disability benefits into account in financial assessments. An investigation by the GMB union in 2018 found that more than 166,000 people are trapped in debt for their social care.[10] On this occasion, the Tories were stung by the public's ignorance of disability, but, as we shall see later, this ignorance has helped conceal the extent of their attacks on disabled people since 2010.

There is a clash between the growing incidence of disability and the direction of government policy to reduce the number of people on disability benefits. Successive governments have obscured this disconnect by exaggerating fraud and maintaining a narrative of policy reform to justify cuts to disability support.

The target set by New Labour to remove 1 million claimants from Incapacity Benefit (IB) has been carried over to Employment and Support Allowance (the benefit that replaced IB) by the Tories. This figure has been conjured for soundbite impact in the deliberate absence of any assessment of levels of need, disability or impairment. It is justified after the economic fact on the purely ideological notion that 'everyone can do some sort of work'. To suggest otherwise, the government argues, is 'outdated', 'patronising and offensive'.[11]

Nearly half of disabled people are unemployed, for reasons to do with both disability and impairment, and the real-world workplace remains exclusionary. With a deliberate disregard for the reality of disabled people's lives, government policies consistently fail to meet their own targets.

Despite the size of the disabled population, we remain a very marginalised group. Research published in 2014 found that two-thirds (67 per cent) of the British public feel uncomfortable talking to disabled people and nearly half (43 per cent) say that they do not know anyone who is disabled.[12]

From the isolation of impairment to the collective experience of disability

Another example of the complexity of disability is the fact that many disabled people do not identify as such. According to government research cited by Slorach, 'a large majority of disabled people, in the UK at least, do not actually consider themselves to be disabled'.[13] Low levels of self-identification can be attributed to the vast array of impairment coupled with the common association of disability with wheelchair use and other visible impairments.

Stigma and a desire to escape the negative connotations of disability in popular imagination also play a role. As Slorach describes: 'Impairments may be physical or mental (or both), single or multiple, temporary or permanent, and acquired before or after birth.' The majority of disabled people – over 80 per cent – are not born with impairments but acquire them over the course of their life, most commonly through disease, injury or trauma.[14]

Despite efforts to reduce disability stigma, including high-profile publicity campaigns around the Paralympics, negative attitudes persist. A 2018 report by the charity Scope revealed the extent of the negative attitudes that are held towards disabled people – and how many non-disabled people do not realise the scale of the problem.[15]

Disabled people are also geographically and generationally dispersed. Being born into a non-disabled family or acquiring impairment without knowing anyone else who is disabled can be a very isolating experience. The low level of public disability awareness and the cultural dominance of negative images of disability mean that a political understanding of disability can generally be accessed only through other disabled people. Further barriers to identification under a shared disability identity can arise through conflicting access and communication needs among people with different impairments: for example, Deaf British Sign Language (BSL) users communicate via a visual language that is inaccessible to blind people, while blind people navigate via tactile paving that causes discomfort to wheelchair users.

In the past, disabled people's collective exclusion from society in segregated institutions provided the basis for group identity,[16] often in opposition to the staff, who held complete power over their lives. It was residents of Le Court, a home run by Leonard Cheshire, who famously founded the Union of the Physically Impaired Against Segregation (UPIAS) in the early 1970s, to which the origins of the present-day disability history movement in Britain can be traced. People with learning difficulties made up and sang songs of resistance to keep going in the inhumane conditions of long-stay institutions, often poking fun at the staff who terrorised them.[17]

It has been suggested that one reason for the decline of the disability movement is the success of the inclusion agenda: greater participation of individual disabled people within the mainstream has removed the basis for collectivisation, leading to atomisation and weaker resistance. The point to take from this is the importance of collectivisation and of not fetishising segregation. The shared identities produced by institutionalisation were limited: hospital and educational structures divided by impairment, imposing hierarchies that shaped attitudes between patients/pupils. The campaigner Baroness Jane Campbell admits: 'I would cross the road rather than be seen with a learning disabled person – when I was a child, I wouldn't be seen dead with one of them.'[18]

Shared characteristics of impairment are almost impossible to identify. The WHO International Classification lists thousands of 'impairments, disabilities and handicaps', from 'Endocrine, nutritional and metabolic diseases' to 'Diseases of the musculoskeletal system and connective tissue', from 'Congenital malformations, deformations and chromosomal abnormalities' to 'Mental and behavioural disorders', among many others, all assiduously categorised and subdivided. Each of these will affect people in very different ways.

Many impairments fluctuate and are experienced relative to environment: for example, mental distress is significantly lessened in an emotionally supportive setting. The experience of impairment as deficit is itself not even consistent. Journalist Steve Silberman became interested in autism after spending time with programmers from Silicon Valley, leading to his award-winning book *NeuroTribes: The legacy of autism and how to think smarter about people who think differently*. Autistic people's brains are wired differently; this is described as neurodiversity, in contrast to the neuro-typical way in which non-autistic people think. Silberman found that, in the tech industry, far from holding people back, neurodiversity is experienced as an asset leading to highly profitable careers.[19]

By contrast, the shared characteristics of disability are wide-ranging and glaring. One consistent and stable characteristic throughout capitalism has been the inextricable link between disability and poverty: disability is both cause and consequence of poverty. The poor are more likely to become disabled due to poor nutrition, lack of medical care, industrial injuries and violence. Once disabled, poorer people are significantly less likely to receive the education or training needed to find employment, or have equal access to social networks, community resources or economic and legal support systems. Approximately 10,000 disabled people die every day as a result of extreme poverty worldwide.[20] Many of the causes and dreadful consequences of disability are entirely preventable.

The intrinsic relationship between poverty and disability is true not only in developing countries. In Britain, disabled people are now nearly three times as likely to experience severe material deprivation as non-disabled people.[21] Disabled people have lower incomes due to labour market exclusion but also because of higher unavoidable expenditures – what journalist Frances Ryan calls the 'Poverty Premium'[22] – as a result of the extra costs of disability. Examples include the costs of specialist equipment, such as wheelchairs or adapted kitchen items, higher transport costs and higher energy bills due to increased needs for heating and laundering. Research for the charity Scope estimates that, on average, disabled people face extra costs of £583 a month, with one in five facing extra costs of more than £1,000 a month.[23] These additional costs are nowhere near covered by disability benefits.

The experiences of disabled people are very different depending on class and access to wealth. As Stephen Hawking wrote in the foreword to the *World Report on Disability*:

> I have benefitted from access to first-class medical care. I rely on a team of personal assistants who make it possible for me to live and work in comfort and dignity. My house and my workplace have been made accessible for me. Computer experts have supported me with an assisted communication system and a speech synthesizer which allow me to compose lectures and papers, and to communicate with different audiences. But I realize that I am very lucky, in many ways.[24]

The social model of disability gives people with different impairments something to unite behind, just as different black, Asian and minority ethnic communities are united by the experience of racial oppression. Focusing on shared barriers experienced across impairment groups gives people the potential to join together in greater numbers with greater shared power. The focus on material barriers is also able to draw in those who may not previously have identified as disabled.

Looking both to the past and to the situation in Britain today, we can see that disabled identities are most clearly defined at moments of struggle for the material resources and conditions people with impairments need in order to survive. These actions, although impairment-specific, convey a sense of what today would be termed 'disability pride'. They also invariably occur concurrently with wider struggles over the division of wealth between the working class and the ruling class. During the Great Depression, the League of the Physically Handicapped fought job discrimination in the United States. Historians Paul K. Longmore and David Goldberger comment: 'The greatest influence on their political thinking and strategizing was the depression-era climate of crisis and desperate activism.'[25]

Since 2010, people who previously may not have self-identified as disabled have become involved in collective action against attempts by the UK government to cut and deny social security payments. Newer activists come from a far wider background of impairment than was present in earlier iterations of the disability movement.[26] In these moments, disabled people find pride in our identities as we transcend the victim role of the oppressed to fight shared injustice.

The scale and depth of the human cost of austerity and welfare reform mean that the stakes are now extremely high. Faced with this, in my experience of activism, it has become far easier to find accommodations between impairment groups and to resolve potentially conflicting access needs or for people to defer these conflicts in the interest of furthering our common struggle.

Uniting against a common enemy

In 2006, controversial disability academic Tom Shakespeare confidently stated: 'Recognition that the majority of people with impairments have no desire to identify as disabled is overdue.'[27] As we shall explore in more detail later, we are now in an age where labour intensification has narrowed the pool of those who can fit the demands of the workplace and work does not pay – certainly not enough to cover the extra costs of disability.

The need for recourse to protections against discrimination at work and for access to social security payments is greater than ever. This has driven up the numbers and proportion of those claiming a disability identity. This presents a challenge for neoliberal governments and local authorities looking to reduce rather than expand public spending, and also a challenge to campaigners: it represents a development with the potential to unite greater numbers in resistance but one requiring a will to fight against a common enemy in spite of the ravages of austerity.

TWO | Justifiable exclusion

Attitudes and othering of disabled people

The idea that exclusion of people with impairments from society is both natural and inevitable is so ingrained as to be widely held as common sense. Professors Mike Oliver and Colin Barnes identified how 'the negative assumptions and ideologies surrounding impairment are so deeply embedded within social consciousness that they have become naturalised as social "facts".'[1] Understanding of disability as a socially created category is thus obscured, blocking development of political consciousness among disabled people ourselves.[2]

Negative ideas about disability are generated by the social and economic structures we live under and reinforced by pervasive cultural references that portray disability as tragedy. Disabled people are both viewed and treated as intrinsically different. The consequence of this 'othering' is widespread hate crime and harassment against disabled people, as well as marginalisation of disability issues even among those fighting for progressive change. Challenging attitudes in the realm of ideas alone can have only limited impact; in order to change disabled people's place in society, we need to confront the socio-economic structures that maintain our oppression.

This chapter examines how the organisation of society and the physical segregation of disabled people exclude and devalue disabled people, giving rise to negative attitudes towards disability and abuse of disabled people. It explains how, according to personal tragedy theory, disabled people are portrayed as objects of pity without our own agency. The exclusion of disabled people is often regarded as a natural state of affairs, with comparisons to qualities of disability and impairment used historically to justify the exclusion of other groups of people. Indeed, disability is so highly stigmatised that the inferiority of disabled people is widely accepted even among many disabled people themselves. The chapter concludes by arguing that there is a prevailing notion that disabled people are worth less than non-disabled people, and that this generates a general disregard for the subject of disability beyond the interests of disabled people ourselves.

Structures that 'other'

Aversion to disability is learned; it is not inherent to the human condition. This is evident in the ways in which people with impairments have been treated differently across societies and throughout history.[3] The segregation of disabled children into 'special' educational settings and leisure activities ensures that many people grow up away from disability. Childhood experience plays an important role in attitudinal development. To illustrate this, social care researcher Maureen Oswin gives the example of a convalescent school for children with tuberculosis and asthma where disabled pupils had been placed. A former non-disabled pupil remembers: 'We never really noticed Mary's handicaps ... we just loved her, we used to quarrel about whose turn it was to push her wheelchair around the playground, and at sewing time we sat round her in a circle.'[4]

Campaigners have long seen inclusive education as the cornerstone for building an inclusive society. In the foreword to the Equality and Human Rights Commission report on disability hate crime, Mike Smith wrote: 'People think of choice of school as parental choice, but it is only when you step back that you can consider the wider impact on our society of segregated education.'[5]

Services for disabled adults are promoted using progressive rhetoric, but too often this just serves to disguise the continuation of practices that disempower and dehumanise. Just one example from a quick internet search finds an adult day service for 'people with complex needs including learning disabilities, epilepsy and autism', which promotes its work providing 'the opportunity to acquire life and vocational skills and with the opportunity to socialise and explore their leisure interests'. The reality of such settings is that individual disabled people too often lack any meaningful choice in how they spend their time.

There commonly exists a sizeable gulf between rhetoric and practice. This was solidly exemplified in undercover footage from the Whorlton Hall scandal of 2019, where staff members met in a room emblazoned with progressive-sounding words including 'person-centred', 'respect', 'inspiring' and 'safe'. In this same room, staff were told by management not to worry about using the approved restraint techniques in which they had been trained but to write up their notes as if they had used them.

Failure to invest in practice that meets rhetorical standards is a consequence of the role that disability service provision plays within capitalist society: essentially, it is not about life opportunities for disabled people but instead about warehousing those less capable of 'productive' work to free up those who are to get on with it unhindered.

The social relations at the core of how these settings function are entirely artificial, contributing to an idea of disability as something 'other' existing outside society. The cliché of 'basket weaving' as an occupation for people society is not sure what to do with has its modern-day equivalent in the form of 'parachute games', where groups of disabled adults are taken to leisure centres to stand around a circle of material, on which they bounce beanbags into the air for hours at a time. I am in no way opposed to finding meaningful activity in ways that defy normative ideas, but much segregated provision can be characterised by attempts to fill time at the least cost with no reference to individual interests or choice.

Without adequate resources to support each individual disabled person to participate in society on an equal basis with others, staff are given the role of 'managing' need. This creates a defining power imbalance between staff and 'service users'. In such situations, disabled people who cannot be contained on minimum resources are experienced as a problem. Staff frustrations are more easily targeted at the behaviour of individual service users (or, in educational settings, disabled pupils) than at the problem of the more nebulous 'system' we live under. Dehumanising approaches develop, where phrases such as 'attention seeking', 'playing up' or 'kicking off' are used to dismiss disabled people attempting to communicate their needs. Scandals such as Winterbourne View, where a 2011 *Panorama* investigation exposed physical and psychological abuse of the disabled residents, or Whorlton Hall, as mentioned above, shock the public but are just extreme examples of a culture that is fostered by the inherent framework of segregated service provision and closed environments.

This is not to point the finger of blame at front-line staff, who invariably work hard under difficult circumstances, but to recognise the role that socio-economic structures play in oppressing disabled people and generating social attitudes towards disabled people as 'other'. The current system expects poorly paid staff to carry out highly complex and skilled roles without adequate resources or training – and, on top of that, to transcend popular social consciousness in how they view the disabled people they work with. The system itself and the staff who work within it are effectively set up to fail.

Segregation creates environments in which abuse is both more likely to happen and less likely to be detected. With the realities of disabled people's lives largely unseen, mistaken assumptions continue unchecked. A common one is that disabled people are safer in 'special services' than in mainstream society. The grandfather of a disabled man who was abused as part of the Longcare residential home scandal, which was uncovered in 1994, told investigative journalist John Pring: 'I didn't even consider the possibility that he could be abused. I never thought that anybody in their right mind could take advantage of a mentally handicapped person.'[6]

Published in 2018 and conducted by researchers at University College London and the Camden and Islington NHS Foundation Trust, the largest ever survey of care home staff in England found abuse in at least some form in 99 per cent of care homes.[7] Disabled children and adults are both at much higher risk of violence than their non-disabled peers. Children with learning difficulties are the most at risk, experiencing 4.6 times the risk of sexual abuse.[8] An investigation into the sexual abuse of adults with learning difficulties published in 2001 suggested that abusers 'may deliberately choose employment in the caring professions because of their vulnerable populations. And the intimate nature of the work.'[9]

Once inequalities experienced by disabled people are revealed, campaigners often find themselves frustrated at how little the public appear to care. Dr Sara Ryan, the mother of a disabled young man who died through neglect in an Assessment and Treatment Unit, commented on Twitter in response to a tweet from the Royal Society for the Protection of Birds: 'Netted sand martins going viral (rightly) in minutes. Preventable deaths and torture of certain people, a gargantuan fight 4 action + attention.'[10]

The House of Commons Petitions Committee experienced this phenomenon recently when none of the footballing organisations they approached responded to their concerns regarding abusive behaviour towards disabled people at football matches. It was suggested that the 'underwhelming' response from readers of the *Slough Observer* to the horrific abuses suffered by disabled people in Longcare was due to a lack of emotional connection.[11] John Pring ends his book *Longcare Survivors: the biography of a care scandal* with his conclusion that such reactions are 'born out of a deeply ingrained indifference – in every nook and cranny of society – to the fate of people with learning difficulties' and that they raise 'something even more disturbing ... the certainty that it would happen again'.[12]

Abuse and indifference to abuse will sadly continue, born out of socio-economic structures that exclude and devalue disabled people, until they are replaced with a society that overcomes oppression.

Better dead than disabled: disability as personal tragedy

The idea of disability as personal tragedy sustains a view that possession of an impairment devalues a person. This approach focuses attention on the negative aspects of impairment and presents disabled people as objects of pity dependent on others for their survival.

Certain impairments do involve experiences of pain and/or distress, and acquiring impairment requires adjustment. However, unequal life chances do not inevitably flow from impairment. Limited employment opportunities and low incomes stacked against higher living costs are the central causes of disabled people's inequality. The focus on adverse personal impacts of impairment diverts attention from the societal barriers that oppress disabled people and, in this way, both flows from and serves the priorities of capitalist society.

Corporate charities with their multimillion-pound industry rooted in the negative portrayal of disability are complicit in this. This charity model dominates perceptions of disability as fundraisers compete for attention, emphasising the worst aspects of impairment to prove that their 'cause' is the most deserving and to solicit donations. A controversial campaign run by the Royal National Institute of Blind People in 2014 (and now apparently removed from the internet) listed health conditions including Alzheimer's and Parkinson's that members of the public claimed they would rather acquire than go blind.

Images of disabled children are a staple in charitable fundraising. This has the effect of infantilising disability, encouraging paternalism and patronising attitudes. Mencap was pressured to drop its 'Little Stephen' logo depicting a crying child many years ago, but the deafblind charity Sense has been using the same footage of a toddler called 'Elliot' for at least the past 10 years, keeping him as a perpetual infant in popular imagination.

The personal tragedy motif is continuously reinforced through cultural reference points that show disabled people as either pathetic victims or as superheroes who have overcome the adversity of impairment. Meanwhile, as identified by Mike Oliver, there is 'little attempt to present the collective experience of disability'.[13]

Disability is also commonly viewed through the perspective of non-disabled protagonists. This reflects an assumption that readers/viewers will be unable to relate to disabled characters, which then perpetuates the widespread inability to connect with experiences of disability. A stark example of this was the decision to cast a puppet rather than an actor as a non-verbal autistic child in *All in a Row*, a play focusing on the difficulties faced by his parents.[14]

The message that it is better to be dead than disabled was perhaps most clearly conveyed by Jojo Moyes' book *Me Before You*, published in 2012 and turned into a film in 2016, which attracted international outrage from disabled campaigners. The plot features a rich young man who enjoys an active life until an injury leaves him paralysed. He struggles to adjust, falls in love with his nurse, then decides to kill himself in order to free her of the burden that a life with him would entail. The fact that the character has the benefit of independent wealth, and thus the ability to meet his own support needs – something this is denied to the majority of disabled people – makes it so much worse.

Author and disability hate crime researcher Katharine Quarmby observes in her book *Scapegoat: why we are failing disabled people* that from the moment disabled people are born, they are told their lives are not worth living.[15] Judgements on quality of life from medical practitioners can encourage negative views. Activist and broadcaster Mik Scarlet writes: 'In my own experience, even though … I made it … with an amazing life … I have still met with a large number of surgeons who have questioned my quality of life.'[16]

Given such prevailing attitudes, it is no wonder that disabled people grow up feeling worthless or that individuals who acquire impairment seek to end their lives, convinced of the impossibility of living a fulfilling life with impairment. Positive portrayals of disability on screen continue to be more the exception than the rule, but where portrayals do occur the input of disabled actors and consultants makes a noticeable difference to the depth of disabled characters.

Disability as a justifiable exclusion

Disability is so highly stigmatised that the inferiority of disabled people is widely accepted even among disabled people themselves. One of the early questions tackled by UPIAS was whether disabled people are oppressed. This was despite prevailing conditions in which the majority of disabled people were incarcerated in institutions. In response to members who claimed to feel 'frustrated' rather than 'oppressed', disability activist Vic Finkelstein argued: 'These "feelings" may be true to *you*, but do not necessarily take us one step forward in understanding the condition of disabled people *in general in society*.'[17]

One of the most striking points to emerge from Quarmby's account of the scapegoating of disabled people is how a number of the torture and murder cases she investigated involved perpetrators who were themselves disabled.[18] She observes that many of the most famous and fervent supporters of eugenics had impairments, including Francis Galton, President Franklin D. Roosevelt and Winston Churchill.[19]

Within a hierarchy of impairment, disabled people with differing impairments have accepted and reinforced stigmatisation against each other. Historically, people with physical impairments consciously attempted to distance themselves from people with learning difficulties and mental distress.

Those with physical impairments were often treated within segregated institutions as if they also had learning difficulties.[20] It is then perhaps understandable that, when they began to organise and assert their rights to equality, they should seek to overturn false assumptions about their minds. In early discussions of strategy, one member of UPIAS argued against participation in protests, reasoning: 'We are not going to convince the general public that to be disabled doesn't mean mental backwardness if we exhibit ourselves in an undignified manner.'[21]

Even at the bottom of the hierarchy there are prejudices and negative assumptions between different impairment groups: in a previous role developing service user involvement across mental health and substance dependency services, I found mental health service users discomforted about association with 'druggies and alcoholics' and substance dependency service users worried about being branded as 'loonies'.

Unconscious acceptance of disabled people as inferior is evident in the way in which disability is often overlooked as a category of oppression. Disabled people are accustomed to being treated in ways that would not be considered acceptable for other equalities strands. It is common practice for the media to seek opinion on disability issues from non-disabled people, often working for non-user-led charities. It is difficult to imagine them exclusively presenting men's opinions on women's issues, for example.

Researcher Fayyaz Vellani highlights another example of this in his article 'David Cameron, the politics of doublethink and contemporary discourses of disability in the United Kingdom'. He observes the bizarre way in which ex-banker Lord David Freud defended himself against criticism after suggesting that people with learning difficulties are not worth the minimum wage: he claimed to 'care passionately about disabled people'. Vellani comments: 'It is remarkable that it is still possible to classify disabled people as a group of citizens about whom a politician cares … It is difficult to imagine this language being used in relation to any other constituency.'[22]

Disabled people are often overlooked as an oppressed group in society. Disabled campaigners were indignant at the complete exclusion of disabled people's resistance from the 'Disobedient Objects' exhibition on protest and civil rights struggles at the Victoria and Albert Museum in 2015. Feedback obtained via culture-sector trade unionists was that this was no deliberate omission but that inclusion of disabled people's struggles alongside those of other oppressed groups simply had not occurred to the curator. It was a shame not to see alongside the Suffragette tea service and protest robots tools of disability protest such as wheelchairs and the type of D-locks used by disabled people to chain themselves to buses in the fight for accessible public transport.

The BBC *Panorama* programme that uncovered the Whorlton Hall abuse was itself guilty of othering disabled people by inviting 'professional experts' and carers to comment without seeking views from any autistic people or people with learning difficulties. It may have been too painful and inappropriate for the victims themselves, but there are plenty of self-advocates who could have been invited onto the programme to confirm that the scenes were unacceptable. As the experts were shown footage of a man with learning difficulties being pinned down and mocked by a team of staff, one of them commented that he must have been confused about what was going on. He clearly wasn't: he was shouting at them 'You bastards'; he knew exactly what was happening and that it was wrong. The injustice was that no one was listening to him, a situation then replicated in the programme's coverage.

One powerful example of disability stigmatisation comes from the work of historian Douglas Baynton. In an examination of three major American citizenship debates concerning women's suffrage, African-American civil rights and the restriction of immigration, Baynton reveals that 'not only has it been considered justifiable to treat disabled people unequally, but the concept of disability has been used to justify discrimination against other groups by attributing disability to them'.[23] The most common disability argument for slavery was that African-Americans lacked sufficient intelligence to participate equally in society,[24] while women's participation in politics was said to be unsafe due to 'much mental disorder' and 'delicate nervous stability'.[25] Such accusations were vigorously denied, but without questioning the hierarchy of human worth on which they were based.

Baynton concludes:

> This common strategy for attaining equal rights, which seeks
> to distance one's own group from imputations of disability and
> therefore tacitly accepts the idea that disability is a legitimate
> reason for inequality, is perhaps one of the factors responsible
> for making discrimination against people with disabilities so
> persistent and the struggle for disability rights so difficult.[26]

Political invective on both the left and the right has traditionally invoked disability to disparage opponents. There is growing awareness of the unacceptability of phrases such as the 'loony
left' or 'economics of the madhouse'. Nevertheless, impairment
is still used as a justification for ignoring the political opinions of
disabled people.

This was a problem encountered by the deafblind activist Helen
Keller in the early twentieth century, causing her continual frustration. She complained: 'I do not mind having my ideas attacked and
my aims opposed and ridiculed, but it is not fair fighting or good
argument to find that "Helen Keller's mistakes spring out of the limitations of her development".'[27] It frustrated her to be presented by
the media as subject to 'exploitation' by 'Socialists' when putting forward her own views.[28] The League of the Physically Handicapped
experienced similar attitudes when officials tried to discredit their
demonstration by claiming that Communists had staged the sit-in
and were using the 'cripples … for dramatic effect'.[29]

Right-wing attacks against the climate activist Greta Thunberg
have similarly used her impairment to question her political
understanding. In one example of this, News Corp columnist
Andrew Bolt provoked an international outcry when he described
her as 'deeply disturbed' and 'strange'.[30]

The treatment of disabled people by right-wing governments
has historically been criticised by left-wing commentators using

language and approaches that reinforce stigma and the idea of disability as personal tragedy. The *Daily Worker* supported the actions of the League of the Physically Handicapped throughout the 1930s in the United States but nevertheless presented their members as objects of pity; descriptions of 'helpless crippled people ... dragging their own lame bodies back and forth' were intended to reflect badly on the authorities that the League was protesting against, but they also represented the same underpinning attitudes they were fighting.[31]

In the age of austerity, disabled people have similarly had cause for complaint about portrayals by the left of victims of welfare reform that play on ideas of 'vulnerability' and contribute towards a pity model of disability.

Hostility towards disabled people is not always straightforward to identify. This is yet another indication of the complexity of disabled people's oppression. A lack of disability awareness combined with learned aversion towards difference has led to the trend of groundless accusations of paedophilia used to justify the harassment, torture and murder of disabled men. All but one of the murders investigated by Quarmby involved victims falsely labelled a paedophile by their murderers.

In the years following publication of her book, another two preventable murders occurred of disabled men by neighbours, involving false accusations of paedophilia. In both cases – Bijan Ebrahimi murdered in 2013 and Kamil Ahmad in 2016 – police failed to act on multiple reports of harassment from the victims leading up to their horrific and avoidable killings; in Bijan's case, the police apparently even sided with the killers.

Quarmby refers to 'problems of perception ... which feed into attacks where disabled men are described as paedophiles and disabled women are routinely sexually abused'.[32] Disabled women are twice as likely to be assaulted or raped as non-disabled women. In April 2014, Majella Lynch, a disabled woman known to services in Southampton, died from a fatal infection following a violent sexual assault in which a shampoo bottle was forced into her abdominal cavity. Myths around disability act as barriers to both prevention and prosecution, including generalised beliefs that nobody would harm a disabled person and that disabled people are not credible objects of sexual attention.

A question of worth

Disabled people are 'maintained in their position of inferiority'[33] by the idea that people with impairments are worth less than non-disabled people. The effect of this is not just to distance non-disabled people from disabled people, but also to generate a general disregard for the subject of disability beyond the interests of disabled people ourselves. In this way, the socially constructed nature of disability and its wider economic significance are frequently overlooked. Disabled historian Hugh Gallagher described 'the land of the crippled', where 'the usual rights and privileges do not apply ... a great wall surrounds this place, and most of what goes on within the wall is unknown to those outside it'.[34]

Disability literature is littered with expressions of frustration at a perceived lack of interest from wider academia and the anti-capitalist left. In 1981, disability activist Allan Sutherland commented: 'It is the general failure of the Left to make such connections between capitalism and impairment.'[35] Fast-forward to 2012 and another disability activist, A. J. Withers, expressed similar experiences about their[36] experiences on the radical left among mainly non-disabled activists: 'After a while I got used to being asked to do workshops and having no one show up ... I got tired of being constantly reminded that progressives didn't think disability or disabled people were important.'[37] Withers acknowledges that this is slowly beginning to change, but surmises:

'Perhaps one of the primary reasons that disabled people have been actively excluded from the left is because there is an unspoken belief, held by other Leftists, that we are broken or flawed.'[38]

Disabled people's oppression powerfully exposes the true, deceitful nature of capitalist society. This compounds the exasperation experienced by disabled activists at the low profile of disability on the wider left. Disability activist-academics Marta Russell and Ravi Malhotra observe: 'Unlike other social movements, the various disability rights movements to date have received relatively little attention from socialists, union activists or academics ... Yet an examination of their various trajectories suggests useful insights that those seeking to challenge capitalism in other struggles can learn from and incorporate in them.'[39]

While frustrations are understandable, this lack of recognition is part of the wider marginalisation of disabled people under capitalism and is itself a product of socio-economic structures that exclude and divide. As Marx wrote: 'It is not the consciousness of men that determines their existence, but their social existence that determines their consciousness.'[40] Ideas change through struggle, and it is through active resistance that disabled people can develop our own political consciousness and fight to make visible the full and complex iniquities of capitalism.

THREE | From asylums to independent living

Disabled people on the edge of society

Knowing our history is important. It helps us understand that what we face in our current time period is socially constructed and can therefore be altered. It gives us greater insights into the workings of the forces that oppress us. It gives us evidence with which to challenge the myths and false assumptions that dominate popular ideas about disability. Lessons from the past can help us shape and build a more effective resistance in the present.

History tells us that disabled people's oppression is incredibly complex and intrinsically bound up with capitalism: capitalism causes impairments through poverty and war; it also creates disability through the discriminatory barriers faced by people with impairments living within a capitalist society. The history of social policy relating to disability shows a series of attempts to manage the disabled population through eradication and exclusion; these attempts include 'eugenics, sterilisation, euthanasia and the institutionalisation of the impaired'.[1]

Disability is an issue that strongly exposes the brutal and exploitative nature of capitalism, and, as such, it has the potential to cause unrest. Capitalist governments are nervous of this and can be pushed to reforms. History also teaches us how fragile any gains are for disabled people so long as we live under a system that puts profit before people; conditions can improve through resistance but they will always be subject to wider economic forces and will always be in danger of being snatched away.

This chapter explores the origins of disability in the rise of capitalism and its function in disciplining the workforce; it provides a brief historical overview of social policies relating to management of the disabled population and their relative impacts on the lives of disabled people; it examines the gains achieved through disabled people's struggle since the 1970s; and, finally, it looks at the decline of the Disabled People's Movement (DPM) under the New Labour government in the years leading up to 2010.

'A very capitalist condition'[2]

Disability is a socially created category, originating in and inextricably linked to capitalism. Discrimination against people with impairments is not a permanent feature of human society. As Slorach explains: 'An increasing body of research strongly suggests that such discrimination did not exist, certainly not prior to the rise of class society, and very likely before the rise of capitalist society.'[3] This is not to claim that everything was perfect for people with impairments in earlier societies, but, prior to the Industrial Revolution, they were part of larger social gatherings, whether families, clans or communities.[4]

Individualism appeared through the rise of capitalism, and those with impairments who could not compete equally in the labour market became a problem for society to control.[5] Categories of disability were developed to mark out less productive individuals. As identified by researcher Deborah Stone, 'The disability concept was essential to the development of a workforce in early capitalism and remains indispensable as an instrument of the state in controlling labour supply.'[6]

Disabled people's position in society is tied to what we represent within capitalism: an 'unproductive' element that cannot earn our own living or, if in work, is unable to produce the same levels of profit for employers as non-disabled workers.

For capitalism to function, our experience of life must be worse than that of non-disabled people.[7] Both the stigma of disability and the material reality of inferior living conditions serve to discipline the workforce, encouraging workers to maximise productivity in their jobs, regardless of workplace conditions or income, lest they face the same fate.

Politically conscious disabled people have been making this connection since at least the early twentieth century. Helen Keller wrote that 'the blind are not debarred from usefulness solely by their infirmity. Their idleness is fundamentally caused by conditions which press heavily upon all working people.'[8]

An analysis of disability as socially created was also developed by the League of the Physically Handicapped in the United States during the Depression era. Their 'Thesis on Conditions of the Physically Handicapped', published in August 1936, explicitly condemned disabled people's oppression, attributing economic disadvantage not to their impairments but to 'job discrimination, unjust policies, and haphazard, unfair rehabilitation and relief programs'.[9]

Capitalism differs in its nature from other, earlier forms of class society – specifically in that capitalists are motivated by the extraction of surplus value and by competition with each other. While the oppression of women and LGBT+ people can be dated back to the rise of class society, the oppression of disabled people is particularly associated with the Industrial Revolution.

The cause of impairment is important to capitalism: it is in the interests of capital to provide for those injured through work or war in order to continue recruiting and exploiting willing workers and soldiers. In practical terms, however, it can prove difficult to restrict provision on this basis. The League of the Physically Handicapped was able to force through an extension of employment opportunities to more disabled people by publicly highlighting the incongruity of the US federal government practice of affirmative action for disabled veterans while maintaining that disabled people born with similar impairments were 'unemployable'.[10]

Hitler's Aktion T4 programme for the killing of disabled adults was officially ended in response to social unrest motivated in part by fears that the killing would be expanded to people who acquired impairments through the course of their lives.[11] The Bishop of Münster, Clemens August Graf von Galen, knew exactly the right buttons to push in his famous sermon against Aktion T4 delivered on Sunday, 3 August 1941, in which he warned of future expansion to the elderly, those injured at work and soldiers.[12] The sermon was reproduced in leaflets dropped by the RAF over German towns and cities, and shortly after this the killing programme was officially ended.

Hitler also faced a major furore over the killings of war veterans: troop morale was seriously disturbed when word reached the Russian front that injured troops sent back to Germany were going to their deaths.[13] Although veterans were officially exempt, this was difficult to maintain in practice as entire hospitals were emptied into the killing centres and the exemption was amended over the course of the programme to spare only veterans who had been either wounded or decorated.[14]

Support for disabled people who have not worked and will never do so 'productively' does not flow from capitalism. It is something that can be fought for, granted in the interests of avoiding discontent among the wider populace, but it is not part of the 'social wage'. The term 'social wage' is applied to spending that keeps the workforce fit, such as healthcare, but, as economist Chris Harman points out, it can also be applied to unemployment benefits for those able to show that they are able and willing to work and to pension schemes dependent on a lifetime of labour. Harman notes: 'The capitalist wants contented workers to exploit in the same way that a farmer wants contented cows. Workers cannot be expected to labour with any commitment to their work unless there is some sort of promise that they will not starve to death once they reach retirement age.'[15] The social wage does not include support for those permanently out of employment.

Analysis of the role that disability plays within capitalism leads to an understanding that full liberation from oppression for disabled people cannot be achieved under a system that puts profit before people. This is not to deny the importance in the here and now of challenging discrimination and campaigning for an equal standard of living for disabled people regardless of impairment. We must fight for improvements, using as leverage the fact that capitalism prefers contented workers.[16]

More disabled people in Britain are living within the community now than in previous generations. As a result, the way we are treated has more of an impact on the wider working class. It can be difficult to raise awareness of what happens to disabled people because disability issues continue to be marginalised within wider society, yet we are a substantial proportion of the population, and we are in close contact with friends, family and neighbours. The public cares sufficiently enough about what happens to disabled people for contemporary governments to be nervous of being seen to mistreat them. This can be used to resist changes that would harm disabled people and to fight for improvements. Ultimately, though, the intrinsic role that disability plays within a capitalist system means that, as expressed by Mike Oliver and Colin Barnes, 'only the transformation of capitalist society will ensure the full inclusion of disabled people and indeed all socially oppressed groups'.[17]

Solutions for the 'unproductive': a brief historical overview

With the rise of capitalism, institutions grew up to house those of the poor who were unfit for work, including 'the sick, the insane, defectives, and the aged and infirm'.[18] A founding principle of any provision of support for these groups was the importance of deterring 'able-bodied malingerers' of feigning impairment to escape wage labour.[19] A survey of urban workhouses carried out by the medical journal *The Lancet* in the mid-1860s found that 'a harsh and repulsive regime intended for the repression of idleness and imposture had been and was still applied to persons suffering from acute diseases, permanent disability or old age'.[20]

Popular pressure led to the development of specialist provision for those unable to work. The first publicly funded 'asylums' had been established under the 1808 County Asylums Act.[21] In 1826, the first year for which statistics are available, fewer than 5,000 people were housed in English asylums; by 1900, there were 77 institutions in which over 74,000 people were confined.[22]

The size and growth of this section of the population came to be viewed as a threat to society by the ruling class. Particular concern was aroused with regard to the 'biological quality' of the British populace when the Boer War revealed that many young men from slum backgrounds were unfit for military service.[23]

A pressure group called the National Association for the Care of the Feeble Minded was set up in Britain in 1886 to bring about the lifetime segregation of disabled people. Influenced by their arguments, Winston Churchill wrote to Prime Minister Asquith in 1910: 'The unnatural and increasingly rapid growth of the Feeble-Minded and Insane classes, coupled as it is with a steady restriction among all the thrifty, energetic and superior stocks, constitutes a national and race danger which it is impossible to exaggerate.'[24] Although a Private Members' Parliamentary Bill to introduce compulsory sterilisation was withdrawn, a Mental Deficiency Act was passed in 1913 that legislated for the lifetime detention of the 'feeble-minded' and 'mental defectives'.

A eugenicist view of disability took hold across the industrialised world. Disabled people were strictly barred from immigration to the United States,[25] and even today applicants applying to obtain a visa waiver for visiting the US have to declare whether they have or have had a 'physical or mental disorder'. In the 1880s, a number of states passed 'ugly laws' to prevent anyone 'diseased, maimed, mutilated or in any way deformed so as to be an unsightly or disgusting object' from being seen in public on penalty of a fine.[26] An exhibition in Philadelphia in the 1920s had a flashing board telling the American public that, every 15 seconds, $100 of 'your money' went on the care of persons with 'bad heredity' and every 48 seconds a 'mentally deficient' person was born in the US.[27] Forced sterilisation of disabled people was legalised in the US as well as in Denmark, Finland, Sweden and Iceland. By 1958, 60,000 American citizens had been sterilised, predominantly women.[28] Compulsory sterilisation continued to be practised in Sweden until 1975 and in Japan until 1996.

Support for eugenics crossed the political spectrum. Speaking in the British parliament in 1912, Labour MP Will Crooks described disabled people as 'like human vermin' who 'crawl about doing absolutely nothing, except polluting and corrupting everything they touch'. The one place where eugenic measures and philosophies were conspicuously absent and marginalised was revolutionary Russia before the 1920s. The Soviet government did away with all existing immigration restrictions, including those pertaining to disability. Writer Keith Rosenthal links this to the fact that disability seems to have been a significant contributing factor to the upheaval, with disabled people playing an important role in the revolution.[29]

The Nazis were responsible for the most extreme application of eugenics. Between July 1933 and September 1939, 350,000 people were sterilised on the grounds of heritable conditions such as 'congenital feeble-mindedness'.[30] This was followed by programmes to systematically murder disabled adults and children. It is estimated that 275,000 disabled people were exterminated through the Aktion T4 programme, although this does not account for killings that occurred after the programme officially ended in August 1941.[31] Around 5,000 disabled children were experimented on and murdered between 1939 and 1945 as part of a programme of so-called *Kinder Euthanasia* (child euthanasia). Killings continued some months after the war ended, until the occupying forces discovered doctors still routinely killing their patients.[32]

The killings were known about outside Germany, and, in some quarters, praised. One officer in the American Eugenics Society declared that the 'euthanasia' programmes showed 'great courage'; a doctor in Virginia, Joseph DeJarnette, lamented that 'the Germans are beating us at our own game'.[33] Helen Keller's fame prompted disabled people to write to her from Germany and Austria, begging for rescue from their deadly fate. To her distress, she could do nothing, since immigration laws barred entry to anyone with impairment. In an impassioned plea to the *New York Times* editor, urging him to highlight the plight facing disabled people and Jews in German-occupied territories, she wrote: 'The letters they send me, – and oh, I receive so many! ... it is impossible to assist these doubly stricken people individually, in view of the fact that other nations will not admit defectives to citizenship.'[34]

During the Nuremberg trials, directors of the Aktion T4 programme quoted in their defence the ruling from the US court that had endorsed compulsory sterilisation. There was never any punishment for the murder of disabled German citizens or compensation paid, and many of the doctors involved continued practising after the war.[35] Artist-activist Liz Crow explains that the Nuremberg courts were 'confused about whether killing disabled people was a public service. The prevailing attitudes about disabled people, that they were inferior, pitiable and burdensome, defined their judgment.'[36] Payment of compensation could in fact be avoided if the authorities could prove that a person was confined in a concentration camp under the black triangle[37] rather than for reasons of ethnicity.[38]

Prevailing attitudes towards disabled people altered relatively little after the Second World War, even as eugenics 'fell from favour'.[39] In Britain, disabled people were excluded from the welfare settlement. The implementation of the Beveridge Report has been credited with creating a 'model system of social citizenship', but it failed to guarantee against the poverty and financial exclusion of disabled people. William Beveridge was himself a keen eugenicist who believed in 'the whip of starvation' to force workers to labour.[40]

By the 1980s, it was widely recognised that the 'supposedly cradle-to-grave welfare state had actually failed millions of disabled people, not least in respect and acceptance from exclusion'.[41] While under the wartime coalition many of the personal social services that supported disabled people had become firmly embedded within local government and non-statutory organisations, the state preoccupation was with universal welfare concerns, such as the NHS.

Some commentators have concluded that the exclusion of disabled people was unintended. In their 2018 article 'From dementia tax to a solution for social care', Peter Beresford, Colin Slasberg and Luke Clements wonder if the welfare state founders may have imagined that the need for social care would dwindle as the system developed.[42] The omission of disabled people, however, is in keeping with the relationship between capitalism and disability. The provision of universal services for family, work and health contributes towards the maintenance of a healthy workforce and, through that, to productivity. Expenditure on disabled people does not.

The only benefits aimed specifically at disabled people through the welfare settlement related to industrial or war injuries. This decision was influenced by fears that any additional payment aimed at disabled people would undermine the employment incentive and betray the contributory National Insurance principle. National Assistance Board cash payments were deliberately set at subsistence level in order to maintain the incentive to obtain employment.[43]

Unlike the NHS, which was founded on the principle of resource following need, Aneurin Bevan established that the opposite would happen for social care, so the extent to which people would be helped 'will depend on our resources'. Thus, '[t]he die was cast from the very beginning: social care never broke free of the poor law principles that the welfare state was supposed to have abolished'.[44]

For the most part, disabled people in Britain remained incarcerated in large 'long-stay' hospitals characterised by degradation, cruelty and neglect until the 1980s. As Maureen Oswin wrote in 1971: 'After the passing of the NHS Act there was no rapid change in hospital building and organisation ... The big old Institutions remained, and over the years they have been up-graded rather than rebuilt.'[45]

Oswin's study of the conditions in which around 12,000 disabled children were living exposed the routine deprivation of children who never left hospital grounds, had never seen uncooked food and rarely saw their parents. On average, they experienced no more than five minutes of personal attention in every 12 hours. Conditions on different wards varied, with cockroach infestations, cold and even murder affecting the worst. The disabled campaigner Ann McFarlane, who was sent to an institution in north Norfolk after the end of the Second World War, witnessed a nine-year-old friend held under bath water by staff as a punishment, causing her to drown. Such deaths were not investigated.[46]

Lack of stimulation typified even the cleanest wards; Oswin described children '[l]ike battery hens, void lives in cot cages'.[47] Incarceration created additional impairments through lack of movement, nutrition and socialisation.[48] Children were often hungry and thirsty. Oswin witnessed 'teenage boys, who were able to drag themselves about on their knees, go into ward courtyards and suck at puddles'.[49] These conditions were normalised to many of the doctors and nurses working within them. Consequently, Oswin's work was met with defensive and aggressive reactions from colleagues and nursing trade unionists.[50] She was blacklisted by her local education authority.[51]

Disabled adults endured similar conditions. Pauline Morris's 1969 study of institutions for adults with learning difficulties found that only 1 per cent had single rooms, with the majority sleeping in large dormitories without personal possessions; only 21 per cent had their own toothbrush or hairbrush; clothing was communal and women were not supplied with bras.[52] There was little to occupy the adults during the day and they had few social relationships. Morris described wards 'where patients are deprived of almost everything which most human beings take for granted'.[53] A lesser value was clearly placed by the state on the lives of adults with learning difficulties. This was demonstrated by the comparative weekly expenditure on food for patients in different types of hospital: in hospitals for the 'mentally retarded', average spend in 1969 per patient per week was £1 19s. 10d., compared with £2 10s. 4d. in chronic sick hospitals and much more in general hospitals.[54]

It is something of a cliché nowadays to talk about care in the community as something of a 'mistake', motivated by cost saving and ultimately leading to disabled people being left without the support they need. The process of moving disabled people out of the institutions and into the community was chaotic and misjudged, motivated by a cost-cutting agenda. Slorach notes that Enoch Powell was the first major UK politician to champion closures in 1961. He had resigned from the previous Conservative administration only three years earlier due to its refusal to make huge spending cuts.[55]

However, I cannot believe that those who blithely repeat this cliché can ever have heard first-hand accounts from those who survived incarceration, witnessed behaviours that communicate experiences of unbearable abuse and neglect, or seen the physical scars, as I did when I began working in the disability sector. Social workers were aware of the physical and sexual abuse endemic within the institutions but also aware of the involvement of high-level figures. State cover-ups concerning high-profile figures such as Cyril Smith and Jimmy Savile evidence the difficulties in bringing such issues to public light. Many practitioners were concerned but felt powerless to act within the existing structures. Developing policy and practice to close the institutions was one way in which they could actively thwart the abuse.

Another barrier to change was public indifference born of the exclusion and consequent 'othering' of disability. So long as disabled people were shut away, the public's level of concern about them was limited. Researcher Pauline Morris commented in 1969: '[T]he public is ignorant and apathetic, and whilst the idea of social euthanasia is theoretically outmoded, few are prepared to bring the problem out into the light of public scrutiny if it means spending money on people who are looked at furtively and with a degree of embarrassment.'[56]

It was only after many years of abuse scandals that the Thatcher government would adopt a new policy of 'care in the community'. From a state perspective, care in the community was just the latest solution for managing the disabled population. There was insufficient investment and planning for community support to replace the infrastructure of long-stay hospitals and to this day the government has failed to meet every target for full closure. Society itself was unchanged in its view of disabled people as inferior and was not ready to accept them into the community.

As disabled people were moved out of the large institutions, abuse and mistreatment followed. Smaller residential units were established but these were often run by people who had previously worked in the long-stay hospitals, bringing with them the same attitudes and practices. The lead instigator of terrible physical, sexual, emotional and financial abuse in the Longcare scandal investigated by John Pring had started his social care career working at Broadmoor, where he learned punitive behaviour management techniques.[57] This is an extreme example but part of a wider story: disabled people may have been physically released from the large institutions but institutional approaches to social care were carried over to the new support settings. Paternalistic and disempowering delivery of social care support for disabled people continues to this day, reflected in the ongoing prevalence of the word 'care' and incidences of abuse scandals.

Prejudice and harassment from within the community also had to be contended with. Quarmby expresses her view that institutionalisation 'was very harmful, and a grave injustice had come to an end. But so too was dumping people back into a hostile society with little thought as to what would happen next.'[58] Campaigns were frequently mounted against planning applications for supported housing by residents of wealthier areas. This, together with the issue of property and land prices, has meant that services and homes for disabled people are mainly sited in the most disadvantaged and higher crime areas.

Harassment and hate crime against disabled people became commonplace. Research by Mencap in 2000 found that almost nine in ten people with a learning difficulty surveyed had experienced bullying or harassment in the previous year.[59] More than half (56 per cent) of respondents to another small online poll carried out by Scope said that they had experienced hostility, aggression or violence from a stranger because they were a disabled person.[60] Quarmby's study of violent murders of disabled people finds a link with areas of poverty and deprivation.[61]

One factor that distinguishes disability hate crime is the level of brutality involved. Torture, burning and urinating on the victim are characteristic, either leading up to or at the point of death. A representative from the Association of Chief Police Officers has described this as different from other crimes: 'It seems to be about seeing the victims suffer,' he said.[62]

Too often, the police present an added danger to disabled people. Deaths in custody of people with mental distress is a persistent injustice. A total of 23 people died in or after detention from 2017 to 2018, with official police figures recording that more than half were people with mental health conditions such as psychosis, depression and self-harm and 18 had drug or alcohol dependency.[63] In one incident in Luton reported by *Disability News Service*, two police officers were eventually found guilty of gross misconduct after attacking and chasing an autistic young man who was putting out wheelie bins at the front of his own and neighbours' homes. In another, police officers in Northampton arrested an autistic man and held him in a police cell for nine hours without medical treatment after he was the victim of a vicious disability hate crime in a local park.

Disabled people have significantly less confidence in the police than non-disabled people and are critical of inadequate sentencing for the perpetrators of violence and abuse against disabled people.

Fighting for equality

Once in the community, disabled people could begin to self-organise to challenge their oppression. The current DPM owes its origins to two organisations formed in the 1970s: the Liberation Network of People with Disabilities (LNPD) and the Union of the Physically Impaired Against Segregation (UPIAS). The latter was established after Paul Hunt wrote to the *Guardian* in September 1972 calling for a new organisation of disabled people to campaign against segregation in institutions.[64] Judy Hunt recalls how '[b]ack then [Paul] and others were seeking answers to why non-disabled society was so contemptuous of disabled people, and why it was so little recognised'.[65] Vic Finkelstein, a disabled anti-apartheid campaigner who moved to Britain, responded. Finkelstein had come to draw a parallel between black people's struggle for liberation and disabled people's fight against institutionalisation.

Through discussions, UPIAS developed a way of looking at disability that formed the basis for what Mike Oliver coined 'the social model of disability'. According to this perspective, 'it is society which disables physically impaired people. Disability is something imposed on top of our impairments by the way we are unnecessarily isolated and excluded from full participation in society. Disabled people are therefore an oppressed group in society.'[66]

The disability movement that developed in Britain was primarily concerned with three areas: promotion of the social model of disability, the campaign for civil rights, and independent living. According to independent living philosophy, independent living does not mean doing everything for yourself; it means disabled people having adequate support to be able to live and participate in the community with the same opportunities as non-disabled people and with choice and control over that support.

The independent living movement can be traced back to Ed Roberts and the Rolling Quads, a group of disabled students at the University of California in Berkeley who campaigned in the 1960s to be able to live on the campus rather than within the university hospital and for support services to be under disabled people's own control. The first Centre for Independent Living opened in Berkeley in 1971, providing peer support, information and advocacy. Following a visit to the US by a number of leading disabled activists, the first centres opened in Britain in 1984 in Hampshire and Derbyshire. Campaigners involved in these then supported centres to be set up across the country.

Organisations and Centres for Independent Living run by disabled people distinguished themselves from organisations and charities run for disabled people but controlled by non-disabled people. An umbrella body, the British Council of Disabled People (later renamed the UK Disabled People's Council) had 80 organisational members representing 200,000 disabled people by 1991.[67]

Alongside this democratically accountable structure was what Oliver referred to as 'the enforcement arm of the Disabled People's Movement', the Disabled People's Direct Action Network (DAN). Their highest-profile action occurred in 1997 when they organised a protest on Downing Street in opposition to plans by the newly elected New Labour government to cut disability welfare payments. A group of activists reached the door of Number 10 and threw red paint over it. The demonstration attracted international media attention and the government's plans were quietly dropped.[68] Protests were also targeted at charity initiatives considered to encourage pity portrayals of disabled people. ITV cancelled its biannual 24-hour 'telethon' fundraiser following a large protest by disabled campaigners in 1992. Key slogans used within the movement to this day include 'Rights not Charity' and 'Piss on Pity'.[69]

One criticism of the movement was its domination by white male wheelchair users, known as 'the wheelchair brigade'.[70] A hierarchy of impairment operated and people with other impairments often did not feel welcome. This is not surprising given the origins of the early movement at a time when disabled people were still segregated and divided within services on the basis of impairment. Finkelstein explained:

> There are, I believe, good historical reasons why people who used wheelchairs did predominate in UPIAS. They tended to be less isolated and so had greater awareness of significant social changes that were already taking place in the health and welfare services as well as political struggles and the general state of the economy. Many had been able-bodied and were familiar with social movements.[71]

One of the movement's biggest outcomes was the passage of anti-discrimination legislation in 1995. The Conservative government was shamed into action after the Minister for Disabled People at the time, Nicholas Scott, was caught lying to parliament about the costs of equal rights legislation. The resulting law, the Disability Discrimination Act (DDA), was not what disabled campaigners wanted, having campaigned instead for civil rights legislation. Provisions in the DDA were then watered down in the Equality Act 2010, which replaced it.

The pursuit of a rights agenda was itself controversial within the movement. As Finkelstein argued, parliament grants legal rights to those it defines as disabled and the focus is therefore 'on identifying characteristics, rather than the nature of society'.[72] Marta Russell highlighted the inadequacies of a rights approach in failing to acknowledge the contradictions of promoting equal opportunities in a class-based (unequal) society.[73]

A less controversial achievement within the movement was the adoption by the United Nations of the Convention on the Rights of Persons with Disabilities in 2006. The wording of the convention was developed and agreed by disabled people's representatives from across the world and is consistent with the social model of disability and the independent living philosophy. Over 160 states are now signed up to it, with the New Labour government pressured into ratification in 2009.[74]

Another pivotal moment for the disability movement in Britain was the passage of the Community Care (Direct Payments) Act 1996. This made it legal for local authorities to give disabled people cash payments with which to purchase their own social care support. Disabled people living in the community could thus exercise greater choice and control over the support they needed. The option to employ and pay their own 'personal assistants' presented an alternative to the paternalistic forms of 'care' provided by agencies and council-run support services. Direct payments radically improved the quality of many disabled people's lives, but it was also, as Vic Finkelstein described, a 'capitalist dream come true'.[75]

This model of independent living differed from the one that developed contemporaneously in Scandinavia in one slight but crucial respect: there, co-operatives led by disabled people act as the legal employer of personal assistants, who are nevertheless recruited and managed on a day-to-day basis by the disabled people they support.[76] In Britain, the part played by Deaf and Disabled People's Organisations (DDPOs)/Centres for Independent Living (CILs) is to support and advise disabled people in their roles as individual employers. Over the years, local government contracts for direct payment support services have steadily decreased in value while non-user-led organisations have undercut and won contracts away from user-led organisations. This has resulted in atomisation and the isolation of disabled employers struggling with legal duties and management responsibilities without adequate support. In this way, independent living represents both resistance and 'an exemplar of the capitalist market penetrating ever deeper into our lives'. We should thus both 'support it and be critical of it'.[77]

By the mid-1990s, the movement had gone into decline to the extent that a number of commentators predicted its eventual demise. Factors to which this has been attributed include:

- a too narrow focus on a rights agenda;[78]
- elevation of the civil rights goal and independent living to the same status within the movement as the social model;[79]
- over-rigid application of the social model;[80] and
- a failure to properly understand the social model by the leaders of the movement.[81]

It has also been suggested that the success of DAN's red paint protest in 1997 left a legacy that was difficult to follow.[82]

One element within the decline was undoubtedly the constant criticism which the social model attracted. Oliver pointed the finger at 'reputations and careers ... built on the back of these attacks'.[83] This undermining of the social model opened the back door to new approaches to disability that were designed to deny eligibility for support and benefits, as examined in Part V.[84] Oliver was not shy in allocating blame. Referring to 'the unfortunate criticisms of [the social model] and the disastrous implications these have had for disabled people',[85] he castigated '[t]hose who have talked down the social model while failing to replace it with something more meaningful or useful', telling them that they 'must bear a heavy burden of responsibility for this state of affairs'.[86]

New Labour betrayal

The New Labour government elected in 1997 promised disabled people much and delivered little. Meanwhile, they set in motion policy developments in social security and social care that were to have a devastating impact when escalated by the Tories after 2010. As Oliver and Barnes noted, 'The coming to power of a new Government seemingly more willing to listen to the voice of disabled people was a problem in itself.'[87] Once in power, Labour denied having pledged to replace the DDA with a bill of civil rights.

The Prime Minister's Strategy Unit produced the *Improving the Life Chances of Disabled People* report, published in 2005. This promised full disability equality by 2025. Among other measures, it set a target for a Disabled People's User-led Organisation on the model of a CIL in every local authority area by 2010 and led to the formation of the government Office for Disability Issues. This was followed by the Independent Living strategy, published in 2008, which aimed at increasing disabled people's choice and control through expanding personalisation beyond social care to services including housing, transport, health, employment, education and training.

During this period, the DPM, then predominantly in the shape of Deaf and Disabled People's Organisations, became accustomed to sitting in meetings discussing policy. Protesting was forgotten. Various disabled people-led engagement networks were set up at national and regional levels, including the Equality 2025 advisory group and the Network of Networks. At a local level, service user involvement mechanisms funded by local authorities and health trusts proliferated.

It is now clear that we were never in the important conversations. At the same time, New Labour was continuing work started under the previous Conservative administration to remove 1 million claimants from Incapacity Benefit and was laying the foundations for the welfare reforms that have caused so much harm to disabled people since 2010.

As Debbie Jolly wrote:

> While successive governments were delivering a stream of white papers, apparently dedicated to improving the life chances of disabled people ... welfare reform (read welfare destruction) was quietly being prepared behind our backs by the state and their market partners.[88]

In social care, too, the seeds were being sown for future cuts that would take disabled people's inclusion back decades. The personalisation agenda was sold to local authorities on the basis that it would bring savings,[89] setting us up for the situation we have now where individual support packages are targeted for cuts. A 2007 report by consultants Melanie Henwood and Bob Hudson recommended the closure of the Independent Living Fund (ILF).[90] This fund, which was established to support disabled people with high support needs to live in the community, sat under the Department for Work and Pensions. Henwood and Hudson identified this as an anomaly and advised absorption into the mainstream 'care and support' system administered by local authorities. As we shall see in the next section, merging the ILF meant cutting it and the essential daily support it provided.

Personalisation paved the way for increasing privatisation of social care services. In 2011, retired policy analyst and researcher on disability issues Jenny Morris published *Rethinking Disability Policy*. In it, she concluded: 'While direct payments (and individual personal budgets) have undoubtedly made a real difference to some disabled people's lives and challenged the assumption that a passive dependency inevitably accompanies impairment, they have also played a role in the undermining of public services, and in the shift towards the marketisation of services.'[91]

Mike Oliver warned the DPM in 1990 of the dangers of getting too close to government.[92] In 2006 he and Colin Barnes noted that this had come to pass: '[S]ince the late 1990s the combination of Government and the big charities have successfully adopted the big ideas of the disabled people's movement, usurped its language and undertaken further initiatives which promise much yet deliver little.'[93] From sitting around the table with campaigners, the government was able to learn the language and key concepts of the DPM. These were then co-opted to create the illusion of progress. Principles that started in the DPM such as 'Nothing About Us Without Us' are now commonly mainstreamed within health policy.[94] The social model was incorporated into the rhetoric used by governments, charities and quangos without any of them making any substantial changes to their practices.[95]

Operationally, DDPOs became consumed by contract culture and service delivery. Some benefited from the opportunities that became available under New Labour, taking on large local authority contracts and accruing annual turnovers in excess of £1 million.[96] This created vested interests in not speaking out against local authorities for fear of losing funding. Other DDPOs lost out, unable to compete against the economies of scale that national non-user-led organisations could offer, and they began to close.[97] Disability activists Theo Blackmore and Stephen Lee Hodgkins have described 'the development of DDPOs and their gradual colonisation, moving from a radical political and social movement to pseudo government agents'.[98]

The disability sector experienced what has been described as a 'disabling corporatism',[99] with those organisations that survived professionalised and de-radicalised. And in the void left by organisations that closed or were weakened to the point of irrelevance, the charities were only too happy to step in and reassert their positions of influence.[100]

Loss of leadership was also a significant factor in the DPM of this period. Co-option occurred, with individuals taking jobs within government or linked to the work of the Office for Disability Issues and the Disability Rights Commission (later replaced by the Equality and Human Rights Commission).[101] Others accepted government honours and took peerages. At the same time, the movement suffered from the untimely deaths and burnout with which we are all too familiar in the disability world for reasons of both impairment and the disabling barriers we face.[102]

De-radicalised, depleted and betrayed: this then was the state of the DPM when the Tories came to power as the leading partner of the Coalition government in 2010.

A history of oppression

The history of disability is marked by violence and deprivation. There is nothing natural about this state of affairs. The brutality and deceit of capitalism are apparent in the successful embedding in social consciousness of the idea that people with impairments are people of lesser worth. This conclusion is only inevitable from the perspective of the profit motive, fixed firm in capitalist social relations.

Whether disabled people are in institutions or in the community, the essential underlying relationship between disability and capitalism is unchanged. From this will always flow marginalisation and inadequate investment, and, together with these, prejudice and discrimination. At different periods and as circumstances change, disabled people will face different configurations of injustice. Our best chance to overcome these is if we are informed with an understanding of how disability fits into the wider political-economic system. To quote Finkelstein, 'We cannot understand or deal with disability without dealing with the essential nature of society itself.'[103]

PART II
TARGETING DISABLED PEOPLE

Retrogressive legislation and policy since 2010

> For the first time in the history of modern social policy things
> are getting worse for disabled people. Independent living
> opportunities amongst the current generations of disabled people
> are diminishing, and will only worsen for future generations
> unless urgent action is taken to reverse current trends.
>
> Jenny Morris[1]

In 2016, the UK became the first country in the world to be found guilty of grave and systematic violations of disabled people's rights. This was the finding of an unprecedented investigation by the UN Disability Committee into the impacts of welfare reform and austerity measures. The Committee was not claiming that conditions are worse for disabled people in the UK than elsewhere in the world; what was of such concern was the large-scale retrogression of the rights of disabled people driven forward by deliberate legislative and policy choices that the inquiry revealed.

As a world leader in disabled people's rights, the UK government was effectively sending a signal across the world that not only is it acceptable to dispense with socio-economic rights in a time of financial crisis, but that this is something governments can get away with doing. Within the limited powers of the UN Disability Committee, the investigation and its findings represented an attempt to counteract the potentially global implications of the example being set by the UK government. Their recommendations were sadly unenforceable, given that the United Nations Convention on the Rights of Persons with Disabilities is not enshrined in UK domestic legislation, and the UK government ignored the report.[2]

Regressive measures, badged as government 'reforms', have been enacted through extensive legislative and policy changes pushed through by the Conservatives in the face of sustained opposition since coming to power with the Coalition government. As a consequence, disabled people have experienced negative changes to all areas of our lives. The UN investigation focused on just three specific and interconnected areas where there was the most dramatic evidence of retrogression (social security, employment and independent living/social care[3]), but adverse impacts have also been experienced in mental health service provision, housing, education and access to justice.

Subjecting the same group of people to multiple cuts has also had a cumulative adverse impact greater than the sum of its parts. In 2018, the Equality and Human Rights Commission warned that '[d]isabled people are falling further behind in many areas, with many disparities with non-disabled people increasing rather than reducing',[4] and they called on the government to urgently adopt an 'acute focus on improving life in Britain for disabled people'.

Austerity in the UK has had a disproportionate impact on disabled people. This is the truth behind David Cameron's lie that 'we are all in it together'. Cuts to benefits (excluding pensions) and local government made up 50 per cent of the 2010 austerity plan. Disability and carers benefits make up about 40 per cent of non-pension benefits and social care makes up 60 per cent of local government expenditure. Thus, the decision to target spending reductions in these two areas automatically led to extensive cuts to income and services for disabled people. By 2021, £37 billion less will be spent on working-age social security compared with 2010, despite rising prices and living costs. Some of the most striking cuts are in disability benefits – the Personal Independence Payment (PIP) and Employment and Support Allowance (ESA) – which together will have shrunk by nearly £5 billion, or by 10 per cent, since 2010.[5]

In social care, spending has shrunk by £7 billion since 2010, with the Association of Directors of Adult Social Services warning in 2018 that social care services were on the verge of collapse in some areas of England. The combination of cuts in benefits and services was found to hit disabled people on average nine times harder than most other citizens in research carried out by the Centre for Welfare Reform. For disabled people with the highest support needs, the burden of cuts was found to be 19 times that placed on most other citizens.[6] Contrary to the government's repeated claim to be 'protecting' and 'targeting resources' on 'the most vulnerable in society', the cuts were effectively aimed at disabled people.

At the same time, decisions were made to benefit the rich and help households with the highest incomes. A 2019 report from the Fabian Society identified how changes to tax and benefit policies since 2010 have contributed to Britain's crisis of inequality and revealed that the government is providing more financial support for the richest 20 per cent of households than the poorest 20 per cent.[7] The UK-wide cost of tax-free allowances for the exchequer was £136 billion in the 2018–19 fiscal year, a rise of 43 per cent since 2012–13 in cash terms. By comparison, the government spent £94 billion on social security for working-age adults and children in Great Britain, a figure that has fallen 0.3 per cent since 2012–13.

The UK corporation tax rate has also been cut in recent years from 28 per cent in 2010 to 20 per cent, with a further fall to 17 per cent promised by 2020–21. In 2018, when Chancellor Philip Hammond received a windfall from the Office for Budget Responsibility, he chose not to end the benefit freeze a year earlier than planned but to change income tax thresholds to help the better-off.

Policy differences between England and the devolved nations show that 'neither the overall scale of spending cuts in England, nor their precise impact on protected groups, was inevitable.'[8] A distributional analysis of public spending impacts carried out for the Equality and Human Rights Commission revealed that disabled people are being hit harder in England than in the other UK administrations. In England, households with 'more disabilities' suffer much larger losses (over £2,900 per year) than those with 'fewer disabilities', largely because of social care cuts. In Wales, the losses are less pronounced, and, in Scotland, households with disabled members 'fare slightly better than non-disabled households, due to increased spending on social care, health and social housing'.[9]

Part II provides an overview of legislation, policy and practice in key areas affecting disabled people's lives since 2010. Chapter 4 focuses on welfare reform and explains changes brought in through the Work Capability Assessment (WCA), which administers ESA, the PIP and Universal Credit, and how disabled people are being failed by each. An overview is also given of other negative changes brought in through the 'bedroom tax', the ending of Council Tax Benefit and the benefit cap.

Chapter 5 looks at independent living and examines the retrogression of disabled people's living standards occurring in social care, mental health, housing, education and employment. It also considers access to justice, which is yet another area of retrogression as well as a tactic that has helped the government achieve its unpopular cuts and changes.

FOUR | Welfare 'reform'

Changes to welfare and tax brought in since 2010, referred to by the umbrella term 'welfare reform', represent the biggest shake-up of the welfare state since its inception after the Second World War. Welfare reform has been characterised by its scale and complexity as well as the ideological determination with which it has been pushed through. It is also notable for the cruelty of its impacts on the poorest and most disadvantaged members of society, including disabled people.

The sheer scale of attacks on disabled people's living standards and the numbers affected were what prompted the heightened concern of the UN Disability Committee. As of February 2019, there were 2.1 million disabled people claiming an incapacity benefit such as Employment and Support Allowance (ESA) and 3.7 million on Disability Living Allowance (DLA) or Personal Independence Payment (PIP), in addition to all those already moved onto Universal Credit (UC). Negative changes affecting receipt of these benefits have impacted on literally millions of people. Figures published in June 2018 show that, since the roll-out of PIP, which was started in 2013, 381,640 disabled people who previously received DLA had been turned down upon reassessment.

Over 1 million sanctions were applied to disabled people between 2010 and 2018. Increased use of sanctioning – where your benefits are stopped for anything between four weeks and six months – is one of the most pernicious aspects of welfare reform. This figure includes over 110,000 ESA and 900,000 Jobseeker's Allowance (JSA) sanctions of disabled people. A further 140,000 ESA and 160,000 JSA sanctions were applied to disabled claimants but later cancelled.[1]

UC was introduced in 2013. It aims to roll into one the six existing, or 'legacy', benefits including ESA, Income Support, Housing Benefit (HB), JSA, Working Tax Credits and Child Tax Credit. It is a programme beset with chaos, confusion and negative impacts for claimants. Once fully rolled out, it is due to affect around 7 million people. Some 58 per cent of households that will be affected contain a disabled member. Despite early Department for Work and Pensions (DWP) assurances that no one would lose out under UC, research conducted in 2012 identified that around 450,000 families containing a disabled member will be financially worse off.[2] This includes 100,000 families with disabled children. In 2018, Esther McVey, then Secretary of State for Work and Pensions, admitted that some people will be poorer under UC amid reports that 3.2 million households will lose more than £2,000 a year.

Welfare reform can be characterised not only by its scale, but also by its complexity. As Mary O'Hara has written, 'the volume and complexity of reforms almost beggared belief'.[3] The proliferation of impenetrable jargon and the technical density of multiple legislative and policy changes deliberately discourage analysis. They make it far harder to draw attention and explain to the wider public what has been happening.

The technical intricacies of the social security system have been further compounded by multiple legal rulings by tribunals and courts that have pushed back against discriminatory policy changes. DWP staff themselves struggle to comprehend and interpret the vast new regulations and guidance. Advice from the

DWP's UC helpline is, for example, notoriously poor. A report for Child Poverty Action Group published in May 2019 found that information provided to claimants about their UC payment and how to challenge a decision if they think a mistake has been made is inadequate and, in some instances, unlawful.[4] The government's own survey of UC claimants found that nearly a quarter (23 per cent) felt that the decision about their claim had either not been explained at all, or had not been explained clearly.

The devolved administrations have invested in various mitigating measures in an attempt to limit the adverse impacts of Conservative policy set in Westminster. The Scottish government has been spending £100 million a year since 2013 'to protect people from the worst aspects of Tory welfare cuts'.[5] Measures include fully mitigating the 'bedroom tax' (discussed later) and restoring cuts made through the removal of Council Tax Benefit.

Passage of the Welfare Reform Bill was blocked in the Northern Ireland Assembly in May 2015 after two and a half years of wrangling that rocked the political process there. Parties opposed to the legislation cited the higher rates of mental distress in Northern Ireland and the potential for even greater adverse impacts than were already being experienced in the other administrations. During this time, Westminster was fining Stormont £2 million per week as a penalty for non-implementation. Eventually a deal was struck and the welfare reform framework was enacted in Westminster rather than in the Assembly via the Welfare Reform (Northern Ireland) Order 2015. One of the mitigation measures agreed by the Northern Ireland Executive was to provide funding so that the bedroom tax would not apply there for four years.

Examples of mitigations by the devolved administrations were reported to the United Nations as part of the reporting process under the United Nations Convention on the Rights of Persons with Disabilities. Bizarrely, they were used within the overall UK government report as evidence of progressing disabled people's rights yet had been implemented in defiance of retrogressive measures enforced by Westminster.

Legislating for welfare reform

The main legislative vehicles for these changes were the Welfare Reform Act 2012, passed by the Coalition government, and the Welfare Reform and Work Act 2016, passed by the Conservatives. A savings target of £18 billion was attached to the Welfare Reform Act, which introduced the benefit cap, the bedroom tax, and UC, and abolished DLA, to be replaced with PIP, among other measures.

Passage of the Welfare Reform Act was repeatedly blocked in the House of Lords due to concern largely centred on the creation of additional child poverty. It was finally pushed through using 'financial privilege', which relates to the principle that the Lords cannot oppose tax and spending decisions agreed by the Commons. A further £10 billion of welfare cuts were then announced in Chancellor George Osborne's 2012 Spring Budget.

After the Tories were re-elected as a majority government in 2015, they passed the Welfare Reform and Work Act 2016. Among other measures, this legislated to lower the benefit cap, introduce a four-year benefits freeze, and cut ESA for people in the Work-Related Activity Group. HM Treasury forecast a total saving of £12.7 billion by 2020–21.

Further changes to policy and practice around receipt of out-of-work disability benefits were introduced through a command paper published jointly by the DWP and the Department of Health in November 2017. This was entitled *Improving Lives: the future of work, health and disability* and followed the *Improving Lives* green paper and consultation initiated a year earlier in October 2016.

The aim of these proposals was clearly expressed as an intention to make savings in the welfare budget through pushing more disabled people into work. The command paper states that 'finding work for an additional 1 per cent of eligible Employment and Support Allowance claimants in 2018/19 would save the Exchequer £240 million, and provide a boost to the economy of £260 million'.[6] The approach taken to achieve this was through greater integration of 'work and health' and the establishment of a government 'Work and Health Unit'. Health services would be increasingly encouraged to treat work as a health outcome and to focus their scarce resources on getting disabled people off out-of-work benefits.

There were suggestions in the original green paper that mandatory work-related activity should be extended to disabled people in the ESA Support Group, who were currently exempt. This was framed positively as remedying a situation in which the '1.5 million people now in the Support Group'[7] were missing out on support from Jobcentres to get into work: 'We are missing a significant opportunity to provide help to people when they could benefit most.'[8] The idea of bringing the ESA Support Group into the scope of conditionality – where receipt of benefits is dependent on engaging in set mandatory activities – was met with overwhelmingly negative criticism in consultation responses. The command paper went ahead with the introduction of a compulsory 'Health and Work Conversation' as a new stage in the application process for ESA; this would be applicable to all, with very few exceptions, but the government appears for now at least to have stepped back from mandatory work activity requirements for people assessed as being the most disabled.

The architects of welfare reform

The nightmare that is welfare reform was produced by the intersection of three different but linked neoliberal agendas: those of millionaire Chancellor George Osborne with his plan to reduce the deficit through harsh cuts to welfare spending, affecting the poorest in society; of Iain Duncan Smith as Secretary of State for Work and Pensions with his personal commitment to overhauling the social security system; and of ex-banker Lord Freud with his determination to continue the work he started for New Labour in drastically reducing the number of out-of-work disability benefit claimants. The impact of any one of these initiatives alone would have been terrible, but together they were calamitous.

The austerity measures inflicted on welfare spending by Osborne amounted to a staggering £40 billion. As Claudia Wood from the think tank Demos observed, 'For anyone, these are substantial sums of money. But for disabled people struggling with spiralling costs of living, such financial losses are life-changing.'[9]

Meanwhile, Iain Duncan Smith had his own vision, influenced by what has become known as his 'road to Damascus' moment when visiting the Easterhouse estate in Glasgow in 2002, an area with a reputation for unemployment, crime and substance dependency. Here, during his period as Conservative Party leader, Duncan Smith conceived an ambition to take people out of poverty by pushing them into employment. He set up the Centre for Social Justice think tank to develop policy proposals underpinned by this vision, which he then took forward as Secretary of State from 2010 until his resignation in 2016 through the huge and costly replacement of the existing social security system with Universal Credit.

Freud has a similar fixation with reducing 'dependency' on the social security system. New Labour appointed him to lead on reforming the social security system, despite the fact that, in his own words, he did not know 'anything about welfare at all when [he] started'. He took just three weeks to research and write the first draft of his influential 2007 report entitled *Reducing Dependency, Increasing Opportunity*.[10] Within this, he advocated for 'a long-term process of transforming the Welfare to Work system'[11] in order to tackle what he saw as the problem of '2.3 million on incapacity benefits and 600,000 lone parents on income support'.[12]

Freud's commitment to this agenda was evidenced by his decision to cross the floor and join the Conservatives in order to continue his work after Labour lost the General Election in 2010.

Employment and Support Allowance and the Work Capability Assessment

One of the areas of welfare reform that has had the most publicity is the notorious Work Capability Assessment (WCA), or 'fitness to work' test, originally administered by the French IT firm Atos. This became the subject of Ken Loach's tragic film *I, Daniel Blake*, released in 2016. The WCA tests eligibility for the out-of-work benefit ESA. Claimants found eligible for ESA are assigned to either the 'Support Group' or the 'Work-Related Activity Group' (WRAG). Those in the WRAG receive a lower benefit and must engage in work search activities in order to receive their payments. ESA is one of the six benefits being merged under UC. In what is sure to cause more confusion among benefit claimants, under UC the Support Group has been renamed the Limited Capability for Work group (LCW) and the WRAG has been renamed the Limited Capability for Work-Related Activity group (LCWRA).

ESA was a new benefit designed by New Labour to replace Incapacity Benefit (IB), with all existing IB claimants subject to reassessment. The Tories chose to roll out ESA without piloting it first or taking into consideration evidence that was already coming to light of, in some cases, fatal impacts on individual claimants wrongly found fit for work. As uncovered by *Disability News Service*, then Employment Minister Chris Grayling and Iain

Duncan Smith made the decision to go ahead with the roll-out of the WCA in the spring of 2011. This was despite a coroner having written directly to the DWP in 2010 calling for a review of the WCA following the suicide of a 41-year-old man from Bedfordshire, Stephen Carré.[13]

Stephen had been out of work since July 2007 due to severe anxiety and depression, which meant that he was rarely able to leave his home or speak to other people. He attended his WCA alone and a healthcare assessor awarded him zero points, with the result that his benefits were stopped. His body was found on 18 January 2010. Coroner Tom Osborne urged that action should be taken to prevent future tragedies. His letter arrived just before the 2010 General Election and was never acted on.

The intention behind the introduction of ESA and the WCA has always been to drastically reduce numbers claiming out-of-work benefits. New Labour set a target of 1 million fewer claimants,[14] which is now mirrored in the Tories target to get an extra 1 million disabled people into work.[15] Although there is no concrete evidence of targets limiting the numbers of claimants that assessors can find eligible for ESA per week, whistle-blowers have described pressure from managers to find claimants fit for work. Dr Greg Woods felt so strongly over one case that he resigned and spoke to the media about his experiences.[16] Secret filming of training given by Atos to doctors to carry out WCAs in 2012 suggested that staff are monitored to ensure that they do not find excessive numbers of claimants eligible; although Atos no longer has the contract to provide WCAs, it would appear that this is still the case.[17]

The DWP has consistently maintained that only 11 per cent of applicants for ESA should end up in the Support Group. This figure was included in information passed to Atos in order to cost their delivery plans for roll-out of the WCA. It was then repeated in the *Improving Lives* green paper in 2016, rounded down to 10 per cent.

Alarmingly, this figure was identified back in 2013 by Annie Howard from Disabled People Against Cuts' (DPAC's) research team to be based on a misreading of data within the DWP. What it actually represents is the percentage that it was assumed would go straight through to the Support Group without needing a WCA – that is, a minimum number of disabled people who would be found unfit for any work-related activity. However, it has been taken to represent the maximum percentage of claimants going through a WCA who should end up in the Support Group.[18] This figure continues to be used as a basis for DWP policy development. It is a significant error but one that serves the ideological goal of reducing numbers of benefit claimants.

In 2016, the government issued new guidance to staff carrying out WCA tests with the specific aim of cutting numbers found eligible. As a consequence, the number of people refused ESA soared to its highest level for three years. Central to the new guidance was interpretation of Regulations 29 and 35. Under these rules, GPs could request claimants be found eligible if they judged them to be at serious risk of, for example, self-harm or suicide if they were denied benefits or forced to engage in work-related activity. These regulations became the basis of more than half of all Support Group awards in 2015. The revised guidance downplays the significance of risk indicators and stresses that such circumstances are 'exceptional'. As journalist John Pring comments: 'The changes appeared to show that ministers had made a calculation that it was worth risking the loss of some lives so that they could cut benefits spending and force more disabled people into their discredited back-to-work programmes.'[19]

Employment and Support Allowance sanctions
ESA claimants placed in the WRAG are subject to conditionality and sanctions. They must sign a claimant commitment setting out

the work-related activity requirements they will carry out each week in return for their benefits. It is at the discretion of their Jobcentre work coach to stop their benefits if they judge that there has been a breach of the commitment.

The DWP has consistently denied that there are targets for sanctioning, but the spurious and arbitrary reasoning behind many sanctions supports the idea that targets exist – or at least some form of pressure from managers. In one example, taken from research carried out for the University of Essex and Inclusion London, a disabled claimant was told by his work coach to attend a training course under threat of sanction, only to return to the Jobcentre for his next appointment after the course to be sanctioned by a different worker. The reason given was that the training too closely matched his existing skills, so he should have been searching for a job instead.[20]

Claimants may have difficulty carrying out work-related activities expected by their work coach for reasons directly linked to impairment, for example completing written forms or using the internet. As of 2015, the largest group within the WRAG were those labelled with 'Mental and Behavioural Disorders' (248,040 people); this includes those with mental distress, learning difficulties and autism. Research by Ben Baumberg Geiger suggests that sanctions discriminate against disabled people.[21]

Conditionality and sanctioning are deeply ideological. Mounting evidence shows that they are counterproductive in the aim of moving disabled people into employment and yet the DWP remains deeply wedded to this punitive approach. Preliminary research carried out by the National Audit Office (NAO) in 2016 showed that ESA claimants who were sanctioned were less likely to gain employment in later months. This picture was supported by research published in 2017 which revealed that, as more disabled people were sanctioned, there was a corresponding increase in the number of disabled people not in work. A five-year project concluded that 'work coaches were too quick to resort to the use of a sanction, and that sanctions were disproportionate to the alleged transgression; there is an imbalance between the amount of support provided and the threat of sanctions ... [B]enefit sanctions, and the threat of them, result overwhelmingly in negative impacts that are counter-productive for both in-work and out-of-work claimants.'[22]

In spite of now overwhelming evidence against the use of sanctions, the government remains committed to a conditionality approach that will be taken even further by UC. It has steadfastly ignored the NAO's recommendation from 2016 to use its own data to evaluate the impact of sanctions in the UK. Mind's former policy officer, Tom Pollard, concluded from an 18-month secondment to the DWP that the department 'is institutionally and culturally incapable of making the reforms needed'.[23] One of the key factors behind this judgement was the DWP's 'misplaced faith in the effectiveness of conditional benefits for this group'.[24]

The Employment and Support Allowance Work-Related Activity Group cut

Another stark example of the deeply ideological nature of Tory welfare reform was the abolition of the ESA work-related activity component. This was a measure that was pushed through in the Welfare Reform and Work Act 2016, amidst fierce criticism and Tory backbench rebellion, and was intended to save £1 billion over four years. From 1 April 2017, new claimants in the WRAG would receive only the same weekly payment as for JSA, a cut of £30 per week.

The higher payment was originally calculated to account for the fact that disabled people are statistically likely to be out of work for longer periods and JSA is set at a level that can provide adequate income for only a short period. As evidence of this, by spring 2010, the JSA caseload had fallen by 700,000, while over the same period the numbers on incapacity benefits including ESA had fallen by just 90,000.

Then Chancellor George Osborne chose to see these figures as proof of a 'perverse incentive' encouraging ESA WRAG claimants to stay out of work for longer than needed. The DWP explained that it was necessary to remove this incentive that acted to 'discourage claimants with potential to work from making the most of opportunities to help them move closer to the labour market'.[25] These claims were supported by a startling lack of evidence. Even the right-wing think tank Reform concluded: 'For some people with severely limiting health conditions the financial rate is unlikely to have any impact on their chances of moving into work.'[26]

Critics of the proposal to cut the ESA work-related activity component pointed to the very real barriers to employment experienced by the nearly 500,000 disabled people in the WRAG. Research was carried out to illustrate the potential harm that the cut would cause: a survey conducted by the Disability Benefits Consortium found that almost seven in ten (69 per cent) of respondents said that cuts to ESA would cause their health to suffer; nearly a third (28 per cent) said that they couldn't afford to eat on the current amount they received from ESA; and 40 per cent had become more isolated and less able to see friends or family after their ESA was withdrawn or reduced.[27]

In response to popular outrage against the ESA WRAG cut, then Minister for Disabled People Penny Mordaunt promised a package of mitigations aimed at reducing the living costs of those in the ESA WRAG, including help with energy, broadband and phone bills. Four months after making this pledge to the Work and Pensions Committee (WPC) in November 2016, the DWP suggested to *Disability News Service* that her only success was ensuring that new WRAG claimants would be told by their Jobcentre work coaches how to secure the cheapest BT telephone tariff.[28] Campaigners have meanwhile wondered whether the government's ultimate goal is to abolish the ESA WRAG itself.

The Work Capability Assessment

The role of private firms in the WCA, which tests eligibility for ESA, is one of its most contentious aspects. This is for three main reasons. The first is the use of public money to fund the accumulation of profit in return for pushing the most disadvantaged members of society off social security and into destitution. The value of the WCA contract held by Atos was £400 million over five years. When Atos quit the contract early, Maximus took over with a new three-year contract due to run from 2015 to 2018 with an estimated value of £595 million. This contract has now been extended until July 2021. Accounts filed for the Centre for Health and Disability Assessments, the arm of Maximus that holds the WCA contract, show an operating profit for the financial year ended 30 September 2017 of more than £26 million.

Second, the culture that operates within the private contractors dehumanises claimants. This is not unique to outsourced providers but is a problem at every level of those organisations, from front-line staff to the boards of directors. Facebook posts discovered by campaigners in 2011 exposed assessors describing claimants as 'parasitic wankers' and 'down and outs'. Assessors are now more careful with their public posts. Evidence from whistle-blowers confirm that management priorities are target- and profit-driven at the expense of accurate assessments and the welfare of claimants. One Maximus whistle-blower told the *Daily Mirror*: 'The US directors treat the UK contract like a cash machine. In the US this would be considered "carpet-bagging".

Working for Maximus was like working for Gordon Gekko. Their attitude is totally incompatible with a contract dealing with vulnerable people.'[29]

The third and perhaps biggest issue of contention is the role of private companies in the actual design of the WCA, in particular the US insurance giant Unum Provident. Unum's involvement and how the company stood to gain from changes to the UK social security system have been examined in detail by disabled researcher Mo Stewart. Stewart demonstrates a clear link between the development of welfare reform policy and aggressive claims management practices adopted within the US insurance industry to deny payouts.[30] Given the well-documented influence of Unum Provident as advisers to the UK government on social security and their relationship with Atos, it cannot be coincidence that there are such similarities between tactics used in the US insurance industry and the obstructions, delays and dismissal of medical evidence common to experiences of the WCA.

Numerous fatalities have been linked to the WCA. In addition to the Stephen Carré case mentioned above, the Mental Welfare Commission for Scotland (MWC) carried out an investigation into a similar case that occurred at the end of 2011 when a woman with mental distress committed suicide following a 'fit for work' decision. The woman, identified only as Miss DE, had a history of depression and was on significant medication, but scored zero points from her assessment by Atos. The MWC report said that it could see no other factor 'in her decision to end her life' and raised numerous concerns about the WCA process.

Serious, systemic problems run throughout the administration of the WCA despite five independent reviews. In oral evidence to the WPC, Dr Paul Litchfield, who carried out the fourth and fifth of these, suggested that the WCA is fundamentally flawed. He said: 'There have been efforts to adjust it and improve it over time, but when it starts from a position which is designed as imperfect, you're lucky if it gets more perfect, it is just as likely to get more imperfect as you adapt it.'[31]

The percentage of decisions overturned at appeal in favour of the claimant has grown steadily. According to figures for July to September 2019, the rate had risen to 77 per cent for ESA and 76 per cent for PIP. This is clear evidence of a failure to make effective improvements. In 2013, the High Court ruled that placing the burden of evidence on claimants 'substantially disadvantages claimants with mental health problems, because the system is designed to deal with a high volume of claimants who can accurately report the way in which their disability affects their fitness to work'.[32] Issues such as difficulties collecting medical evidence to support a claim and inaccuracies in assessment reports remain as problematic as ever.

GPs can be reluctant to provide medical evidence for benefit claims, and many levy a fee. A survey of GP surgeries carried out by Citizens Advice in 2014 found that 29 per cent of respondents did not provide medical evidence as standard to all patients, 15 per cent turned down all requests, and 50 per cent of those who did provide evidence charged their patients for doing so. Of these, 61 per cent charged sums between £10.01 and £50. Once a case goes to appeal, the courts request and pay for medical evidence. Provision of additional evidence at this stage accounts for the high percentage of decisions overturned at appeal. Knowing this, the DWP has failed to make changes to the application process to remove or significantly ease the burden of evidence for claimants. It is unclear what if anything the government has done to action recommendations in this regard given by the High Court in 2013.

Even if claimants do provide full, indisputable medical evidence at their assessment, there is no guarantee it will be taken into consideration or even understood. The WCA is not a medical assessment but a functional assessment. It is carried out by a generalist healthcare professional who may not be qualified or have knowledge relevant to the particular conditions of the claimants they assess. A report from the Public Accounts Committee highlighted that assessors have 'an incomplete understanding of particular conditions, especially fluctuating and mental health conditions' and recommended the DWP ensure it has 'well-trained, knowledgeable assessors sensitive to the complex issues that claimants are dealing with, particularly those with mental health conditions'.[33] In May 2016, the government accepted the Committee's recommendation to make significant progress with a target date of spring 2017. To date, there is no evidence indicating improvement.

Assessment contractors have also consistently struggled with quality standards. In 2016, the NAO found that not one of the companies carrying out the assessments met the government's quality standards threshold, and, while the cost of providing assessments was rising, providers were still struggling to meet expected performance standards. In 2018, an analysis of the government's own figures by *Disability News Service* raised concerns that tens of thousands of applications for ESA could have been decided by civil servants on evidence from WCA reports that should have been rejected because their quality was 'unacceptable'. Poor disabled access to many of the assessment centres used by the outsourced contractors continues to be an issue for claimants, with wheelchair users having to travel many miles for their nearest accessible centre in some cases.

Personal Independence Payment
In June 2010, Chancellor George Osborne announced plans to cut DLA expenditure by 20 per cent by replacing it with PIP.

The government's own figures for 2010–11 showed benefit fraud at just 0.5per cent, so this target could only be achieved by denying benefits to genuinely disabled people. Every disabled person in receipt of DLA was expected to undergo reassessment as the new benefit was rolled out. While the stated aim of PIP was to 'target support at those who need it most', the intention from the outset was clearly about budget savings, regardless of human cost. The DWP predicted that once PIP was fully rolled out, 428,000 fewer people would qualify for the higher-rate mobility element than they would have under DLA, with total savings of £2.17 billion. Meanwhile, private companies would profit from administering the assessments. In 2017, Capita and Atos received nearly £255 million between them to perform PIP assessments.

Scrapping DLA was a deeply unpopular move. The government consultation launched in December 2010 received more than 5,500 responses, overwhelmingly against the proposals and warning of the dangers of pushing an already disadvantaged group deeper into poverty, yet these were roundly ignored by government.

DLA and PIP are benefits designed to cover the extra unavoidable costs of being disabled. They also act as a passporting benefit, giving access to other entitlements such as a blue badge for parking and Carers' Allowance. Neither are means-test so disabled people in work should be equally eligible.

There are two components: mobility and care. Whereas under DLA there were three levels of award under each component (lower, middle and higher), under PIP there are just two (standard and enhanced). Claimants in receipt of the higher-rate mobility element for DLA or enhanced mobility for PIP are eligible to exchange cash payments for a vehicle through the not-for-profit scheme Motability. This provides essential assistance with accessing the community, including travel to health appointments, for those unable to use public transport or who face severe mobility restrictions.

The assessment process for PIP is similar to ESA in that it involves completion of a questionnaire followed by face-to-face assessment with a generalist healthcare professional. Awards for the two components are decided on a points basis, which scores whether claimants meet a set of criteria called 'descriptors'. These descriptors and the guidance for assessors on how to interpret them have been subject to various challenges concerning unfair restriction of eligibility. Whereas under DLA it was possible to get a lifetime award for conditions that do not change over time or are progressive, the big idea with PIP was to constantly reassess claimants. Officially this is to check if claimants' conditions have improved and if they consequently no longer need the payments. In reality this is experienced as an exercise in hounding disabled people off benefits.

Both the roll-out of PIP and the assessment process itself have been beset with difficulties and have been criticised for their severely detrimental impacts on claimants. The scale of trying to reassess all DLA claimants without adequate planning or resources led to delays and backlogs for new applicants in desperate need of access to the benefit. In 2014, the Public Accounts Committee labelled the government's handling of the situation 'nothing short of a fiasco' that has caused distress to thousands of sick and disabled people. Atos was singled out for criticism for misleading the DWP about its capabilities when bidding for the £1 billion contracts. The Committee's report found that many claims were delayed by more than six months, with some claimants taken to hospital due to the stress of the process and being unable to afford medically prescribed diets.

To date there have been two independent reviews of PIP – one carried out by Paul Gray, former chair of the Social Security

Advisory Committee, and one focused specifically on the roll-out in Northern Ireland – yet the same fundamental problems with the system remain unchanged. The rate for PIP decisions overturned at appeal has now risen to 76 per cent.

Contempt for claimants and disregard for their welfare form one of the fundamental problems with the assessment process. Disbelief of claimants' own accounts of the disabling barriers they face is built into the design of the system. From this flows a dehumanisation of the disabled people being assessed and a disregard for safeguarding. As a consequence, claimants understandably now have an 'inherent distrust' of the system, as found by the WPC.

Undercover filming by Channel 4 in 2016 exposed a culture of contempt among PIP assessors employed by Capita.[34] Footage showed one assessor, Alan Barham, boasting that he would largely complete assessment forms before meeting the claimant. He told the reporter that he would 'completely dismiss' claimants' explanations for why they needed disability benefit, and rely instead on his own 'informal observations' to 'catch them out'. Barham also mocked a disabled claimant, telling the undercover reporter that her disability was 'being fat'. 'She asks for help to wipe her arse because she's too fucking fat to do it herself,' he said. Barham, who was subsequently found guilty of gross misconduct and sacked by Capita, argued that he had been made a scapegoat. He contacted *Disability News Service* to say that nearly everything he was caught saying by *Dispatches* was standard practice and was therefore 'driven by Capita'. His claims are supported by the fact that little changed following his dismissal.[35]

Similar issues are experienced by claimants undergoing PIP assessments, whether at the hands of Capita or Atos. This indicates that the root of the problem lies deeper than with the respective outsourced providers – at the level of the fundamental intention and design of the system. PIP assessment reports from both providers are notoriously inaccurate, commonly riddled with factual mistakes and bear little or no relation to the actual assessment that took place. One explanation for this is that assessors are under pressure to complete reports within time frames that are simply too short. An Atos whistle-blower speaking out in 2018 said that assessors are given as little as 15 minutes to read claimants' medical history before interviewing them. She described the process as a 'relentless conveyer belt', with assessors googling medical conditions and copying and pasting between assessment reports to save time.[36] Denying assessors the time to conduct thorough assessments is itself contemptuous of claimants, whose lives literally depend on their receipt of social security payments.

The full truth appears even darker: the scale of errors in assessment reports, including statements that are the complete opposite of what claimants have told assessors, has led to accusations of deliberate dishonesty and lying. Eight months after an investigation by *Disability News Service* (DNS) began, DNS had a database of more than 200 cases in which disabled people described – in varying levels of detail – how assessors lied in their written reports. Examples included a woman disabled as a result of stage three breast cancer and awarded zero points who said that she was 'utterly shocked' when she read the report because it was 'full of complete lies', including the assessor stating that her daughter takes her shopping every week, when she lives in Northern Ireland and her daughter has lived in England for the last 16 years. Another, who stayed in his wheelchair throughout his PIP assessment, was said by his assessor to have got up from the wheelchair and walked about. The DWP, Atos and Capita all refused to launch an investigation into the claims of widespread dishonesty.[37]

The roll-out of PIP has been dominated by attempts to limit eligibility: that is, to take benefits away from those already in receipt of them and to deny new claims. In contrast to the government's oft-repeated claim to be protecting the 'most vulnerable', this target-driven approach dismisses the needs of disabled people and their families, for whom help with extra costs provides a lifeline.

The government failed to make the savings it intended from the introduction of PIP, but not for want of trying. One example of their determination to restrict eligibility in the face of widespread opposition and evidence of the detrimental impacts on claimants was the decision to introduce a '20-metre rule'. This had not been mentioned in the original PIP consultation. Under DLA, if you struggled to walk more than 50 metres you qualified for the higher rate. Under PIP, this was reduced to 20 metres to qualify for the enhanced rate. According to government figures, with the criteria set at 20 metres, the number of people receiving higher rates of mobility support was set to plunge from 1,030,000 (if DLA had not been replaced by PIP) to just 602,000 by 2018. They also predicted that 548,000 of the 892,000 working-age people who were receiving the higher rate of the DLA mobility component in February 2013 would not receive the enhanced mobility rate of PIP once they were transferred to the new benefit.

A judicial review launched against the introduction of the 20-metre rule forced the DWP to rush through a consultation in 2013. Only five individuals out of the 1,142 organisations and individuals who took part in the second consultation agreed with the reduced mobility criteria. It was nevertheless retained. The judicial review, which could only be conducted under the technicality of whether the government had paid due regard to impact, and not on the merits or otherwise of the policy itself, was dismissed: the government had fulfilled its obligation to consult and was fully aware of the objections but chose to ignore them.[38]

A very public U-turn and embarrassment for the Tories were the outcomes of another attempt to limit eligibility in March 2016.

The government planned to halve the number of points a claimant was awarded if they used specially adapted aids and appliances. Their argument was that the use of aids and appliances reduces the extent to which a person is disabled and thus decreases their level of need. According to the Spring Budget, the policy change would save £4.4 billion by 2020. Disabled campaigners and charities were united in their opposition to a measure that would result in 370,000 disabled people losing an average of £3,500 a year. Within the same budget, tax giveaways were promised to the richest members of society, with noticeable gains for the top 50 per cent of earners.[39]

In the midst of the outcry, Iain Duncan Smith resigned his long-held position as Secretary of State for Work and Pensions – more likely prompted by upheaval within the Tory party over Brexit as opposed to a newly discovered conscience. He claimed that he was not in favour of the welfare cuts to begin with and that the Chancellor's economic strategy was 'deeply unfair'. In a public resignation letter, he wrote: 'I have for some time and rather reluctantly come to believe that the latest changes to benefits to the disabled and the context in which they've been made are a compromise too far.' The proposals were promptly axed. The Chancellor refused to apologise but the fiasco badly damaged his reputation.

Other attempts to limit eligibility have been overturned as a result of legal action initiated by claimants. The case with the largest implications was taken in response to changes to regulations to restrict eligibility for those with psychological distress under the 'Moving Around' and 'Planning and Following a Journey' descriptors. These were predicted by the DWP to affect around 164,000 disabled people. They were vociferously opposed by campaigners and rushed through by the government in such a way as to deliberately avoid scrutiny by parliament in February 2017.

In December 2017, the High Court ruled that the changes were 'blatantly discriminatory' and commented that the wish to save money could not justify such an unreasonable measure.[40] The judgement gave no room for the government to appeal.

The future of PIP as a non-means-tested benefit helping with the extra costs of disability is under threat. This was brought sharply into focus by the announcement made by the Work and Pensions Secretary, Amber Rudd, in March 2019 concerning government plans to merge the assessments for ESA and PIP. She claimed that this would ease stress for claimants by reducing the number of assessments they are required to go through. Campaigners are fearful that the plans are the latest aspect of a long-held intent by government to do away with DLA/PIP altogether.

Mandatory Reconsideration

Mandatory Reconsideration (MR) is a calculated tactic used by the DWP to discourage claimants from challenging wrongful benefit assessment decisions. It was introduced in April 2013 for UC and PIP claims, and in October 2013 for all other benefits administered by the DWP, including ESA. The high rate of decisions overturned at appeal had been the subject of negative publicity in the years preceding the introduction of MR. MR creates a stage that claimants must go through before they can appeal a benefits assessment decision at tribunal where the case is reviewed by a DWP 'decision maker'.

Figures cited by the WPC show that of the almost 1 million MRs of PIP and ESA decisions since 2013, 82 per cent of PIP MRs and 89 per cent of ESA MRs upheld the original decision. This is consistent with a performance indicator, uncovered through a Freedom of Information request, which the DWP has since publicly claimed to have dropped, that 80 per cent of MRs should uphold the original decision. MR is thus little more than a rubber-stamping exercise in support of the assessor's finding and designed to block access to justice. Between 2013 and September 2017, 557,000 people who were turned down at MR failed to then go on to appeal.

During MR, claimants are not entitled to receive the benefits they are contesting. The process can take over six weeks and has been consistently criticised as a way to ensure that claimants wrongfully denied benefits will drop out of the system rather than go through to appeal. Once claimants go on to appeal, they are then entitled to 'ESA pending appeal'. However, this is not paid automatically and claimants need to provide fit notes (as sick notes have been rebranded) from their GP to their local Jobcentre. Campaigners have recently exposed how misleading letters sent by the DWP to GPs have blocked access to ESA pending appeal for untold numbers. The WPC has been critical of MR, stating: 'The claim made by the government that MR has not restricted access to the appeals process (for welfare benefit decisions) is un-evidenced. Anecdotally we hear from many Disabled people who cannot cope with going through both MR and an appeal and give up despite the impoverishment it results in.'[41]

Universal Credit

Universal Credit (UC) is the Tory flagship welfare reform programme. Billions have been invested in it already and according to the current target it will have taken over 13 years to roll out. It is an utter disaster that critics believe to be unsalvageable. You might imagine that a programme due to affect around 7 million people would be subject to comprehensive planning and impact assessment. Instead, the roll-out has been implemented through a 'test and learn' approach that is only suitable for smaller projects. The result has been almost unbelievably poor planning and a considerable waste of public money at a time of supposed austerity.

The people who have suffered most from this have been the poorest and disabled members of society, people reliant on the social security system who have lost out and, in too many cases, whose lives have been destroyed by their experiences. On his visit to the UK in 2018, the United Nations Special Rapporteur on extreme poverty and human rights, Philip Alston, wrote:

> [T]here seems to be an unacknowledged risk that this approach could treat vulnerable people like guinea pigs and wreak havoc in real people's lives. 'Test and learn' cannot be a decade-long excuse for failing to properly design a system that is meant to guarantee the social security of so many, and it does not remedy the damage done to those who were thrown into debt or out of their houses, or made to rely on food banks before the improvements kicked in.[42]

UC is promoted as a simplification of the existing social security system. At face value this may sound like a good idea, but in practice this is an incredibly complex endeavour that involves attempting to align the systems of two different government departments – Her Majesty's Revenue and Customs (HMRC) and the DWP – so they are capable of sharing up-to-date information.

In January 2019, the High Court ruled that the DWP's method of assessing earned income under UC is unlawful, and there continue to be flaws in how HMRC's Real Time Information system interacts with the DWP, leading to incorrect benefit reductions. The view from UC service centres that deal with the administration of the new system is one of chaos. An anonymous case manager blogging about his and his colleagues' experiences across several offices writes: 'Universal Credit is an expensive, badly organised, error-strewn, easy to defraud shambles.'[43]

UC was the big idea within former Work and Pensions Secretary Iain Duncan Smith's vision of a system that stops people ending up trapped in 'worklessness' and 'dependency'. It is deeply ideological with a strongly embedded principle of conditionality – that claimants must demonstrate required activity in return for their benefits. The introduction of mandatory 35 hours per week job search requirements forces claimants into a charade of activity of questionable value for finding appropriate work. Claimants have spoken of endless CV writing workshops, training that is below their existing skills levels and pressure to take up self-employment. For the first time, under UC, claimants in part-time employment will be expected to look for extra work at risk of being sanctioned. Estimates have indicated that 40 per cent of DWP staff may themselves be affected by in-work conditionality under UC, raising questions from the PCS trade union (Public and Commercial Services Union) about who would manage their claims.

Sanctions have rocketed under UC: in December 2017 around 0.3 per cent of JSA claimants were experiencing a sanction compared with 8.2 per cent of UC claimants required to search for work. The system that has been created is highly punitive and disempowering for claimants with no proven benefits to justify it. The NAO stated: 'Both we, and the Department [DWP], doubt it will ever be possible for the Department to measure whether the economic goal of increasing employment has been achieved.'[44]

The roll-out of UC has been beset with difficulties, delays and waste due to poor planning. Implementation of the system was found to be 'extraordinarily poor' by the WPC in 2013. The chair at the time, Margaret Hodge, criticised the way in which the 'failure to develop a comprehensive plan has led to extensive delay and the waste of a yet-to-be-determined amount of public money'. It was estimated that at least £140 million of IT assets would have to be written off. Implementation costs, initially forecast to be around £2 billion, later grew to over £15 billion. More than 3 million recipients of the legacy benefits were expected to have transferred to the new system by 2017, but the full move will not now be completed before 2023 at the earliest.

Using Freedom of Information requests, campaigner John Slater is attempting to piece together the strategic and operational failings of the UC programme. Slater believes that UC was a 'total mess' in its early years, before the DWP brought in outside experts to assess what was going wrong, leading to a major 'reset' in 2013. Although he considers there to have been some improvements since then, he suspects that it can never be made fit for purpose. Slater told *Disability News Service*: 'Once something on this scale has gone so horribly wrong, I don't think you can ever fully recover it and get it to the place it would have been if it had been run properly from the start. I've seen this with other programmes and projects.'[45]

The failure of the DWP to grasp the enormity of the task has had a direct adverse impact on claimants. From January to October 2017, 40 per cent (20,000 households) waited in total around 11 weeks or more for full payment, nearly double the target waiting time. The majority of claimants do not have the money to manage over this period and go into debt as a result. Just a third of new claimants whose award included a payment for disability received their UC award on time and in full, according to an inquiry by the WPC in 2018.[46]

The design of UC actively disadvantages claimants in a number of ways, with a disproportionate negative impact on those who are disabled. UC claims are made and paid by household. This means that claimants must keep the DWP informed of their relationship status and living arrangements at all times; if not,

their benefits are sanctioned. This raises issue of privacy and surveillance but also, for people with particular impairments, a need
for clear and accessible communication of UC rules that differ
from legacy benefits. There is concern that treating income by
household can lead to individuals becoming financially trapped
in abusive relationships. Disability is also a factor here, with disabled women twice as likely to be victims of domestic abuse.[47]

UC is paid monthly in arrears direct to the claimant. This is a
deliberate design choice that differs from legacy benefits, which
were paid more frequently and with Housing Benefit going direct
to the landlord. The intention was to create an experience more
similar to being in work in order to teach budgeting skills. What
this approach has failed to recognise is that low-paid work is also
commonly paid more frequently. Research suggests that most
of the one in three UC claimants who are working receive their
pay cheques on a weekly or fortnightly basis instead of monthly.
It is much harder to budget on a low income; for example, if
your child has holes in their shoes and you have enough money
in your account, are you really going to deny them a new pair
even though it risks leaving you without money at the end of the
month? People with certain impairments may never learn the
maths skills needed to budget.

Unsurprisingly, the roll-out of UC has seen a dramatic increase
in rent arrears. Nearly three-quarters (73 per cent) of UC tenants
are in debt, compared with less than a third (29 per cent) of all
other tenants. A report published in October 2017 by Southwark
Council found that UC has the potential to be 'catastrophic' and
lead to a spiral of debt for claimants.[48] The report found that, 20
weeks after transferring from the legacy benefit system to UC,
the average claimant had accrued £156 of arrears. In Southwark
alone, where 12 per cent of council tenants had moved onto UC,
rent arrears totalled over £5.3 million, and one food bank in the

London borough reported an increase in the number of referrals by 94 per cent.

The other key feature of UC is its 'digital by default' approach, which is inaccessible to many disabled people. Disabled people are statistically less likely to use the internet for reasons linked to both impairment and cost: according to the Office for National Statistics (ONS) in 2017, 80.8 per cent of disabled people used the internet compared with 95.8 per cent of non-disabled people. Being able to complete complex forms online is yet another consideration. Lloyds Bank UK Consumer Digital Index 2018 found that 21 per cent of the UK population did not have five basic digital skills and 16 per cent were not able to fill out an online application form. Disabled people will be disproportionately represented within these groups. According to a DWP survey in June 2018, only 54 per cent of all claimants were able to apply online independently without assistance. Although there are options available such as face-to-face visits for claimants, there is no evidence of central data modelling undertaken to ascertain the level of need for reasonable adjustments. A written Parliamentary Question on this was effectively unanswered, which is a clear indication that it did not happen;[49] in meetings with DWP officials they say that accessibility arrangements are the responsibility of local Jobcentres.

In the expectation that over 80 per cent of claimants will eventually manage all benefit-related aspects of their claim online, over 100 Jobcentres have been closed with a loss of around 750 jobs. However, mandatory personal attendance at Jobcentre interviews remains a core requirement of UC. The closures are not only short-sighted but represent one among a number of aspects of UC that have disproportionate detrimental impacts on disabled people.

Ongoing contact with the Jobcentre via the UC online system is a condition of continuing to receive benefits, yet research by the

Government Digital Service that set up the system showed that 30 per cent of UC claimants cannot set up the online account that UC uses. As the WPC pointed out: 'Some disabled people – for example, people with severe learning disabilities – will never be able to use all online systems independently.' It is barely believable that an issue as basic as accessibility could have been so badly misjudged within the development of a system costing billions of pounds. The DWP was so busy focusing on the type of people they want to change claimants into that it seems to have forgotten to look at who they actually are.

There is considerable concern about how disabled claimants will be safely moved onto UC, given the inaccessibility of the system in addition to reductions in support for disabled people through cuts to local services. 'Managed migration', the process of moving claimants of legacy benefits onto UC, will see over a million ESA claimants needing to transfer. The DWP says that it will safeguard claimants moving from ESA to ensure that no one has their benefits stopped before they have made a successful claim for UC, but it has been criticised for providing next to no detail on how it will manage this. The charity Mind has warned that 750,000 disabled people could be left without any income if they are not sufficiently safeguarded during the transition.

There are many points at which the transition could go wrong – from claimants not receiving or understanding letters telling them that they need to reapply under UC to claimants not having the support to do so within the time limits. Mind pointed to the well-documented difficulties experienced by disabled claimants who have already moved onto UC to suggest that many more will be at risk of 'slipping through the net' during the migration, potentially leaving them without any income and exacerbating their impairments. Despite this, at the time of writing, the government refuses to entertain the idea of allowing automatic transfer, whereby the

DWP would be responsible for transferring claims from legacy benefits onto UC without requiring claimants to take action.

Several key groups of disabled people lose out financially under the new system, including 100,000 disabled children who stand to lose up to £28 a week; 230,000 severely disabled people who could receive between £28 and £58 a week less; and up to 116,000 disabled people who work who could be at risk of losing around £40 per week. In this latter category are disabled people in receipt of Enhanced and Severe Disability Premiums (EDP and SDP), neither of which exist under UC.

Transitional protections were put in place to protect existing EDP and SDP claimants from financial loss but these applied only to claimants moving onto UC through 'managed migration'. The transitional protections did not cover claimants moving onto UC through a change of circumstance: for example, moving from an area where UC has not yet been rolled out to one where it has. The WPC put this down to 'serious error' within the DWP. Whether oversight or otherwise, once the limitations of transitional protection were raised, the DWP fought against compensating claimants negatively affected in this way. Two disabled men who had lost over £170 per month when they were moved onto UC took a judicial review and won. The High Court ruling found that the Secretary of State for Work and Pensions had unlawfully discriminated against them.[50]

A week before the judgement was handed down, Esther McVey announced that no one in receipt of SDP would be made to move onto UC until transitional protection were in place. The High Court did not find that removal of EDP and SDP under UC was itself discriminatory, so new claimants will still not be able to receive these additional payments. The implication of the ruling was that around 10,000 disabled people who had already been moved onto UC and had lost out financially were owed back payments. The DWP consulted on and passed regulations providing a flat rate of £80 per month in compensation, despite calls for full losses of £180 per month to be recompensed. Again, the Secretary of State for Work and Pensions was taken to judicial review and again the High Court ruled in favour of the claimants.

Through UC, disabled people are required to have more frequent contact with front-line DWP staff, who often lack the understanding and skills to work appropriately with people with different impairments. This raises safeguarding concerns, in particular for claimants who live with mental distress, are neurodivergent or have learning difficulties. A survey by PCS union published in February 2018 revealed that nearly three-quarters of front-line UC staff believe that they have not been sufficiently well trained to do their job properly and feel ill-equipped to 'deal with some of the most vulnerable members of society'.

Jobcentre staff are supposed to provide support with applications but they may not have the necessary skills. According to DWP research cited by the NAO, 'some staff found it difficult to support claimants because they: lacked the time and ability to identify claimants who needed additional support; lacked the confidence to apply processes flexibly and make appropriate adjustments; and felt overwhelmed by the volume of claimants reporting health problems'.[51]

It is increasingly common for advocates, friends and family to accompany disabled claimants to Jobcentre appointments in an attempt to protect them from inappropriate treatment by front-line staff who either do not understand or refuse to make reasonable adjustments for impairment. In just one example of this, the Deaf and Disabled People's Organisation Inclusion London was contacted by a woman in North London desperate to find support for two separate neighbours, both with a long history of serious and enduring mental distress, who had become too frightened to attend their Jobcentre appointments alone. One, who had anorexia, was told by his work coach to go shopping for food in order to develop his social skills.

UC is a major embarrassment for the Tories. There is a constant flow of stories in mainstream and social media about people whose experience of UC is that they have had the social security safety net snatched from under them. DPAC released a report compiling hundreds of stories collected across just 16 weeks from January to May 2019 evidencing impacts including homelessness, debt, hunger, survival crime, prostitution and suicide.[52]

At the same time, the programme is failing to meet the government's own objectives. The NAO concluded in its highly critical report that 'the project is not value for money now, and that its future value for money is unproven'.[53] As a consequence, UC is an area where the government is extremely nervous and where they can be pushed to make concessions. Examples of this include the announcement in October 2017 that the UC helpline would be moving to a freephone number following a public outcry against the high charges claimants were incurring on the previous 0345 number; and the announcement in the 2017 Autumn budget that the waiting time for new UC claimants to receive their first payment would be reduced from six weeks to five. In 2019, in her first landmark speech as Work and Pensions Secretary, Amber Rudd outlined a number of changes designed to make UC fairer, including pilot schemes to provide more frequent payments for new claimants, a new online system for private landlords and a more flexible approach to childcare provisions.

The *Telegraph* wrote in 2010 that UC 'will be the reform, above all others, against which the success of this administration will be measured'. This is likely to be true, but not in the way Iain Duncan Smith envisaged. The government remains committed to driving UC forwards despite its many well-evidenced failings. Given the amount of money and time invested, it would be highly embarrassing to admit how poorly managed it has been. The punitive approach of UC also serves the government's economic agenda of ensuring a flow of workers into rising numbers of badly paid, insecure jobs. The more they push on, the greater the mess becomes.

For disabled people already hit by the introduction of ESA and PIP alongside cuts to independent living support, UC represents yet more hardship, stress and financial loss. There are a number of ways in which UC is particularly problematic for disabled people. It is all the more concerning, therefore, that the DWP is not able to systematically identify and monitor the progress of disabled people who have started the UC process as it does not collect data on these groups within its systems. Conveniently for the DWP, this ensures an absence of information that would be needed to evidence discriminatory impacts on disabled claimants. The only hope is that disabled people can unite with other groups adversely impacted by UC, such as low-paid workers and single mothers, to build a stronger resistance.

Housing-related changes
There are a number of additional key legislative and policy changes related to housing that have adversely affected disabled people on such a scale as to need mentioning. Many people are hit by all or a number of them at the same time and they provide further evidence of the depth and complexity of the changes brought in through the welfare reform programme.

'Bedroom tax'
One of the most notorious Tory welfare reforms is what is commonly known as the 'bedroom tax'. This is the name given by critics to what the government calls the 'removal of the spare room

subsidy', also sometimes referred to as the 'under-occupation penalty'. It came into force on 1 April 2013 and deducts Housing Benefit from those living in social housing who are deemed to have a spare room according to set size and occupancy criteria. The reduction is 14 per cent for one spare bedroom and 25 per cent for two or more. When the United Nation's Housing Rapporteur visited the UK just six months after the deduction came in, she was disturbed by the extent of unhappiness caused by the bedroom tax and struck by how heavily this policy was affecting 'the most vulnerable, the most fragile, the people who are on the fringes of coping with everyday life'.[54]

Justification given by government was that this measure would remove 'unfairness' from the current housing system whereby those in the private rented sector receive Housing Benefit capped at Local Housing Allowance (LHA) rates. LHA was introduced in 2008 and is calculated based on the number of rooms the claimant's household is deemed to need according to set criteria, not the number of rooms in the property or the amount of rent charged by the landlord. Tenants can be caught with a significant discrepancy between their LHA and available rentals.

The DWP claimed that the bedroom tax provides 'an economic incentive for working age tenants to move to smaller properties where their accommodation is considered larger than necessary'. Disabled adults who needed an additional bedroom for an overnight carer were exempt from reductions for that room.

The biggest issue with this policy is that there are not sufficient numbers of smaller properties available for everyone affected to move to, leaving individuals and families stuck in a situation where their Housing Benefit is not enough to cover their rent. The government recognised in its own equality impact assessment that there may be insufficient properties to downsize to. A year after the bedroom tax came in, housing associations reported the scale of this problem. In England alone there were 180,000 tenants under-occupying two-bedroom homes, but only 85,000 smaller homes available. The scarcity of smaller accommodation was especially striking in rural areas.

Many of the individuals and families pushed into this situation did not have the option of moving into employment or taking on extra work to cover the difference: more than two-thirds of those affected by the bedroom tax are disabled people. As of May 2017, there were 414,000 households in Great Britain who had a deduction made from their Housing Benefit due to the removal of the spare room subsidy. Of these, there were 278,000 where the claimant or partner was receiving DLA, PIP or ESA. These figures do not account for disabled people not in receipt of those benefits, so the actual percentage is likely to be much higher.[55]

Additional factors affecting disabled people include the general chronic shortage of accessible properties, narrowing still further the pool of available accommodation for downsizing, as well as the particular barriers linked to a person's impairment that a move could present. This is all aside from the question of whether everyone, regardless of their income level, has a right to a secure tenancy and a home for life.

As a mitigating measure to assist those struggling to pay their rent, the government contributed additional funding to the Discretionary Housing Payment (DHP) fund, which tenants can access through their local council. This fund was designed to provide short-term payments and so tenants caught by the bedroom tax must continuously reapply with no guarantee of success. A few months after it came in, a survey by Papworth Trust found that three in ten disabled people (29 per cent) hit by the tax had been turned down for a DHP.

Despite widespread opposition and a number of forced concessions, the bedroom tax remains in place to this day, contributing to rising poverty and immiseration. The campaigns against it nevertheless played a valuable role in exposing the wider iniquities of the welfare reform agenda. There was popular support in the early years of the Coalition government for the idea of needing to 'fix a broken welfare system'. The clear unfairness of the bedroom tax, imposed on people the government knew would neither be able to afford it nor move away from it, acted as a wake-up call to the public. This opened the way to a wider appreciation of the dark reality behind reasonable-sounding government rhetoric. A poll by ComRes for the National Housing Federation carried out in September 2013 found that 59 per cent of the public believed the policy should be abandoned, up from 51 per cent when it was introduced in April. Ed Miliband's Labour felt so confident in levels of popular opposition to the bedroom tax that they pledged to scrap it if elected in 2015.

David Cameron was forced to make a U-turn even before the bedroom tax came into force after claiming in Prime Minister's Questions on 6 March 2013 that there was an exemption for families with severely disabled children. At the time, government lawyers were busy trying to quash this possibility. A week later the exemption was confirmed along with a list of others applying to parents of young armed forces personnel and foster carers.

A legal challenge resulted in further exemptions for disabled couples who need separate bedrooms and families with disabled children needing an additional room for an overnight carer. Four other cases, heard at the same time, were dismissed as arising from social rather than medical needs associated with the claimants' impairments. As such, the judges ruled that the option of applying for a DHP provided adequate mitigation. The court also refused to overturn the introduction of the bedroom tax itself, objecting to the level of interference in the policymaking process that this would entail.

Abolition of Council Tax Benefit

The government abolished Council Tax Benefit (CTB) in 2013. In its place every council was tasked with designing its own local scheme, called a Council Tax Reduction (CTR) scheme, to provide financial support to working-age residents on low incomes. Working-age disabled people in receipt of certain disability benefits could have the benefit replaced with up to 100 per cent support from the local schemes. For many, however, this meant receiving a Council Tax bill for the very first time. Some areas were not publicising their local schemes and so many disabled people were not aware that they could claim, while not all disabled people are eligible for relief and for those who are it is yet another system to navigate.

Unsurprisingly, local authorities chose to reduce the generosity of the CTR relative to the national system of CTB that preceded it. When central government introduced the CTR in 2013, the funding it provided to local authorities for the scheme was only 90 per cent of what maintaining the generosity of CTB would have cost it, despite requiring that support for pensioners was maintained at its previous level. In principle, councils were free to top up this funding from other sources, but with budgets already tight, four-fifths of English councils cut back support. Working-age entitlements in England were 24 per cent lower in 2018–19 than they would have been under CTB. For that year, this equates to an average loss of £196 for the 3.6 million households who would have been entitled to CTB.[56]

These cuts have fallen almost entirely on low-income households. As a direct consequence, Council Tax debt in England rose by nearly 40 per cent in six years.[57] Analysis of government figures found the total amount of Council Tax arrears across England in the 2017–18 financial year was £944 million, 37 per cent higher than in 2012–13, when it was £691 million.

Benefit cap

The benefit cap is one of the most clearly ideological policies of welfare reform and one that has consistently proved popular with the general public. The basic idea is that working-age adults should not be able to receive more in social security payments than another person can earn in work. Hence a cap is imposed to supposedly make things fair.

As a solution to rising benefit levels, this approach conveniently overlooks the role of soaring housing costs in the absence of a rent cap. In 2013, the year when the benefit cap was introduced, Housing Benefit accounted for the biggest benefit spend after State Pensions, at a cost of £16.94 billion. This was not money squandered by claimants choosing a 'lifestyle on benefits', as the media and politicians portrayed them, because it was paid directly on rent, with a substantial proportion of this public money going straight into the pockets of private landlords. In 2016, £9.3 billion of Housing Benefit was going to private landlords, nearly double the amount from 10 years previously, according to a study by the National Housing Federation.[58]

When the benefit cap was introduced in 2013, the Coalition government predicted that it would reduce public expenditure by £225 million by April 2015. The cap was set at £26,000 per year (£500 per week), which was the average income of a family in the UK, and at £18,200 per year (£350 per week) for single people with no children. By 2014, a total of 36,471 households were having their payments reduced by the benefit cap, of which 17,102 were in London where rents are 61 per cent higher than the national average.

With effect from 7 November 2016, the cap was lowered to £20,000 for couples and lone parents outside Greater London (£13,400 for single adults with no children) and to £23,000 for couples and lone parents in Greater London (£15,410 for single adults with no children). Exempt from the benefit cap are DLA, PIP and the support component of ESA. Disabled people in the ESA WRAG are affected by it even though they have technically not been found fit for work and so are not in a position to easily take up work or increase their earnings to mitigate their losses.

This is yet another example of a policy with a disproportionate impact on disabled people. According to the government's equality impact assessment, it expected roughly half of the households who would lose from the policy to contain someone who is disabled. After the cap was lowered, more than 10,000 disabled people had their benefits slashed in just one month. Figures released by the DWP showed that more than 10,000 households that included someone claiming ESA had their benefits cut in February 2017 because of the cap, about 15 per cent of the total affected.

Pulling apart the safety net

Welfare reform was not a necessity arising from rampant benefit fraud or the financial crash. It was a deliberate, ideologically driven choice intent on increasing inequality and punishing anyone of working age not in work, for whatever reason. The government has been forced to make minor concessions to its plans due to particular popular and political pressure, but it has never swerved from its direction of travel. This is despite the fact that budget savings are not being realised and that there is plentiful evidence that its policies are pushing disabled people further from employment.

Polly Mackenzie comments:

> [S]uccess has evaded policy makers. The assessments used to transfer people from IB to ESA have been expensive, inaccurate, and deeply traumatising for millions of those forced to undergo them. The whole process has led to only a small reduction in

the number of people claiming these benefits. The disability employment gap remains stubbornly high. And, according to a new measure of poverty, more than half of those below the poverty line have a disabled family member.[59]

In addition to those examples cited by Mackenzie, the roll-out of UC is a long list of missed deadlines and spiralling costs; the projected savings of replacing DLA with PIP have thankfully not materialised, with the Office for Budget Responsibility assessing that it would have cost less to keep DLA; mounting evidence proves that conditionality and sanctions are counterproductive in moving people closer to the labour market; and the intention to drastically reduce numbers in the Support Group of ESA and move ESA claimants off benefits and into work has not been realised.

All of this adds up to a lack of success only if the government's stated targets are taken at face value. What has been achieved is the wrecking of a social safety net that millions rely on. This was clearly the goal all along.

FIVE | Independent living cuts

There have been cuts and negative changes affecting every area of disabled people's lives since 2010, although it is welfare reform that has received the most media attention. Hard-won progress in eroding segregation, moving away from institutionalisation and extending the right to disabled people to live and participate in the community has been reversed. The situation continues to deteriorate in an absence of will from the Tories to reverse cuts and in the deepening of trends that have an adverse impact on disabled people.

Many of the cuts and changes are the result of local government funding shortfalls that impact on the availability of essential day-to-day support for disabled people. Cuts in one area then make cuts in another harder to bear, producing a cumulative impact that compounds disadvantage still further. As one important example of this, cuts to social care and front-line community services have removed support that could have helped disabled people understand and navigate benefit changes; without this support, people unable to survive without welfare benefits are more likely to lose them and this has made the effects of welfare reform more serious and severe.

Cuts to disability-specific services and entitlements have been experienced on top of factors that are making life increasingly difficult for all working-class people and which have a disproportionate impact on disabled people. A few examples of these are rising energy prices creating fuel poverty (there are a number of reasons why a disabled person may have higher than average energy bills, including a need to stay warmer for health-related reasons and a lack of support to go out, leading to more time spent at home), library closures (disabled people are less likely to have online access at home and more likely to need support to use computers; however, public services and welfare benefits are increasingly provided on a 'digital by default' basis) and railway privatisation (staff cutbacks carried out in the interests of profit negatively affect disabled people's ability to travel by removing assistance to board and use public transport).

Attacks on disabled people's independent living have not been carried out directly by Westminster but via cuts to funding for local authorities and public health and through the privatisation of services. This has enabled the government to wash its hands of responsibility and to blame councils and private providers for failing in their duty of care towards disabled people. At the same time, new legislation has been passed, including the Care Act 2014 and Children and Families Act 2014, which, rather than improving things, have been used by the Tories to attempt to conceal retrogression behind a veneer of progress.

In England, there is a deliberate lack of monitoring of local authorities to check that they are meeting their statutory duties and fulfilling disabled people's rights under the Convention on the Rights of Persons with Disabilities. The government is, of course, well aware what is happening. In 2017, Tory-led Surrey County Council threatened to hold a referendum on proposals to raise Council Tax by 15 per cent to fund social care. Council leader David Hodge backed down amidst rumours of a back-room deal with central government that benefited Surrey without improving the overall situation in England.

This chapter provides an overview of legislation, policy and practice in social care, mental health services, housing, education and employment. Many of these areas are in crisis. It also explains the closure of the Independent Living Fund (ILF) and the scandalous situation regarding the incarceration of autistic people and people with learning difficulties in Assessment and Treatment Units. These are all key aspects of disabled people's right to live independently and to be included in the community that have suffered under successive Conservative governments.

Social care

The crisis in social care has had a profound impact on disabled people, one that threatens our very place in society. Without support for basic daily tasks such as eating and drinking, using the toilet, washing, dressing and leaving the house, many disabled people are unable to take part in society or enjoy any quality of life. Denial of such support is a denial of the most basic of human dignities.

Disabled people of working age make up around one-third of all adult social care users, while nearly half of all social care expenditure is spent on working-age as opposed to older disabled people, yet the mainstream narrative on social care presents it almost exclusively as an ageing population issue. This suits a government interested in finding ways for people to pay for their own social care; whatever the rights or wrongs of it, this may be an option for older people who acquire impairments in later life after having worked, saved and bought their own home, but not for working-age disabled people who are statistically much less likely to have those chances.

At the time of writing we are still waiting for a long anticipated green paper on future funding for social care. Continuous delays have been attributed to Brexit, but this masks a more fundamental dilemma for the government, which has been under pressure not just to focus on older people but to include issues relating to social care for all disabled adults. To do this would mean acknowledging their own role in starving local authorities of the funding needed to meet their statutory responsibilities. Meanwhile, disabled people are stuck in the middle as central government and councils argue over who is to blame.

Under the excuse of austerity, the Conservatives have destroyed local authorities by slashing their funding and pushing many towards bankruptcy. Northamptonshire County Council became the first local authority in over 20 years to effectively declare itself bankrupt by enforcing a Section 114 notice in 2018, banning all new expenditure with the exception of 'statutory services for protecting vulnerable people'. It has been predicted that others will follow. The National Audit Office (NAO) revealed that one in ten local authorities could run out of reserves by 2021.

Local authorities should not be exempt from criticism for choosing to pass on funding cuts to disabled people and failing to take a stronger and more rebellious stance against Westminster, but, at the same time, central government cannot deny culpability for the consequences of its hefty reductions to local government funding. Local Government and Social Care Ombudsman Michael King said: 'While I appreciate the challenges councils are dealing with, we cannot make concessions for failures attributed to budget pressures and must continue to hold authorities to account against relevant legislation, standards, guidance and their own policies.'

Adults' and children's social care are by far the biggest areas of expenditure for local authorities – with some London boroughs spending over 70 per cent of their budget on social care. It was therefore inevitable that disabled people would suffer from a 49 per cent cut in government funding for English local authorities from 2010–11 to 2017–18 alongside rising demand.

Social care spending in England has shrunk by £7 billion since 2010. Half of local authorities overspent on adult social care budgets in 2017–18, with half of these drawing on council reserves to meet the overspend. The Local Government Association estimates that adult social care faces a £3.5 billion funding gap by 2025 just to maintain existing standards of care, while figures show that councils in England receive 1.8 million new requests for adult social care a year – the equivalent of nearly 5,000 a day.

Additional pots of funding for social care loudly announced by government have been far from sufficient. These include the Better Care Fund, which is intended to improve integration between health and social care to prevent hospital admissions, and allowing councils to levy an extra social care precept on top of Council Tax. Research published in June 2018 showed that, despite these meagre measures, social care services are on the verge of collapse in some areas of England. The Association of Directors of Adult Social Services has stated that councils 'cannot go on' without a sustainable long-term funding strategy to underpin social care, and warned that continuing cuts to budgets risk leaving thousands of people who need care being left without services.

Despite rising need, the number of disabled people receiving social care support has fallen dramatically. Between 2009 and 2017, the number of people receiving adult social care in England fell by 50 per cent from 1.8 million to 0.9 million, with cuts continuing in the following years. In 2015, the government changed the data collection system for adult social care, thus disguising the real situation. It was estimated in 2017 that there were 1.2 million disabled people unable to get the support they needed, almost double the number in 2010. This can be attributed partly to the Care Act 2014, which established a new national minimum eligibility threshold set at 'critical' and 'substantial' levels. In 2013, the Care and Support Alliance warned that setting the threshold at this level would mean that 340,000 disabled people may be without support to do things as basic as getting up, getting washed, getting out of the house and managing bills.

In a bid to make budget savings, English local authorities have targeted individual social care support packages in ways that appear to breach the Care Act. Legally, decisions on support allocations should follow assessments and respond to need. It is nevertheless common to see budget proposals passed by councils that aim to make a targeted saving across social care packages. Social workers are then sent in to conduct reviews with the goal of identifying support they can remove. Examples include replacing support to use the toilet with incontinence pads when the disabled person is not incontinent, replacing support to shop and prepare meals with an expectation that the disabled person can live off microwave meals, and blanket removals of overnight support, leaving many people unable to evacuate in case of fire.

Legally, cuts can only be made through a reassessment as opposed to a review, but the distinction is frequently and deliberately blurred. In one high-profile case, Southampton Council outsourced its reviews to Capita. A whistle-blower revealed evidence that freelance social workers contracted by Capita were offered financial bonuses if they increased the cuts to disabled people's support packages by 20 per cent. Both Capita and the council deny that these bonuses were ever paid but did admit that one out of every five reviews carried out by the Capita team resulted in a cut.

Both local authorities and NHS organisations have sought to cap expenditure for individual disabled people living in the community where enforced placements in residential institutions would be cheaper. Cost capping is potentially unlawful as it sets a blanket policy that applies before individual assessments are carried out. However, legislation does allow local authorities to take resources into account when they make support planning decisions, and these decisions can legitimately override disabled people's personal wishes.

In March 2018, the Equality and Human Rights Commission (EHRC) threatened to judicially review 13 Clinical Commissioning Groups (CCGs) over their policies on Continuing Healthcare (CHC), which placed arbitrary caps on funding and failed to consider the specific needs of individual patients. CHC supports people with medical needs to live in the community and can be used as an alternative or a supplement to local authority social care support. The issue came to light through an investigation undertaken by campaigner Fleur Perry, who initially identified 37 CCGs that had set cost restrictions that could force disabled people into residential care. As a result of the action by the EHRC, all 13 CCGs that were in breach of the law agreed to review their policies. This is a small victory within a wider picture where resources are prioritised over disability equality.

Savings plans announced in Barnet in 2019 threatened to force disabled people into residential care against their wishes. Barnet Council proposed saving more than £400,000 in 2019–20 by creating more 'cost-effective support plans', such as using residential care rather than funding support packages that allow disabled people to live in their own homes. The Conservative-run council said it wanted to consider 'the full range of care options … rather than offering community-based placements by default'. This meant a new 'assumption that new clients are placed in cheaper accommodation settings where appropriate'. One of disabled people's greatest fears is having the right to live in your own home taken away.

Social care charges are placing yet further strain on disabled people as local authorities look for ways to mitigate their social care budget shortfalls. As Jenny Morris writes, 'Local authorities do not have to charge for community care but, as their budgets have been progressively cut back, they have increasingly been opting to use their discretionary powers to charge.'[1] Freedom of Information requests submitted by GMB union in 2018 showed that at least 1,178 people had been taken to court over social care payment arrears and more than 78,000 had debt management procedures started against them by their local authority. The true figure was likely to be higher as not all local authorities responded.

Over the past few years, councils have followed each other in passing increasingly harsh charging policies, branded by campaigners as a 'tax on disability', that risk pushing disabled people out of the social care system altogether. In this situation, people's needs are likely to escalate, resulting in crisis and extra costs for the NHS.

English local authorities are largely failing to follow the Care Act but avenues to challenge this are severely limited. The appeals process legislated for in the Care Act is not due to be implemented until April 2020. In the meantime, for those disabled people who do understand their rights and have the resources to make a complaint, it is often only through the threat of legal action that wrongful decisions are reversed. This hinges on eligibility for legal aid but also, more and more frequently, on the chances of finding a community care solicitor with capacity to take on any more work. Disabled people who find legal support can often end up in cycles of reassessment: their local authority makes an inadequate and unlawful support award, their solicitor sends a pre-action letter, the local authority withdraws the support offer pending reassessment, and so the cycle continues. Meanwhile, the disabled person and the personal assistant(s) they employ have no security for the future.

Where cases have escalated to the High Court, the limitations of judicial review have been clearly demonstrated, with judges unwilling to question social work practice. In the case of Luke Davey, a severely disabled former ILF recipient who lost a legal challenge against Oxfordshire County Council over its plan to cut his care package by over a third, the judge ruled that 'the courts should be wary of overzealous textual analysis of social care needs assessments carried out by social workers for their employers with the risk of taking them away from front-line duties'. He added: '[I]t is not for the Court to be prescriptive as to the degree of detail in an assessment or a care plan – these are matters for the local authority.'[2] Disabled people and their families are left without redress while their quality of life is rapidly and often unlawfully diminished.

Independent Living Fund

One social care policy change, fiercely opposed by campaigners, was the closure of the Independent Living Fund (ILF). The ILF was set up in 1988 to enable disabled people with high support needs to live in the community when the alternative was residential care. The fund was administered by a non-governmental body under the Department for Work and Pensions (DWP) rather than the Department of Health and as such was seen as an 'anomaly'. The solution to this, which was proposed in a review commissioned by New Labour, was to close the ILF and transfer full responsibility for meeting social care support needs to local authorities. This was taken forwards by the Coalition government through a two-step process: first, the fund was closed to new applicants in December 2010; then, in 2012, a consultation was launched on proposals to close it permanently in 2015, affecting around 18,000 disabled people.

ILF recipients were overwhelmingly against closure. The ILF consistently had high user satisfaction ratings (98 per cent at its final annual report) and, according to the final ILF annual report and accounts, just 2 per cent of the budget was spent on administration. By contrast, experiences with local authority-administered social care support were patchier. Overall, the latter was known to be less efficient and more onerous for the recipient and to prioritise risk aversion over equality and choice for disabled people. Local authorities that responded to this first consultation were largely in favour of closure. Unlike disabled campaigners, they appear not to have twigged that the government was not intending to transfer long-term funding to them along with the additional responsibilities.

Legal action supported by Disabled People Against Cuts (DPAC) and Inclusion London successfully challenged the government over a failure to adequately consult on the proposals. This bought a three-month delay to the planned closure. The government then simply repeated the consultation in 2014 and retook the decision to close the fund. A subsequent legal challenge was dismissed on the grounds that this time the minister was fully aware of 'the inevitable and considerable adverse effect' that closure would have on disabled people. It was therefore lawful. In passing judgment, Mrs Justice Andrews emphasised that the ruling did not concern the rights or wrongs of closure but whether the government had discharged its legal duties to evaluate the impact of the policy decision. She concluded that the assumption on which the Minister for Disabled People Mike Penning based his decision was that 'independent living might well be put seriously in peril for … most (or a substantial number of) ILF users'.

In response to high-profile protests, the government conceded to awarding English local authorities with a further four years' worth of funding for a 'former ILF recipient grant' following an initial post-closure transition year. This amounts to some £675 million but does not match the full costs of replacing the ILF. The funding, like the transition grant, was not ring-fenced even to adult social care, leaving local authorities free to spend it wherever they chose. Given the wider financial picture and the low public profile of adult social care, it is not surprising that many local authorities quickly disregarded any responsibilities towards former ILF recipients that the award of this funding might imply and immediately cut support packages from ILF levels.

One year after the ILF's closure, Freedom of Information requests revealed that eight London boroughs had made cuts to individual support packages of 50 per cent or more. Ironically, given that one justification for closure of the ILF was a need to get rid of a 'postcode lottery' in social care, the post-ILF approach was found to dramatically vary between areas: 10 boroughs reported no cuts to any packages, while four boroughs reported reductions for over half of all disabled people previously in receipt of ILF money.

The devolved administrations all took measures to protect former ILF recipients in their nations. Following the closure of the fund, Scotland, Northern Ireland and Wales each set up equivalent schemes to continue to protect the support packages of disabled people previously in receipt of the ILF. The Welsh government originally intended that the Welsh Independent Living Grant (WILG) would run only until April 2019, but following a fierce campaign led by Nathan Lee Davies and other Welsh activists, Julie Morgan, the Deputy Minister for Health and Social Services in the Welsh Assembly, announced just two months before the planned closure that she had written to council leaders to ask for an immediate 'pause' in the transfer of WILG recipients onto local authority-funded support.

Mental health

Mental health is one area that the Conservatives have chosen to publicly recognise as a problem but without any acknowledgement of the role of their own policies in creating and exacerbating the crisis. In Theresa May's first major speech on health as prime minister, she highlighted 'the burning injustice of mental health and inadequate treatment that demands a new approach from government and society as a whole'.

The measures she announced to tackle the situation are unable to address the scale of the problem or the root causes of rapidly escalating incidences of mental distress. These included £15 million allocated for community services such as crisis cafés, which works out at just £23,000 per constituency. Other measures represented an attempt to shift responsibility away from overstretched mental health services onto equally overstretched teachers and potentially uninterested employers: the plans included offering mental health first aid training to all secondary schools and carrying out a review into the support employers can offer employees who have had to take time off work. Proposed interventions such as an increase in the availability of online support are not appropriate for effectively addressing complex trauma and mental distress.

Mental health services have experienced significant cuts at a time of rising demand. Numbers seeking treatment went up from 500,000 in 2010 to 1.7 million in 2016 at the same time as £600 million was slashed from Mental Health Trust budgets. Over this period, 34,000 beds in acute services vanished, leading to patients sometimes being sent hundreds of miles from family, friends and home for treatment in whatever bed can be found. In August 2017, a senior judge spoke out in one case of a 17-year-old girl, telling society it should be 'ashamed' for not protecting a suicidal girl and warning the nation that there would be 'blood on our hands' if a suitable placement could not be found for her.

The closure of front-line community mental health services has removed day-to-day support for people living with mental distress and it is unsurprising that acute incidences have risen sharply at the same time. In 2017 it was reported that detentions under the Mental Health Act had risen by 47 per cent in 10 years.[3] This has a disproportionate impact on people from black and minority ethnic communities, with black patients four times more likely to be detained than white.[4]

The shortage in provision within the mental health system has led to an increase in the use of police cells to detain people experiencing mental distress who are considered to be a danger to themselves or to others. This is highly inappropriate and unsafe. In July 2018, according to official figures released by the police watchdog, deaths in police custody were at a 10-year high, with experts citing the impacts of austerity and the crisis in mental health services as the reasons why.[5] A total of 23 people died in or after detention in 2017–18 (up from 14 the previous year), with official police figures recording that more than half were people with conditions such as psychosis, depression and self-harm and 18 had drug or alcohol issues.

The situation for children and young people is particularly concerning; a failure to receive appropriate support for incidences of mental distress early in life can impact badly on a person's life chances, leading to lifelong distress and suicide. The number of referrals by schools in England seeking mental health treatment for pupils rose by more than a third between 2014–15 and 2017–18. Fifty-six per cent of referrals came from primary schools. Teenage suicide is on the increase, with provisional data compiled by the Office for National Statistics in 2018 showing that the rate has almost doubled in eight years.

Waiting times have been heavily criticised. Figures from June 2019 showed that the number of young people waiting more than a year to access treatment had more than trebled in a year. Over the course of long waiting times, mental distress worsens. The charity YoungMinds estimated in 2018 that three-quarters of young people referred to NHS mental health services waited so long to be seen that their condition had deteriorated further by the time they got to see a doctor.

The NAO warned in October 2018 that even if current government plans to spend an extra £1.4 billion on the sector are delivered, there will still be 'significant unmet need' because of staff shortages, poor data and a lack of spending controls on NHS CCGs. The NAO report said that only one-quarter of young people who required mental health services were able to access help from the NHS. The Department of Health and Social Care hopes to increase the proportion to 35 per cent – estimated to be equivalent to treating an additional 70,000 children and young people per year between 2015–16 and 2020–21 – but this will still leave nearly double that number without support.

The provision of appropriate therapeutic interventions for adults has been adversely affected by welfare reform and the drive to get disabled people off benefits and into work. Mental distress is the most common condition that affects participation in work. Of 2.4 million disabled people claiming Employment and Support Allowance (ESA) in 2017, 49 per cent reported mental distress as their primary condition. It is also the leading cause of sickness absence; according to figures cited by the Mental Health Foundation, '70 million work days are lost each year due to mental health problems in the UK, costing employers approximately £2.4 billion per year'.[6]

Tackling mental health has been a priority within Tory welfare reform, with a focus not on well-being but on reducing numbers out of work. This has manifested through investment in increasing the availability of short-term, low-intensity interventions targeted at supporting people back to work. This was encouraged by Professor and Labour peer Lord Richard Layard on the basis that the investment would pay for itself through tax dividends, and has led to the establishment of the Increasing Access to Psychological Therapies (IAPT) programme.

Mental service users and psychologists are deeply critical of the IAPT approach, which has taken funding away from more effective longer-term support at a time of escalating need. There is criticism that many IAPT workers lack in-depth training and experience of severe mental distress. Limiting interventions to just a few sessions or providing therapy online does not allow a relationship to develop between client and therapist, which is the route through which a person with mental distress may gradually make meaningful change. Psychologist Paul Atkinson writes that 'IAPT is not a psychotherapy. It is an assembly line of behavioural adaptation and a perversion of the counselling and psychotherapy profession.'[7]

Targeting therapeutic roles at 're-engaging' clients in employment is considered by many to be unethical. In one example of this, G4S advertised jobs for cognitive behaviour therapy (CBT) practitioners accredited by the British Association for Behavioural and Cognitive Psychotherapies with job descriptions stating that the roles were '[t]argeted on the level, number and effectiveness of interventions in re-engaging Customers and Customer progression into work'.

Campaigners such as Mental Health Resistance Network also point to a lack of recognition inherent in this approach that, for many people with mental distress, work is 'simply unfeasible', which 'constitutes a dangerous level of pressure and coercion'.

IAPT has failed to live up to the success rate that was promised. Figures from 2016 show that half of 'low-intensity' CBT patients relapse in 12 months; the outcomes are even worse in areas of high deprivation. The government has pushed on regardless in its determination to subsume mental health support within an overriding employment agenda. Under current plans, the number of employment advisers in mental health settings will double.

Meanwhile, support for those experiencing the most serious distress is dangerously under-resourced. The body of Julian Gaunt was discovered by a dog walker in a Norfolk field on 23 November 2018, four days after he was reported missing by his family. The 46-year-old had been in contact with various medical professionals, who had recommended he be referred for more long-term psychological support. He took his own life while waiting for a date to begin receiving treatment. At the inquest into his death, a senior coroner said that she had 'major concerns' about the length of time he may have waited for support and stated that she was particularly concerned that 'people with less serious problems could receive treatment from the county's wellbeing service faster than those with more complex conditions'.

An independent review of the Mental Health Act established by Theresa May in 2017 will not lead to the level of change needed within the system nor reverse damage enacted through cuts and the influence of the welfare reform agenda. Campaigners raised objections to the appointment of Professor Sir Simon Wessely as chair of the review, arguing that his 'body of work on ME [myalgic encephalomyelitis] (or "chronic fatigue syndrome") demonstrates his lack of honesty, care and compassion for patients' and highlighting his role in 'devising the theories of "malingering and illness deception" which underpinned the Work Capability Assessment'.

These objections were ignored, as were calls for greater involvement of mental health survivors and service users, in particular those from black and minority ethnic communities, given the serious racial inequalities operating within the mental health system. The final review, which was published in December 2018, recommended 'incremental steps toward a better situation', including 'proposals on advance directives, nearest relatives, access to advocacy, better safeguards and a new right of appeal against compulsory treatment'.[8] All of these are welcome to improve what is currently in place, but, as expressed by the National Survivor User Network, 'they aren't the end point for the change needed'.

Assessment and Treatment Units

One area where mental health legislative change is urgently needed but not on offer is the continuing detention of autistic people and people with learning difficulties without a mental health diagnosis under the Mental Health Act. Currently they can be detained within mental health settings, including Assessment and Treatment Units (ATUs), if they are considered to pose a risk to themselves or others. Despite being designed for temporary care and assessment while long-term support is organised, many residents can be detained for more than two years.[9]

Conditions within such settings are associated with the overuse of medication, physical restraint and isolation, and with the wishes of the person and their family often dismissed. Figures disclosed by Radio 4 in 2018 demonstrated growing use of physical restraint in mental health units, despite ministers telling NHS trusts to use such techniques less often. Staff in NHS mental health hospitals deployed restraint on patients 22,000 times in 2017, up almost 50 per cent from 2016. Use of face-down or 'prone' restraint, which is particularly dangerous, increased by around 40 per cent.[10]

In the worst cases, such as that of teenager Connor Sparrowhawk, neglect has resulted in avoidable deaths. Southern Health NHS Foundation Trust was eventually fined a record £2 million following the deaths of Sparrowhawk, who drowned in a bath following an epileptic seizure in an NHS care unit in Oxford in 2013, and of another patient, Teresa Colvin, who died in hospital in 2012 after she was found unconscious at a Southampton Adult Mental Health Hospital. Following a campaign by Colvin's husband to uncover the truth, Southern Health NHS Foundation Trust admitted failing to protect her from serious self-harm. A subsequent NHS investigation into the deaths of 13 patients with learning difficulties found that failures to provide adequate, safe and prompt care contributed directly to their deaths.

The government has consistently missed targets to move autistic people and people with learning difficulties out of institutional settings and back to their communities. Institutionalisation and abuse of disabled people are nothing new, but in a different climate, where there was less to fight, this particular injustice would have arguably received much greater attention. After the 2011 Winterbourne View ATU abuse scandal, the government promised to move all inpatients into community-based housing within three years under its transforming care programme. That target was missed. Latest figures show that 2,350 people still live in ATUs. According to figures from 2015, around half are directly run by the NHS with the rest operated by private providers, including the ATU at the centre of an abuse scandal in 2019, Whorlton Hall.

Meagre government efforts to move people back into the community have been undermined by underfunding in social care and the interests of private providers. Figures seen by the *Guardian* in 2019 show that, at one ATU in the two years up to April 2018, almost 50 per cent of residents left to go into privately owned 'independent hospitals'. Only around 30 per cent went on to either supported living or residential care in the community.

Campaigners are calling for more scrutiny over where people go after ATUs, but, without investment in the development of community social care support services, private institutional settings are too often considered the only viable option. The owners and shareholders who profit aren't interested in questions of how such provision perpetuates the oppression of disabled people and its incompatibility with building a truly inclusive society.

Housing

Housing for disabled people is yet another area described as being in crisis, with a chronic shortage of accessible properties. Disabled people are twice as likely as non-disabled people to live in social housing, so a lack of availability in this sector is a particular problem. It is the reason why disabled people with mobility impairments were housed on the upper floors of Grenfell Tower, unable to evacuate in the case of fire. One of the victims to die in this horrific way was Sakineh Afrasiabi, a woman described by her sister as a 'vulnerable, physically disabled and partially sighted pensioner' who was deprived of her 'human right to escape'. The inquiry into the Grenfell fire heard how Kensington and Chelsea Council placed the woman near the top of the 24-storey block and threatened to remove her from the council housing list if she refused the offer.[11]

There were 365,000 disabled people in England with unmet housing needs according to government figures released in 2016. In 2018, the EHRC published the report from its inquiry into disability and housing, entitled *Housing and Disabled People: Britain's hidden crisis*. The report evidences very strong and unmet demand from disabled people in the social housing sector, where the average waiting time to be housed in accessible accommodation is over two years and, in one case, 20 years. Evidence heard by the inquiry reflects shared experiences across the country of disabled people trapped in their homes, or having to eat, sleep and bathe in one room, or of adults having to be carried around their homes by family members due to the lack of appropriate access.

Journalist Frances Ryan writes of the similar picture she found when she started talking to disabled people about their housing over the last few years, with examples such as 'a wheelchair user washing in a paddling pool in his kitchen with a hose because he couldn't use his bathroom. A mother falling down concrete steps carrying her son's wheelchair. A young woman forced to use a commode in the living room because the toilet was upstairs.'[12] The EHRC report concluded: 'Increasing the availability of social housing needs to be part of the solution to the shortage of accessible homes.'

Despite this recommendation by the EHRC and the prevalence of disability among social housing tenants, the government's green paper on social housing published in August 2018 almost entirely omits disability and access. In 2015–16, 49 per cent of households in the social housing sector had at least one disabled member, yet housing for disabled people is mentioned only in the context of 'supported housing' and the word 'accessible' appears in the 78-page document only four times, on each occasion relating to the need for accessible information or complaints procedures. This is alarming because it suggests a ghetto approach to housing for disabled people.

Concerns about re-segregation of disabled people within the community have been raised in response to similar approaches taken by local authorities, which invest in large units of 'extra care' housing as opposed to improving the availability of accessible accommodation within the community. Southampton Council invested a reported £21 million to build a complex of up to 100 flats to provide 'housing with care' for residents who are elderly or disabled. At the same time, Southampton City CCG brought in a new NHS CHC policy which argued that the needs of disabled people who require more than eight hours of long-term healthcare a day 'would be more appropriately met within a residential placement'. In this way, the wishes of disabled people to live in the community alongside non-disabled people are being overlooked in the development of both housing and health/social care policies.

Inclusive education

Access to education improves the individual life opportunities of disabled people, but, more than that, at a societal level, education that is inclusive of both disabled and non-disabled learners plays a role of fundamental importance in building cohesive communities where disabled people are accepted rather than shunned. While educational opportunities for disabled pupils have fallen since 2010, inclusive education has come under particular attack. Since the General Election in 2010, the government's own statistics show that there has been a gradual increase in the numbers of disabled children and young people being redirected into segregated education. The education watchdog Ofsted's 2016–17 annual report stated that the proportion of pupils with a SEN (Special Educational Needs) statement or EHCP (Education, Health and Care Plan) attending a state-funded special school, rather than mainstream provision, had risen from 40 per cent in 2010 to 45 per cent.

The decline in numbers of disabled children and young people being included in mainstream education can be linked directly to plans under the Coalition government to reverse what they called 'the bias towards inclusion'. Under pressure from campaigners, the 'presumption for mainstream' principle made it into the 2014 Children and Families Act but was significantly undermined by Clause 33, which allows the exclusion of disabled children from mainstream education if their inclusion is judged to be 'incompatible with (a) the wishes of the child's parent or the young person, or (b) the provision of efficient education for others'.

At the same time, provision for disabled learners in mainstream settings has been badly hit. In 2017, it was reported that special needs education in England had lost out on £1.2 billion over two years because of shortfalls in funding increases. Interim findings from a survey carried out by the National Education Union showed that one in five teachers were aware of illegal exclusions of disabled students within their educational setting. In that same year, Ofsted warned that some parents were being asked to educate their disabled children at home because their schools claimed that they could not meet their needs. The number of disabled pupils without any educational placement was found to have risen to 4,050 in 2017 in England, up from 776 in 2010. More recently, Ofsted has highlighted the disproportionate representation of disabled pupils among permanent exclusions. In 2018, Ofsted said that it was 'concerned' that, in secondary schools, pupils with support for Special Educational Needs and Disability (SEND) are five times more likely to have a permanent exclusion than pupils without such support. Over the 2017–18 school year, 27 per cent of pupils with SEND support had a fixed-term exclusion, amounting to 93,800 pupils.[13]

Examining the unprecedented growth in exclusions and unlawful off-rolling of disabled pupils, the Education Select Committee stated in July 2018 that:

> An unfortunate and unintended consequence of the Government's strong focus on school standards has led to school environments and practices that have resulted in disadvantaged children being disproportionately excluded … There appears to be a lack of moral accountability on the part of many schools and no incentive to, or deterrent to not, retain pupils who could be classed as difficult or challenging.[14]

In 2019, three families took the government to the High Court over its funding policy, which was leaving councils across the country without enough money to fulfil their legal obligation of providing education for disabled pupils. They branded this situation a 'scandal', with campaigners supporting the action using the hashtag #SENDnationalcrisis. In October, the application for judicial review was rejected on the grounds that there was 'no unlawful discrimination' in the way the government made provision for SEND funding.

An additional attack on disabled people's access to education was made through cuts to Disabled Students Allowance (DSA). Cuts to DSA were first proposed in 2014 in an announcement by then Universities Minister David Willetts, but then deferred to the start of the academic year in September 2016 in response to protests by the National Union of Students. Government plans to transfer responsibility from central government for meeting the learning support needs of disabled students to universities and colleges will inevitably result in needs going unmet and increasing barriers to education for disabled learners. Areas targeted for cuts included assistive technology and support workers for non-medical support, such as note-takers. Figures in 2015 put the number of students who would be affected at 70,000. A report from the Department for Education in England, released in 2019, revealed that 60 per cent of eligible students had never heard of DSA.[15]

Employment
The Tories justify their entire record on disability with the fact that, from 2013 to 2018, an additional 930,000 disabled people reportedly entered work. What this figure does not tell us is whether those people are financially better off, healthier or happier. There is also no evidence to directly attribute this increase to

government policy, as opposed to, for example, general employment trends that have seen employment figures rising over this same period or the demographic increase in people who identify as disabled. If we analyse three key areas of disability employment policy (Access to Work, the Work Programme and the Disability Confident scheme), we find a notable lack of success and, in some cases, measures that have actively pushed disabled people out of employment.

Given the emphasis on employment running throughout Tory disability policy and welfare reform, limited progress made in this area can only be judged as policy failure. The UK has a persistent disability employment gap – the difference in employment rates between disabled people and the rest of the working-age population – of around 30 percentage points, and this has not shifted significantly. An initial pledge in 2015 to halve the disability employment gap was quietly dropped after it was calculated that, at the current rate of progress, it would take almost 50 years to achieve; this was then replaced with a target of 1 million more disabled people in work by 2027.

Campaigners are concerned that this emphasis on employment is leading to disabled people being pushed into unsuitable work that cannot provide an adequate standard of living, and causes additional distress while exacerbating existing conditions. Nearly half of the increase in disability employment between 2013–14 and 2017–18 was due to disabled people becoming self-employed or taking part-time jobs. During this period, the number of disabled people in self-employment increased by more than 22 per cent, while the number of non-disabled people who were self-employed rose by just 9 per cent. The increase in the number of disabled people in part-time self-employment increased even faster, by about 25 per cent. Research findings published in 2017 found that more than half of all self-employed people were failing to earn a decent living.[16] Once the extra costs of disability are taken into account, the likelihood increases still further that at least a significant proportion of those additional disabled people counted as being in work are struggling financially.

Negative changes to Access to Work (AtW), the government's disability employment support programme, occurred as a result of the DWP trying to increase numbers of disabled people using the scheme within an only marginally increased budget. In order to achieve this, they were, in the words of the Work and Pensions Committee, 'bearing down on the awards of current service users who happen to require relatively high cost support, to the detriment of meeting their needs effectively'.[17]

Despite fierce campaigning by the StopChanges2AtW campaign founded in 2013 by Nicky Evans and Geraldine O'Halloran, the situation with AtW is another issue that arguably would have received more attention in a different climate. The bottom line is that removal of AtW support leads to stress, ruined careers, job losses and debt, but the removal of disability benefits leads to distress, death and suicide; with cases abounding of the latter, the very real suffering experienced by victims of AtW pales in comparison and gets overlooked.

The political significance of DWP policy in this area is that it gives the lie to the government's stated interest in getting more disabled people into work and confirms an overriding priority to reduce state-funded support irrespective of associated impacts on employment opportunity. A blog post on the DPAC website from 2014 stated that:

> Despite the government's well publicised extra investment in the scheme Access to Work's clear direction of travel is to cut individual packages, with the result that the employability of Deaf and disabled people is being seriously undermined. It is difficult to summarise all the changes: AtW is awarded on

a discretionary 'case by case' basis and the programme has always denied the existence of any blanket rules for particular impairment groups. What we have seen emerging are some clear patterns around the cutting of packages, lack of information and hostility to AtW customers alongside growing inefficiency and cuts to AtW service delivery.

Research published in 2017 highlighted a number of policy and operational issues. Almost half of survey respondents had experienced changes to their AtW package, with 'cuts' or 'cost-cutting' the most frequently given reason for this. Nearly all of those experiencing changes reported negative impacts on their work. In the worst cases people had lost their jobs, turned down work or reduced their income as a result of the changes. Many respondents reported a personal, as well as professional, impact from the changes through stress, poorer health, and loss of self-esteem or confidence.[18] The scale of administrative and payment errors has led to an unevidenced suspicion among campaigners of a deliberate ploy to render engagement with the scheme unworkable and reduce the ongoing caseload. Lost paperwork has become a routine part of the process, as have late payments, non-payments and payments to the wrong customer, leading to considerable financial stress. It is rare to find anyone who uses the scheme who doesn't have a list of similar stories. A meeting in parliament in October 2017 heard how some AtW customers and their interpreters/support workers had been left thousands of pounds in debt due to financial errors.[19] The DWP has denied Freedom of Information requests from campaigners to make public reports from internal audits of the scheme.

Amidst such controversy, the DWP conveniently changed the way in which it records AtW statistics, so it is no longer possible to compare with previous years; instead of counting customer numbers, what is now recorded are 'approvals' of support provision. This does not include those who continue to receive AtW support without the need for reassessment, nor does it show how many people lost their support or had it cut after being reassessed, making it impossible to know how many disabled people are currently receiving AtW compared with previous years, or whether and by how much the average level of support packages has risen or fallen.

Specific policies affecting Deaf BSL users have been ameliorated in response to pressure, but other negative changes remain in place. The controversial '30-hour rule'[20] was scrapped in 2014 but a cap on individual awards was announced instead. Shortly after the cap's introduction, it was increased in March 2018 by £15,000 after the launch of a legal challenge. Although something of a win for campaigners, around 80 mainly Deaf BSL users were still hit by the new cap, limiting their ability to perform their job roles.

Stricter eligibility criteria for those in self-employment continue to act as a barrier, with new applicants required to demonstrate long-term business sustainability. Enforced personal contributions towards wheelchair costs, said to reflect the days of the week when a person is not at work, mean that wheelchairs more suitable for a work environment are now out of reach for many disabled people.

The government chose to attack AtW, an existing disability employment scheme with an excellent track record for successfully supporting disabled people not only into jobs but into careers; its own disability employment initiatives brought in since 2010 have conspicuously failed to deliver. The Work Programme, introduced in June 2011 with the aim of supporting benefit claimants into work, cost billions in public money paid to private providers and was proven to have worse outcomes than doing nothing. Rates for supporting disabled people into employment were particularly bad, underpinned by a 'payment by results' model that encouraged providers to concentrate on those claimants with the highest chances of finding work. Just 3.4 per cent of disabled claimants on out-of-work benefits who started on the scheme in December 2013 had a spell of at least three months in work a year later. This is barely a third of the number who would have been expected to get a job through their own devices without any compulsory 'help'.

By March 2016, the Work Programme had implemented 175,000 sanctions against disabled people in the Work-Related Activity Group (WRAG) of ESA, while at the same time only moving 36,986 into work. It was terminated in 2017. The Work and Health Programme that replaced it has an annual spend that is just one-fifth of the Work Programme funding, leading campaigners to question how effective it can be.

Disability Confident is a scheme that government ministers talk about loudly and often. Additional numbers of disabled people in work cannot be attributed to it and there is no evidence of any tangible disability employment benefits from what is little more than a communications campaign. Esther McVey proudly claimed credit for designing the scheme during her run in the Tory leadership election in 2019, when under pressure over her record on disability as Secretary of State for Work and Pensions and a former Minister for Disabled People.

Launched in summer 2013, Disability Confident has become something of a laughing stock within the disability sector. Speaking at the 2014 Conservative Party conference, Iain Duncan Smith, then Work and Pensions Secretary, claimed that 'over 1,000 employers' had signed up. The following year, the DWP was forced to admit in response to a series of Freedom of Information requests submitted by *Disability News Service* that the true figure was fewer than 400 employers, while only 68 were 'active partners'. Later analysis found that, in the three years since it was launched, only about 40 mainstream private-sector employers without a financial interest in disability had signed up. One of those was a small café in Cornwall. Not only were employers largely uninterested, it was also essentially meaningless when they did sign up, requiring no commitment to change their current practice.

Disability Confident was then effectively merged with the Positive about Disability (Two Ticks) scheme: the DWP approached all employers who had an active registration with Positive about Disability to invite them to migrate to a new Disability Confident scheme, which was then relaunched in November 2016.

Critics have continued to argue that it is too easy for employers to sign up to the scheme and then continue to discriminate against disabled people or to sign up without even employing a single disabled person. The DWP itself is a case in point: staff at Caxton House, DWP headquarters, wear lanyards branded with 'Disability Confident' but behind the façade disability discrimination has been steadily rising for years. In October 2018 it was revealed that the employment tribunal had dealt with almost 60 claims of disability discrimination taken against the DWP by its own staff over a 20-month period. Civil Service figures published in 2019 showed that the proportion of DWP staff who said that they had been victims of disability discrimination at work in the previous 12 months had risen by about 50 per cent in just four years. The figures suggest, according to calculations by *Disability News Service*, that more than a third of disabled DWP staff experienced disability discrimination at work in 2018. That the department responsible for disability employment policy is not even bothered enough to get its own house in order is a clear indication of the Tories' absence of genuine commitment towards inclusive employment for disabled people.

Barriers to justice

While disabled people's living standards have been deliberately rolled back, barriers to justice have been increased. The two main ways in which this has been achieved are through passage of the Legal Aid, Sentencing and Punishment of Offenders Act 2012, commonly known as LASPO, and the introduction of 'Mandatory Reconsideration' as a new stage within the appeals process for benefit assessment decisions, as detailed in Chapter 4. A third measure, the introduction of fees for employment tribunals in 2013, leading to a marked decrease in the number of disability discrimination claims brought, was overturned by the High Court in 2017. These examples demonstrate how, instead of reversing policy changes with an adverse impact on disabled people's lives, the government chose instead to subvert justice to avoid challenge.

LASPO reduced the scope of legal aid, excluding many areas of law including welfare benefits, alongside changing rules on eligibility. This has had a direct impact on restricting access to justice for disabled people at a time of enormous upheaval within the welfare system. The EHRC stated that it considers 'the reforms to legal aid to raise issues for the protection and promotion of disabled people's rights under the [Convention on the Rights of Persons with Disabilities] and undermines redress in relation to these rights'.[21] Figures published by the Ministry of Justice in October 2017 showed that just 440 claimants were given legal aid assistance in welfare benefits cases in 2016–17, down from 83,000 in 2012–13. This represents a drop of 99.5per cent.

As a consequence of LASPO, many advice and law centres have closed, dramatically reducing the availability of legal aid lawyers to take cases on behalf of those who remain eligible. In July 2019, the *Guardian* reported that the number of legal advice centres in England and Wales had halved since 2013–14. Some disabled people who cannot afford legal costs are also now excluded from legal aid by the revised eligibility criteria, which take assets as well as income into account. This affects those who, for example, own their own home, perhaps through inheritance, but who are dependent on social security payments for their income. This leaves them unable to challenge wrongful social care decisions under the Care Act 2014.

Losing the gains of generations

Britain once had a complex and targeted social safety net. It was far from perfect but it gave disabled people a platform from which to push for further progress. Much of that has been swept away by deliberate legislative and policy choices since 2010. What is left is in chaos. This has taught us a lesson in how relatively quickly the gains of generations of disabled campaigners can be snatched away. Frances Ryan sums up the situation: 'Despite decades of progress, the intricate threads that make up disabled people's safety net are always vulnerable to those in power who wish to cut them away ... It is not hyperbole to say that the stakes have rarely been higher than now.'[22] As explored in the next chapter, the impacts have been terrible and profound on many levels, but had the system been simpler, how much more damage could have been done even more quickly?

Keeping pace with policy changes over nearly 10 years has been and continues to be exhausting – overwhelming campaigners, watchdogs, disability organisations, public lawyers and journalists, and arguably dividing forces in defending against multiple attacks. But there has been a fightback every step of the way. Not as much as we needed to stop the onslaught, but, as explained in Part I of this book, there are material reasons why disability issues remain so marginalised within a capitalist society and attract less attention than we think they deserve. Campaigners have educated ourselves to become experts in technical policies and procedures, legal rights and the analysis of statistics, operating in networks to share information and ideas for resistance, as recorded in Part IV. We certainly have not let the Tories have it all their own way – and from that we must take heart.

We must also be prepared for things to get even worse.

Against a backdrop of ever diminishing support and decreasing living standards for disabled people, the question of legalising assisted suicide keeps coming up through successive legal challenges and attempts to pass legislation via private members' bills.[23] The lobby behind this has substantial resources and considers itself progressive. There is nothing progressive about making people's lives unbearable and then offering them a way out.

In 1912, Russian revolutionary Yevgeni Preobrazhensky wrote: 'It seems to me that all suicides in circumstances of hunger and need have the undoubted character of murder ... The question of a right to suicide will only make sense in a future society where no material motives for suicide will exist. Only in a society that has guaranteed to all its members the means of existence will the question be appropriate.'[24] This remains as true today as it was then.

PART III
'HUMAN CATASTROPHE'

The impact of austerity and welfare reform on disabled people

> Evidence before us now and in our inquiry procedure as
> published in our 2016 report reveals that social cut policies have
> led to a human catastrophe in your country, totally neglecting the
> vulnerable situation people with disabilities find themselves in.
>
> Theresia Degener, Chair of the United Nations
> Committee on the Rights of Persons with Disabilities[1]

These words were addressed to representatives of the UK government during the concluding session of a routine public examination of the UK under the United Nations Convention on the Rights of Persons with Disabilities (UN CRPD). It took place less than a year after the government dismissed the findings of the Committee's special investigation.

The sizeable government delegation sent to Geneva, comprising representatives from a number of departments and all devolved administrations, suggested that the government was intent on overturning the inquiry findings. They argued that because the investigation focused on just three areas (welfare reform, employment and independent living), it provided an unrepresentative picture of the overall situation and that progress was being achieved in other areas of disabled people's lives. Long lists of policy initiatives and legislative measures were put forward without any evidence to support the claim that they had effected positive change, as the government attempted to obscure its avoidance of any of the substantive issues raised by the Committee in its questioning.

At the same time, Deaf and Disabled People's Organisations presented extensive, robust evidence of the adverse impacts of government policy affecting all areas within the scope of the CRPD. The final Concluding Observations published by the Committee showed that they had not been taken in by the government's smoke and mirrors. The government was free to simply ignore all their recommendations but it was a relief to disabled people across the UK to have had our reality formally acknowledged and documented.

Since 2017, the situation has deteriorated even further. When under pressure, the Tories have conceded minor mitigations as detailed in the preceding chapters. This confirms that they are fully aware of the impacts of their policies but choose to push on regardless. Theresa May claimed that austerity was over in her 2018 Conservative Party conference speech, but the continuing roll-out of Universal Credit and the failure to reverse the cuts mean that the relative incomes and living standards of the poorest and most disadvantaged in society continue to decline. In other words, *things are worse now than they were when the UN investigation was carried out and are continuing to get even worse.*

The complex interplay between the impacts of multiple negative changes is entrenching inequality ever deeper within society. The Equality and Human Rights Commission highlighted disabled people as one of the groups most at risk of 'being forgotten and becoming trapped in disadvantage' in its 2018 report on equality and fairness in Britain. A press release accompanying the report announced: 'Prospects for disabled people, some ethnic minorities, and children from poorer backgrounds have worsened in many areas of life. This inequality risks becoming entrenched for generations to come, creating a two-speed society where these groups are left behind in the journey towards a fair and equal country.'[2]

The war on disabled people must be understood within the context of a wider attack on the working class in Britain, which is enriching the wealthiest at the expense of the poorest. In May 2018, the Equality Trust warned of an inequality crisis, as the richest 1,000 people in the UK increased their wealth by £274 billion over five years. This took their total wealth to £724 billion, a sum that was significantly more than the wealth of the poorest

40 per cent of households at £567 billion. In 2018, there were 27.6 million households in the UK. This means that the combined wealth of the richest 1,000 people was more than 127 per cent greater than that of the poorest 11 million households.

Rising inequality is a direct result of regressive tax and benefit changes. According to the Office for National Statistics, the average income of the poorest fifth of the population after inflation contracted by 1.6 per cent over 2017–18, while the average income of the richest fifth rose by 4.7 per cent. In 2019–20, new tax and benefit changes will enrich the wealthiest fifth of households by an average of £280 – which represents 0.4 per cent of the median disposable income for that quintile – while the poorest fifth will lose £100 or 0.8 per cent of average household disposable income. More than a third of the £2.8 billion package of tax cuts for this year will go to the richest 10 per cent of households. The harm inflicted on disabled people is all the more shameful when we consider that others – those who were already well off in life – have benefited at the same time.

Part III looks at the individual and social impacts of government measures attacking disabled people. Chapter 6 explores the human cost of government legislation and policy affecting disabled people since 2010, including rising poverty, benefit deaths and psychological harm. It examines evidence that disabled people have been pushed further from paid work as a direct consequence of measures justified on the basis that they would incentivise employment, and argues that current policy is escalating future need, with damage being done from which it will take generations to recover.

Chapter 7 looks at the social impacts of policies and practice that threaten disabled people's continued existence in the community alongside non-disabled people. Funding cuts to education and social care and a failure to invest in accessible social housing are leading us towards physical re-segregation and institutionalisation. At the same time, there has been a fuelling of attitudes that 'other' and thereby marginalise disabled people: on the one hand, growing disadvantage, resulting from cuts to state-funded support and leading to greater reliance on charity, has encouraged a pity view of disability; on the other, hatred and hostility towards disabled people have been enflamed by anti-benefit-claimant rhetoric used by the government to justify welfare reform. Chapter 8 explores the political fallout from the government's war on disabled people and argues that disability cuts have contributed to the social polarisation that characterises the current political landscape. Bitter divisions have been created between those who have been exposed to the government's treatment of disabled people and those who are so removed that they don't realise or believe what is happening.

SIX | The human cost

Once a week, Mark and Helen Mullins would undertake a 12-mile round trip on foot to their nearest food kitchen in Coventry. Helen had a learning difficulty and was refused Jobseeker's Allowance (JSA) on the grounds that she was not fit for work; however, she had no medical diagnosis so she was also refused Incapacity Benefit. Living off Mark's £57.50 per week JSA, they could only afford to heat one room of the house and kept food in plastic bags in the garden as they could not afford a fridge. They became frightened that instead of receiving the support they needed, Helen would be sectioned. After they were found lying side by side in an apparent suicide pact, friends spoke to the media of the couple's struggle to access the correct benefits.

This was one of the first benefit death stories that came to public attention in the early years of the Coalition government. It tragically encapsulates the aspects of needless individual suffering and increasingly Kafkaesque bureaucracy within the social security system that have come to characterise welfare reform: Helen and Mark Mullins were in touch with services, they were in genuine need of support and yet, because they needed support, they were unable to navigate a social safety net rendered too complex for the very people who need to access it.

The incident sticks in my mind because it happened at a time when benefit deaths were a newly emerging phenomenon. Such stories are now media fodder on a near daily basis. It is right that we remember every person who dies unnecessarily as a direct result of government policy and that we call out each injustice, but it is also significant to note how desperation and suffering have grown to become part of everyday experience. As Frances Ryan writes, 'Death has become part of Britain's benefit system.'[1]

It is simply now impossible to give all the support that is needed as a result of cuts and benefit changes. Any organisation or individual vaguely linked to disability whose contact details come into the public domain now finds itself deluged with communications from distressed individuals desperately searching for someone to help, unable to believe what is happening to them, not knowing how they will survive. The vast majority of contacts are received by people and organisations that have no funding or capacity to provide advice, information or support in any form. Even those that are able to do so are unable to meet the level of demand that exists.

Death is the most extreme example of the human cost of austerity and welfare reform, but there are many other terrible impacts, including rising poverty, food-bank use, debt, survival crime and homelessness, in addition to widespread mental distress. The policies that have inflicted such harm have failed to deliver their stated policy aims and therefore have an aspect of needless cruelty about them. Research conducted over five years 'found that the [welfare] reforms were not only largely ineffectual in terms of boosting employment, but that they had indeed been actively harmful and were linked to a sense of social disengagement, a rise in poverty and destitution, a take-up of survival crimes and an exacerbation of ill health and impairments.'[2]

This chapter also looks at how disabled people's quality of life has been eroded by cuts to social care and community support services. These have led to increased isolation, anxiety and stress in addition to the removal of dignity and opportunities to participate in the community. Disabled people who employ personal assistants have been put at legal and financial risk by cuts to infrastructure support. Again, deaths and suicides have occurred as a consequence of government policy and practice in these areas.

Rising poverty

Poverty is rising as a direct consequence of welfare reform and austerity measures. The Tories continue in steadfast denial of this. In June 2019, Chancellor Philip Hammond told BBC *Newsnight*'s Emily Maitlis: 'I reject the idea that there are vast numbers of people facing dire poverty in this country ... I think that's a nonsense. Look around you, that's not what we see in this country.' Maitlis replied: 'I beg to differ. We're in Downing Street so if I look around me I'm not going to see a lot of poverty. But if I went to other parts of the country, I would see that poverty.' The BBC has been heavily criticised by disabled campaigners over the years since 2010 for providing the Tories with a platform to conceal the true nature and impacts of their policies, but Maitlis's point here was well made.

According to a new measure of poverty that takes into account costs such as housing and childcare, 14 million people in the UK – a fifth of the population – now live in poverty. In 2017, 1.5 million people experienced destitution, meaning that they had less than £10 a day after housing costs, or they had to go without at least two essentials such as shelter, food, heat, light, clothing and toiletries during a one-month period. Terms largely unheard of a decade ago, such as 'food poverty', 'fuel poverty' and 'funeral poverty', are now commonplace.

Rising poverty levels have a disproportionate impact on disabled people, the Department for Work and Pensions' (DWP's) own figures show that poverty among disabled people is rising steeply. In just one year, between 2016–17 and 2017–18, the number of disabled people living in poverty rose by 200,000. Figures also show that as many as 600,000 more disabled people are now in absolute poverty compared with 2010. Once housing costs have been accounted for, the number of disabled people living in absolute poverty has risen to 5 million.

Disabled people are disproportionately affected by food poverty. A report by the Equality and Human Rights Commission (EHRC) in 2017 found that 18 per cent of disabled people aged 16–64 across the UK were living in food poverty, compared with 7.5 per cent of non-disabled people – showing that the disabled community is more than twice as likely to struggle to pay for food as the rest of the population, in what the EHRC described as a 'failure' by government.[3]

Food-bank use has exploded under the Tories. In 2018, the country's largest food-bank provider, Trussell Trust, distributed a record 1.6 million emergency food parcels across its network, representing a 19 per cent surge in usage over the course of just one year. Pointing to data showing that its emergency food supplies had grown for five consecutive years – a 73 per cent increase overall – the charity warned that food banks could not keep expanding indefinitely to cover for a failing social security system. Three-quarters of households using food banks contain someone with a health condition and/or impairment and one-third contain someone with mental health support needs.

Research by the Trussell Trust found that people using food banks were also experiencing multiple forms of destitution. Fifty per cent had gone without heating for more than four days in the past 12 months, 50 per cent couldn't afford toiletries, and 20 per cent had slept rough in the last 12 months. Over 78 per cent of households were severely, and often chronically, food insecure. Universal Credit (UC) is unsustainably fuelling food-bank dependency. In areas where UC has been rolled out for a year or more, there is an average increase of 52 per cent in food-bank usage. This compares with a 13 per cent increase in areas either without full roll-out or where UC roll-out has been in place for only up to three months.[4]

While denying that 'vast numbers of people' in Britain live in 'dire poverty', Hammond did acknowledge in the BBC interview that people are 'struggling with the cost of living'. It is deeply ironic for a millionaire like Hammond to be passing judgement on what constitutes poverty as opposed to minor financial hardship. There is clear evidence of multiple negative social impacts arising from the removal of essential income from people unable to earn an adequate income through safe and legal means. At the same time that Hammond was rejecting the notion of widespread impoverishment, the Work and Pensions Committee (WPC) was carrying out an inquiry into UC and survival sex.

One woman spoke to journalist Frances Ryan about how she and many of her disabled friends 'started sex work for the ease and flexibility it offered to those who are too unwell for traditional employment – or, as she puts it, whose energy levels are sometimes too low to function properly but "who need money to survive in the world"'. Ryan comments: 'The use of sex work as a last option for marginalized women is not a new phenomenon, but as benefit cuts were rolled out, evidence pointed to austerity measures exacerbating women's reliance on sex work.'[5]

Other negative impacts include debt and homelessness, with disabled people disproportionately represented in rising levels of both. A study of 30,000 cases helped by Citizens Advice found that nearly half (48 per cent) had a long-term health condition or disability, with many falling behind on household bills like Council Tax or water rates.[6] According to official figures collated by the Department for Communities and Local Government, homelessness among disabled people increased by around 75 per cent between 2010 and 2017. Research by the homeless charity St Mungo's found that 80 per cent of rough sleepers who died in London in 2017 lived with mental distress, up from three in ten in 2010.[7]

Unless current policies are reversed, the situation is set to become even worse. Analysis by the charity Shelter suggested that a million households in Britain could be put at risk of homelessness by 2020 as a direct consequence of the freeze on Local Housing Allowance rates.[8] Of these, 211,070 contain a member who claims a disability benefit.

Multiple hits

Disabled people have been hit by multiple cuts and negative changes at the same time. For each one of these there is evidence of serious adverse impacts affecting large numbers of people. Many of these relate to having to cut back on necessities as a result of inadequate income. As the WPC heard through its disability employment gap inquiry, which took place from 2016 to 2017, benefit levels for disabled people were already falling short of meeting the support and living costs that claimants faced *before* the removal of entitlements including the Employment and Support Allowance (ESA) Work-Related Activity Group (WRAG) component and Severe and Enhanced Disability Premiums under UC. A few months after the bedroom tax came in, Papworth Trust found that nine in ten disabled people who had been turned down for emergency housing payments were having to cut back on food or on paying household bills, and more than a quarter (27 per cent) were cutting back on medical expenses such as medication, therapies and monitoring health conditions.

Reductions in income following assessment for Personal Independence Payment (PIP) have hit disabled people particularly badly. A major survey by more than 80 organisations reported that more than a third of those whose funding had been cut said they were struggling to pay for food, rent and bills.[9] By 2018, over 75,000 disabled people across Britain had lost their cars, power wheelchairs and scooters after losing eligibility for the higher-rate mobility component of PIP, leaving many isolated and trapped in their homes. This figure represented 43 per cent of the 175,000 Motability clients who had moved from Disability Living Allowance (DLA) to PIP at that point. At the same time as PIP claimants were losing out, Motability continued to do well financially. Motability Operations Group's chief executive Mike Betts took home £1.7 million in salary, benefits, pension, bonus and incentives in 2017, while the not-for-profit scheme was also revealed to have some £2.4 billion of public money in reserves.

Local government cuts to community support services have also forced disabled people to go without essentials. In 2014, two-thirds of councils were offering a daily hot meal to support older and disabled residents in their own homes. Two years later, that figure had gone down to less than half. The findings of a survey published in 2018, found nearly half (43 per cent) of respondents had to cut back on their food spending to pay for social care support, and 40 per cent said they had to cut back on heating costs. The effect of charging increases is often to 'drive disabled people into care poverty and to create confusion, stress and complexity in an already overly burdened bureaucratic system through what is effectively an unhelpful and unnecessary tax on disability and old age'.[10] Anecdotally, we hear about disabled people pushed out of the social care system through charges they cannot afford. Without regular low-level support, people's conditions are at risk of escalating to crisis point.

The same group of people has been hit by multiple cuts and changes and yet the government has consistently rejected calls by disabled people and the UN Disability Committee to carry out a cumulative impact assessment (CIA). Their initial claim that such an exercise is not feasible was undermined by the Institute for Fiscal Studies, which confirmed in 2014 that they think it is possible to assess the cumulative impact of tax and benefit changes for the disabled population as a whole. In December 2018, a backbench business debate was secured by Labour MP Debbie Abrahams on the government's continuing failure to undertake a CIA. In a briefing for the debate, Simon Duffy, Director of the Centre for Welfare Reform, highlighted 'the utterly self-contradictory claim that [the government] cannot carry out a CIA, but that its policies will have a beneficial impact on disabled people'. He commented: 'The only plausible reason is that the Government knows that any such analysis will show that its policies have caused considerable harm to disabled people and to other disadvantaged groups.'[11]

In the absence of government action, non-government agencies stepped in to attempt cumulative analysis. In 2013, the think tank Demos assessed the combined effect of 15 disability benefit-related cuts. They found that individual disabled people would be hit by up to six different cuts at once, while, overall, 3.7 million disabled people would experience some reduction of income.

The EHRC commissioned its own CIA of welfare and tax changes from 2010–11 until 2021–22. The findings confirmed that negative impacts are particularly great for households with more disabled members and for individuals with higher support needs. On average, disabled lone parents with at least one disabled child lose almost £3 of every £10 of their net income: almost £10,000 per year. The researchers concluded:

Our analysis shows that, overall, changes to taxes, benefits,
tax credits and Universal Credit (UC) announced since 2010
are regressive, however measured – that is, the largest impacts
are felt by those with lower incomes. Those in the bottom
two deciles will lose, on average, approximately 10 per cent of
net income, with much smaller losses for those higher up the
income distribution.[12]

Benefit deaths

In March 2019, the relatives of eight disabled people who died
due to DWP failings backed a petition to MPs calling for an
independent inquiry into deaths linked to DWP actions. In the
case of Jodey Whiting, a young woman who committed suicide
in February 2017 after her out-of-work benefits were stopped for
missing a Work Capability Assessment (WCA), the Independent
Case Examiner concluded that the DWP had failed five times to
follow its own safeguarding rules and was guilty of 'multiple' and
'significant' errors in handling her case. The response from the
DWP made it clear that they had no intention of changing their
practice following Jodey's death and confirmed that they 'currently have no plans to hold an independent inquiry into deaths
relating to actions taken by [the DWP]'.

Campaigners continue to be frustrated by the lack of accountability for any of the numerous deaths or suicides directly linked
by coroners to the removal of benefits. As the DWP has pointed
out, in Jodey's case there was no finding of 'any evidence of misconduct by Civil Servants or Ministers'. The removal of benefits
from people in vulnerable positions is a deliberate political choice
and an injustice so far without consequence for those responsible.

Deaths and suicides are associated with many if not all of the
welfare reform measures targeted at disabled people. At the time
of writing, the website Calum's List includes the names of over 60

people whose deaths have been publicly attributed by family and friends to the removal of benefits by the DWP. The true number will never be known. A phenomenon that started with the WCA has steadily continued with each new benefit cut. Meanwhile, nearly a decade after the first tragedies emerged, avoidable loss of life continues to be associated with the WCA.

A few years after the suicides of Stephen Carré and Miss DE (mentioned in Chapter 4) were linked to the WCA, the suicide of another man, Michael O'Sullivan, was ruled by a coroner to have been triggered by intense anxiety caused by his experience with the WCA process. Michael worked as a builder until severe mental distress made it impossible. Despite being signed off work by his GP, he was found 'fit for work' at the age of 60. He killed himself on 24 September 2013.

In 2016, as a result of legal action taken by *Disability News Service*, the DWP was forced to release redacted information from 49 Civil Service peer reviews carried out following deaths linked to benefits. The majority of these involved the WCA and reassessment for ESA.

Alongside the suicides, the removal of benefits has been held responsible by a number of families for hastening the deaths of their loved ones. In 2013, Mark Wood, who lived with complex mental distress, starved to death after a WCA found him fit for work and his ESA was stopped. This in turn triggered the stopping of his Housing Benefit, leaving him with just £40 per week to live on. Concerned about his patient's condition, Wood's GP wrote a letter stating that he was 'extremely unwell and absolutely unfit for any work whatsoever'. The letter, presented to the inquest, also stated that his anxiety disorder and obsessional traits had been made 'significantly worse' because of the pressure put on him by benefit changes. It is unclear whether Wood ever managed to pass the letter to the Jobcentre. When Wood died, he was markedly underweight and malnourished, with a body mass index described by his GP as 'not compatible with life'.

Moira Drury's daughter Nichole believes that a seven-month delay in processing her mother's benefit claim hastened her death in 2015. Moira, who was disabled and a survivor of domestic violence, worked as a nurse to bring up her three children. After missing two WCAs due to illness rendering her bed-bound, her ESA was terminated. While she attempted to navigate the system to reapply, her Council Tax Benefit was stopped, leading to a build-up of Council Tax debt and a court summons. For the last seven months of her life, as her health deteriorated, she received no income. Nichole concludes: 'I am absolutely certain that the stress she endured caused her to give up her fight against her illnesses. Without the stress this caused she would have had a little more precious time.'

A number of suicides have been linked to the bedroom tax. Stephanie Bottrill took her own life just one month after the bedroom tax was first introduced in 2013. She walked into traffic on the M6 road near her home in the early morning on 4 May, leaving behind a note that blamed the government for her death. In 2015, another mother hit by the bedroom tax, Frances McCormack, was found dead by hanging. She received an eviction notice on the same day her body was discovered. She was charged bedroom tax after her son killed himself, leaving her deemed to have a 'spare room'. Part of the note she left was addressed to David Cameron, describing the hardship that the bedroom tax was causing. An assistant coroner ruled that it was unclear whether she intended to take her own life or just to send a strong message to the authorities dealing with her case.

One in five of the Civil Service peer reviews whose release into the public domain was secured by *Disability News Service* involved the death of a benefit claimant who had been sanctioned.

The admission came in response to a Freedom of Information request submitted by the Disabled People Against Cuts (DPAC) research team. The DWP told DPAC that 10 of the claimants covered by the 49 'peer-reviewed cases' had had their benefits sanctioned at some stage. This suggests that claimants who have been sanctioned are far more likely to suffer a death linked to their benefit claim than those who have not.

One death linked to sanctioning that received media attention was that of David Clapson, a former soldier who died from lack of insulin 18 days after his JSA was suspended in July 2013. His sister, Gill Thompson, spoke out after he was found dead with just £3.44 in his bank account. His electricity card had no credit, meaning that the fridge where his insulin was kept chilled was not working. The petition started by Gill calling for a benefit inquiry attracted more than 177,000 signatures. Many years and deaths and much public and political pressure later, the government still refuses to carry one out.

The same pattern has now begun with Universal Credit (UC). One piece of written evidence submitted to the United Nations Special Rapporteur on Extreme Poverty and Human Rights on his 2018 visit to the UK was from a woman named Maggie whose brother died a month after attempting to take his own life. The brother, who had learning difficulties and cerebral palsy, was left hundreds of pounds in debt following a move onto UC. Maggie wrote:

> He had money worries and had received huge bills from DWP and housing after going on Universal Credit. Before this John had very good mental health and was a positive happy person ... I do not understand why my brother on Universal Credit and who did everything he was told to do, received huge frightening bills due to the fact that neither Universal Credit, or Working Tax Credit Benefit has not re-assessed him in a timely manner. John was a

very law abiding person and did everything that DWP, etc. told
him to do but was seriously let down by this department. His
benefits had been in chaos for several years but no one cared from
the various departments that John and myself contacted.[13]

John was not just hit by UC and the struggle of navigating DWP
systems but also by the removal of Council Tax Benefit and the
difficulties of communicating with the local authority:

At the same time John also tried at least six times to get a refund
of Council Tax he had overpaid but each time he visited the LB
[London Borough] Hammersmith and Fulham to say he was not
working they said he had the wrong form or piece of paper. They
did not help at all and fobbed off my obviously special needs
brother, and he never received a refund from them.[14]

Cuts to social care have also led to avoidable deaths. A study
carried out by health economics researchers and published in
November 2017 linked austerity to nearly 120,000 excess deaths
in England, with the over 60s and care home residents bearing the brunt.[15] Researchers warned that, going forwards, there
could be an additional toll of up to 100 deaths every day unless
trends in public spending were reversed. Campaigners' concerns
about the potential dangers of removing overnight support from
disabled people were tragically validated by the death of Amanda
Richards in Coventry in December 2013. After her 24-hour social
care support was cut she burned to death in a house fire, having no support to escape the blaze. The serious case review carried out after her death found that the cut in healthcare support
had played a major role in the events. The report showed that
there had not been an adequate risk assessment carried out into
the dangers of leaving Amanda unsupervised and that relatives'
concerns about the sustainability of the care plan had not been
properly considered.

Another death, in 2017, similarly provides evidence of the risk that disabled people with high support needs are being placed in as a result of failings in the social care system. Julie Cleworth, who needed assistance to drink, clothe and feed herself, died from starvation because a care worker failed to check on her. Julie starved to death after being left on her own for three days with no access to food, water or medication. The care worker was jailed in August 2019, but the bigger social justice issues about inadequate support and dehumanising living conditions for disabled people seem not to have attracted attention. Julie was apparently in receipt of support five times a day for periods ranging from just 15 minutes to an hour. Her mobility was severely restricted following a series of strokes, she was unable to walk, had learning difficulties and lived with mental distress. Given the level of her needs compared with what she received in support, her life must have been severely restricted. These are conditions comparable to the long-stay institutions where disabled people's most basic human needs were routinely neglected.

The government continues to deny a direct 'causal' link between government policy and benefit deaths. Their argument is that suicide is complex and cannot be attributed to any one thing: even if a person leaves a suicide note citing the removal of their benefits as the reason behind their decision, the government argues that the balance of their mind in choosing to kill themselves must also have been a contributing factor. It is a disingenuous argument, as Frances Ryan explains:

> Suicide is complex but it is not hard to predict what the impact might be on someone of losing their only income. Remove social security from a disabled person too disabled or ill to work and it's like pushing someone off a cliff and feigning surprise when they hit the beach.[16]

There is strong evidence of the harm and distress that welfare reform measures are causing and yet the government has chosen to push on in the same direction, continuing to roll out the same policies to greater numbers of people. Due to difficulties in obtaining evidence, campaigners are not able to robustly evidence that there have been tens of thousands of deaths and suicides, but even one death in avoidable circumstances should be considered too many and should warrant action to prevent a recurrence. It is clear that the government has been repeatedly warned by coroners and their own civil servants that their policies are putting the lives of disabled people at risk. They have consistently ignored these warnings. Thus we can say that this government has blood on its hands.

Psychological harm

Measures introduced through welfare reform, including benefit assessments and the intensification of conditionality, subject a significant proportion of the population to extended periods of extreme stress and anxiety. This inevitably aggravates existing conditions but also causes mental distress for disabled people who may not have experienced it previously.

Both quantitative and qualitative research document the impact of 'mad-making' aspects of welfare reform. A study by academics from Liverpool and Oxford Universities published in 2015 found that reassessments for Incapacity Benefit from 2010 to 2013 were associated with an extra 590 suicides, 279,000 additional cases of self-reported mental health problems and the prescribing of a further 752,000 anti-depressants.[17]

Non-disabled people have been made disabled by benefit cuts that cause significant distress and anxiety. Research published in 2016 concluded 'that reducing housing support to low-income persons in the private rental sector increased the prevalence of depressive symptoms in the United Kingdom'.[18] This was found to undermine the cost savings that changes to the Local Housing Allowance within Housing Benefit (HB) were intended to achieve. The researchers noted:

> [T]hese reforms ... (by increasing the level of depressive symptoms among recipients of the HB) potentially counteract policy initiatives in other areas that were designed to reduce reliance on disability benefits by reducing the generosity of incapacity benefits ... [T]he costs incurred in treating persons whose mental health has deteriorated may offset any potential savings resulting from cutting the HB.[19]

Processes of assessment/reassessment place strain on a number of levels. Considerable effort is required to understand and complete the application form, collect medical evidence and attend the face-to-face assessment. Many can only manage this with support. Owing to the level of inaccuracy in assessment reports, it is advised that a person should never attend an assessment alone but that they have someone with them who can verify what happens if required at a potential appeal stage. Only a small minority of people will be able to access formal support for this process. Those agencies that provide welfare information, advice and support concentrate their extremely limited capacity on help for appeals.

For assessments, those who have family, friends or neighbours will need to rely on them for support. This then places a burden on those around the disabled person who may themselves be subject to benefit assessments or to working conditions with little free time and difficulty obtaining time off work. There is no choice in the date or time of a face-to-face assessment, and arriving even just a few minutes late counts as non-attendance without good reason. This can result in the termination of benefit claims, necessitating starting a new application from scratch – a process that can take many months without any income.

Assessments themselves can be both mentally and physically traumatic. Analysis of NHS figures by *Disability News Service* showed that the proportion of people claiming out-of-work disability benefits who attempted suicide doubled between 2007 and 2014 following introduction of the WCA. Some claimants report tests by assessors not qualified in their particular conditions that put their physical safety at risk. The blogger Kitty S. Jones recalled her own experiences of a PIP assessment, which she described as 'dehumanising, degrading, very distressing and potentially harmful'. She wrote: 'No one should be made to feel worse because of an assessment for support. The activities I was asked to do should have been stopped when it became clear I was struggling. I stated I was in pain, I was visibly sweating, trembling, weak and clearly in a lot of pain with the effort.'[20]

Assessment approaches may vary between assessors but claimants consistently report feeling violated by the experience. If an assessor appears friendly and helpful, it can be even more upsetting to find that they have written a very critical assessment report essentially accusing the claimant of lying about their impairment. Aggressive questioning by assessors whose attitude openly suggests suspicion that the claimant is being dishonest is equally upsetting. There was outrage on social media when one claimant living with mental distress and suicidal ideation tweeted that she had been asked why she hadn't killed herself yet in her PIP assessment. Many others responded to say that they had been asked the same thing and inquiries to Atos and Capita revealed that this is a standard question. Approaching the question of suicidal thoughts in such an insensitive way risks triggering distress and self-injury.

Many disabled people get through life by focusing on the positives of what we can do, refusing to define ourselves by the pain or distress and barriers we face. Within the assessment process the disabled person must acknowledge and represent the full range of debilitating effects with which they live. Only then do they stand a chance of being found eligible by assessors looking for any opportunity to deny a claim. A concerted focus on the negative aspects of our lives can be extremely distressing. Undergoing repeated reassessments compounds this trauma.

Many disabled people are subject to multiple assessments. Around half of ESA claimants also claim PIP. Everyone on ESA needs to reapply for UC as it is rolled out. Each experience of an assessment confronts disabled people with extreme anxiety and stress, which are capable of aggravating our existing impairments. Research into understanding the impact of welfare reforms in Scotland for individuals living with mental distress found evidence that assessments cause permanent psychological damage. The researchers concluded:

> The WCA experience for many caused a deterioration in people's mental health which individuals did not recover from. In the worst cases, the WCA experience led to thoughts of suicide. People felt that there was an inconsistency in terms of GP recommendations and the WCA recommendations. Many people were subject to further upset and distress due to communication from DWP being lost in the post.[21]

It is not uncommon for individuals to be repeatedly called up for WCAs, stuck in a never-ending cycle of assessment, denial of benefits, and reinstatement on appeal, only to then be called again for reassessment. This places a persistent and intolerable strain on a person. One disabled woman found dead in her home in 2018, surrounded by unpaid bills and letters from the DWP, had been subject to annual WCAs. Over a five-year period, Sandra Burns was repeatedly found ineligible for ESA, then won on appeal each time – getting into debt during the process.

Her brother Ian told the local newspaper that the stress of the process had a degenerative impact on his sister, ending with the massive heart attack that killed her. He said:

> She could walk small distances and couldn't stand for long. Every time ATOS assessed her, they judged her fit for work. She described how one man said, "I've been watching you walk from the waiting room and as far as I'm concerned, you're fit for work." These appeals would take six to eight months. Every single time, she won the appeal and got a backdated payment. But in that period, she would get into debt and lose her credit rating. And then she'd get back on an even keel until the next year, when the same thing would happen.'[22]

Such hounding adds to the impression that disabled people are being vindictively targeted through welfare reform.

Conditionality and sanctions are so harmful that the WPC has called for disabled people to be exempt. A study carried out by researchers at the University of Essex found that, rather than incentivising work-related activity as conditionality is intended to do, there is evidence that it is literally 'mad-making'.[23] Under conditionality, participants are driven by a range of perverse and punitive incentives, being expected under threat of sanctions to engage in activity that undermines their self-confidence, such as removing their qualifications from their CVs in order to be more employable for jobs that are available.

The impact of sanctions was life-threatening for some participants as well as psychologically damaging. One participant described what led him to attempt to take his own life:

> The problem I had with that was the woman [working in the Jobcentre] who sanctioned me was in the same place and it made me extremely nervous. I now have a problem going into the jobcentre because I literally start shaking because of the damage that the benefit

> sanction did to me ... So yeah that was part, the sanction was one of
> the reasons that triggered the mental health and problems I'm having
> now ... it was awful and I ended up trying to commit suicide.[24]

Participants in the study described living in a state of constant anxiety due to the ever present threat of sanctions. Anxiety was exacerbated by the unpredictable way in which conditionality was applied, leaving participants feeling helpless and unsure how to avoid sanctions. This state of chronic fear is unlikely to enable people to engage in work-related activity.

The harm caused by punitive, burdensome and unfair welfare reform measures extends beyond individual claimants themselves. Family and friends are also subject to anxiety and distress as they experience the suffering of their loved ones at the hands of a system that is meant to provide support. The following open letter to Atos, the company that administered the WCA until 2015, sent to DPAC in 2012, powerfully captures the trauma and anger:

> To ATOS: where to start? Let's start with my son's father who
> was sent to you through his work. He was very, very ill. He could
> not work because of his condition, which by the way you did not
> assess properly. In fact, I don't think you did a proper medical
> on him! You told him that he was 'fit for work' and were signing
> him off sickness and that he would have to return to work after
> his last interview with him. He died. You, ATOS, called him to
> ask where he was as he had an appointment with you. I told you
> that he died the day before and you slammed the phone down on
> me. Not one word of condolence or sympathy for our loss. Just
> empty silence. Did you know what was wrong with him? Did
> you actually look at him properly? I think not! He worked hard
> all his life and was never on sickness till he began to get ill ... So
> Rest in Peace my poor Davy. This government failed you. You
> were a hard-working man who tried his best to keep his family
> and home together. After putting into the system for all those
> years, the system failed you when you needed help!

The government is fully aware of the devastating impacts of its welfare reform policies. Relevant consultations and inquiries have been overwhelmed with responses as individuals and organisations endeavour to make known the scale and impact of the cuts: the DWP was inundated with around 6,000 responses to its *Improving Lives* consultation on the future of disability, health and work, 'including 1,300 submissions via [DWP's] online platform Citizen Space, and over 3,000 emails'. The unprecedented response level to the WPC inquiry into benefit assessments included around 3,000 comments on the Parliament.uk website and 550 written evidence submissions; the United Nations investigation was itself informed by interviews with over 200 individuals and 'voluminous documentary evidence (more than 3,000 pages)'.[25]

The lack of available support for those seeking to navigate benefit assessments has placed a considerable additional workload on MPs' case workers, which also means that MPs from every elected party are well acquainted with the consequences of the policies that have been voted through in parliament. Once out of office, former Work and Pensions secretaries have gone on the record to criticise the harshness of the benefit assessments they were previously responsible for rolling out. During his short-lived bid to become leader of the Conservative Party, Stephen Crabb remarked in a TV interview: 'I see this in my surgeries, every single MP in their surgery sees this – people who felt that the assessment procedure has been traumatic, intrusive, hasn't been a comfortable experience at all. And that's what we've got to fix.'[26] One of the architects of welfare reform, Iain Duncan Smith himself, told a meeting: 'It was quite obvious to us that the system was far too narrow, was acting in a far too harsh manner and was making judgements about people.'[27] He added that, despite independent reviews that helped 'soften' these effects slightly, the system remains flawed.

Crisis in social care

Reductions in social care support packages restrict disabled people's ability to participate in the community while also causing immense stress and anxiety. Disabled people who require social care support to live in the community fear their social care assessments every bit as much as their benefit assessments, if not more. Cuts to support can place people in very real danger as well as prolonged discomfort, isolation and boredom on a daily basis. In June 2019, the Local Government and Social Care Ombudsman slammed Bolton Council for causing 'considerable distress and harm' to a disabled woman following a 60 per cent cut in her support package carried out by an assessor intent on reducing the hours of support she received. It was found that the cut from 67 to 25 hours a week left her unable to keep herself safe and properly medicated at weekends, harming her health and well-being. She recorded having 75 accidents over the 12 months after her care was cut. The ombudsman also raised concerns that other disabled people 'had similarly been caused significant injustice' by the council. Such practices are by no means limited to this one council.

Assessments for funding to pay for day-to-day support that enables disabled people to live in the community can be just as intrusive and distressing as the benefit assessments for ESA and PIP described earlier. Support assessments are undertaken by social workers for local authority 'care and support', or by Continuing Healthcare (CHC) assessors where there is a medical need. Support assessments are more convenient than benefit assessments in that they routinely take place in the disabled person's own home. The person also has more room to negotiate a time or day for the appointment that better suits them and any family, friend or advocate attending (although it is never an option to arrange an appointment outside working hours). However, the assessments can be just as confrontational if the disabled person is not compliant with suggestions for meeting their support needs in cheaper ways. Examples of this include replacing personal assistance hours with incontinence pads (when the person is not incontinent) or urinary catheterisation (which is painful and has a high level of risk attached, particularly for women).

Under the Care Act, assessments should be 'carer blind', but pressure is commonly brought to bear on disabled people to use friends, family, neighbours or anyone else for unpaid informal assistance in place of local authority-funded support. One woman was told that if she wanted to keep attending her community choir, she could ask the other participants to help her take her medication and use the toilet.

Social workers can make referrals for CHC funding and may want to be present during CHC assessments. It is not uncommon for social workers to argue with the CHC assessor in front of the disabled person as they try to offload as much cost onto each other as possible. CHC assessments are especially lengthy and ask about the most personal areas of a person's life, including incontinence and mental lucidity. The CHC system has been criticised as 'an intensely complicated and unfair system with big local variations in access and long delays in decisions that cause distress to patients and their families'.[28]

The general approach taken by cash-strapped local authorities is to scratch around for any possible savings that can be made from an individual support budget. This process can include referrals for other linked assessments, such as to Occupational Therapy, and can involve increasing levels of scrutiny aimed at identifying potential cuts. At least one local authority has suggested placing sensors in disabled people's homes to monitor the movements of personal assistants – if the assistant is deemed to be insufficiently active, the hours will be cut. Disabled people's own judgement about their conditions and support needs are not trusted. There is also an underlying attitude that people in receipt of state-funded support are not entitled to privacy or dignity.

When a person has high support needs, cuts to their daily support will have a major impact on their quality of life. Support assessments therefore provoke intense anxiety and stress. One former Independent Living Fund (ILF) recipient working for a Deaf and Disabled People's Organisation told Inclusion London:

> Before I was referred for funding from the Independent Living Fund I lived without having my most basic needs met, spending hours unable to have a drink or go to the toilet, without dignity and without any quality of life, existing between TV and hospital ... Unfortunately, in my job I see many people who are suffering the dreary lifestyle ... One client says that she feels she is treated 'worse than a dog – at least dogs get taken for a walk every day' – as she spends all but a couple of hours a week in bed ... The hour that she can spend in [her wheel]chair, while the care worker is doing housework, she drives from room to room like a caged animal.[29]

For disabled people who missed out on the ILF, lack of support for meeting even the most basic needs steadily became more and more common after 2010. Journalist Kate Belgrave reported on the experiences of one disabled woman, Angela:

> Angela's afternoon carer had been off sick the day before, which meant that Angela had not had anything to drink since 2pm the previous afternoon. She finds getting a drink for herself very challenging: the involuntary movements of her head and arms makes co-ordination and turning on the water taps difficult ... So Angela woke up at about 4am, thirsty. By about 5am, Angela was so thirsty that she decided to get out of bed, climb into her motorised wheelchair and travel down the road to the 24-hour Asda to buy a drink.[30]

Anecdotally, deaths and even one suicide have been linked to fears of support cuts and the stress of reassessment following ILF closure. One disabled woman told *Disability News Service* that being offered just seven hours a week to leave her home and access the community had added to her 'distress and feelings of panic, fear and dread and loss of control over her day-to-day life'. Another former ILF recipient told Inclusion London that he had taken a break from his employment due to the stress: '[T]he ongoing impact and stress of continual assessment and re-assessment, having to fight for basic things, has been a major contributor in me dropping out of the workforce, at least temporarily, in order to take a career break.'[31]

For disabled people living in the community, the ongoing management of individual support packages has also become increasingly stressful. This is due to the impact of cuts in eroding the infrastructure that was designed to support disabled people in managing their support budgets and employing personal assistants as personalisation was rolled out. Contracts for personal budget support services have been cut to the bone. Little more than payroll services are now commonly offered, leaving disabled people without support to understand and meet their legal obligations as employers of personal assistants. This becomes a problem of even greater significance when local authorities then bring in changes, charges and cuts as part of budget-saving measures.

Social workers themselves often lack awareness of employment obligations and commonly attempt to make cuts to support hours without honouring legal notice periods for personal assistants employed by the disabled person. Other disabled employers have had to battle with their local authority to be able to pay their personal assistants the national minimum wage. Her Majesty's Revenue and Customs (HMRC) confirmed that individual disabled employers would not be exempt from a scheme set to recover back pay owed as a result of a legal ruling on overnight support pay. This is an unhappy situation for both disabled employers, who are increasingly placed at financial and legal risk, and their personal assistants, who deserve secure jobs paid at a decent rate.

Mental health service closures

The closure of mental health community services by local authorities and Clinical Commissioning Groups (CCGs) is yet another way in which disabled people's lives and well-being have been put at risk by cuts. Closures are directly linked to the worsening of mental distress among former service users, which can then require more expensive interventions by acute services. In this way, a short-term cuts agenda represents a refocusing away from low-level prevention towards higher spending in more specialised treatment.

Powerful resistance led by service users in Cambridge in 2014 was able to save one mental health service from closure, but sadly many others across the country have shut. After almost four months continuous occupation of Lifeworks, a community-based drop-in and crisis centre, Cambridgeshire and Peterborough NHS Foundation Trust relented and a contract to keep Lifeworks open for at least another five years was signed. One service user, Alex Jones, told journalist Ros Wynne-Jones: 'I've been sectioned around 12 times. But since I've been coming here, I haven't had one hospital admission.'[32]

The type of barriers that people living with mental distress face can make it more difficult to be heard and to organise the kind of high-level resistance needed to get cuts overturned. The closure of a well-respected, life-saving residential unit for women with mental distress in Croydon went ahead despite opposition from former service users and their families. They argued that, instead of shutting the service, there were long-term preventative benefits to be gained from investing in rolling out the service model to neighbouring boroughs.

The fears of service users concerning the planned closure of Highgate Day Centre were similarly dismissed and the proposals went ahead in 2015. In 2017, Camden and Islington NHS Foundation Trust and Camden Council then issued a joint apology after the 'unacceptable' impacts of the cut were evidenced in a damning report by Healthwatch Camden.[33] By then, the damage had been done. The report said that dozens of people living with mental distress who used the centre in Highgate Road had been 'failed' by the cost-cutting move and that many reported suicidal thoughts that 'were not only perceived but real'. Three residents tried to kill themselves after the decision was taken. 'Anxiety, uncertainty, depression, isolation and sense of loss were caused by the changes,' the report said. 'The very high number of reports of negative mental health, including suicidal thoughts, give cause for serious concern.' Over seven months, Healthwatch obtained 'evidence of increased use of emergency services, hospital and crisis house admissions that appear to be a direct consequence of changes'.[34]

Pushing people further from employment

Welfare reform and austerity measures have pushed disabled people further from employment. The government has consistently justified its approach to disability by repeating its view that the best way out of poverty is through work and that its policies are targeted at supporting more disabled people into employment. Evidence of success rests entirely on the numbers of additional disabled people in work. Sixty per cent of people living in poverty are in a household where someone works,[35] so what this figure does not tell us is whether those additional people in work are earning an adequate living. There is also no tangible evidence that the increase is directly attributable to government policies.

Negative changes to Access to Work as well as the closure of Remploy factories (see Chapter 11) have created unemployment and have undermined disabled people's employment opportunities. It is also becoming more difficult for disabled people to stay in employment, with disabled people over-represented in redundancies and with performance management systems having a discriminatory impact on disabled workers. Official figures analysed by Scope in 2017 indicated that more disabled people were leaving employment than entering it. Between October 2016 and March 2017, 123,000 disabled people left employment. This represents 114 disabled people leaving employment for every 100 entering it. This compared with an equivalent of 100 non-disabled people moving into work and just 97 leaving.

Impoverishing people creates barriers to employment. Job searching requires access to the internet and phone credit. A person also needs to be able to keep smart and clean and to be well nourished. The WPC heard evidence from witnesses about how 'the greater the poverty a jobseeker is living in, the harder [it is] to find sustainable work'. One specialist employment provider explained: 'Poverty leads to unstable housing, mental health conditions, worsening physical health, debt and, at best, can provide a major distraction from the business of finding work.'[36]

Research found that benefits paid to disabled people in the ESA WRAG were inadequate even before the £30 per week cut introduced for new claimants from April 2017. Almost seven in ten disabled people surveyed (69 per cent) said that cuts to ESA would cause their health to suffer. A third (28 per cent) of survey respondents said that they could not afford to eat on the current amount they received from ESA. Forty per cent of respondents reported that they had become more isolated and less able to see friends or family after their ESA was withdrawn or reduced. Almost seven in ten (69 per cent) said that cuts to ESA would cause their health to suffer and almost half (45 per cent) said that the cut would probably mean they would return to work later.[37]

Conditionality and sanctions also push disabled people further from the labour market. Researcher Ben Baumberg Geiger concludes: 'Sanctioning may have zero or *even* negative impacts on job-related outcomes.'[38] Even the government's Behavioural Insights Team, whose flawed behavioural economics model underpins the idea of conditionality, has questioned the 'costs of depleting a person's psychological resources' through punitive approaches.[39]

Conditionality creates a disempowering power dynamic with work coaches that is mentally undermining for jobseekers. A study by researchers at Herriot-Watt University found that '[t]he WCA and other mandatory structures work against individuals developing or retaining employability skills as voluntary work is seen as demonstrating fitness for work; education is also not possible whilst receiving ESA. The system fails to recognise that for many, volunteering is good for well-being and may be "as good as it gets".'[40]

Cuts to daily living support for disabled people have a negative impact on employment opportunities. If a person lacks the support to get out of bed, get washed and dressed and leave the house, they will not be able to do a job even from home. In their response to the government's *Improving Lives* consultation, Inclusion London stated: 'A conversation between health and work that leaves out social care will unquestionably fail to deliver the Government's vision.'[41] This is not an issue that government is prepared to address.

Research by the MS Society into the impact of the 20-metre rule for PIP found that disabled people had been forced to reduce their working hours or leave employment altogether as a result of losing their Motability vehicle after being denied higher-rate PIP. They calculated that 927 people with MS had left work as a result of the 20-metre rule over three years and 905 had reduced their working hours.[42]

Creating problems for the future

In addition to the immediate harm caused by current government policy, far-reaching negative impacts will be experienced into the future. This is a consequence of permanent damage to the mental and physical health of a substantial proportion of the population requiring long-term support. Where cuts to public services and welfare reform have negatively impacted on children and young people, the damage to their life opportunities will have repercussions in terms of inequality, social cohesion and demand for adequate provision of support services for generations to come.

Austerity has fuelled an increase in the numbers of children taken into care. It is estimated that 75,480 children were in care in 2017–18, which represents an increase of 24 per cent in 10 years. Speaking on behalf of the Association of Directors of Children's Services, Stuart Gallimore said: 'A decade of austerity has, undoubtedly, impacted on children and families ... The cumulative impact of cuts, over many years, to the vital services children and families rely on is now being ever more sharply felt.'[43] Looked-after children – children in the care of their local authority and often living with foster parents – are known to face additional barriers throughout their lives, including increased risks of depression, anxiety, substance dependency and criminal convictions. This impact will therefore have a bearing on the need for support services into the future.

Cuts to social care are being compensated for by many children and young people whose parents are disabled. Forty per cent of respondents to a survey by the Children's Society reported that their children were spending more than 15 hours a week assisting their parents and 60 per cent were doing so for more than 10 hours a week. In 70 per cent of households with at least one child aged 10 or over, children were assisting their disabled parent for more than 10 hours each week. The responsibilities placed on children and young people in this situation can have negative impacts on their education and social inclusion.

Disabled young people are being caught up in gang exploitation and unjust government responses to youth crime as a result of disability cuts. Disabled young people are five times more likely to receive permanent exclusions from school. Cuts to mainstream education budgets resulting in inadequate learning support provision explain the dramatic increase in exclusions and off-rolling of disabled pupils. Options for pupils who fall out of education are slim, with many units and alternative provision providers chronically oversubscribed. As a result, many excluded pupils are taught for only a few hours each week. Evidence suggests that gangs are deliberately targeting disabled young people.[44] Measures introduced by the government to demonise young people and blame 'feral' youths for social problems are destroying the lives of disabled young people who happen to be in the wrong place at the wrong time. A number of young people who have been convicted with life sentences under Joint Enterprise legislation are disabled.

Compassion replaced with contempt

The level and range of harm inflicted on the lives of the most disadvantaged members of society by the Conservative Party are extraordinary – beyond what anyone would have imagined when the Tories took power in 2010. Following his visit to the UK, Philip Alston, the UN's Special Rapporteur on Extreme Poverty and Human Rights, described the way in which:

> British compassion for those who are suffering has been replaced by a punitive, mean-spirited, and often callous approach apparently designed to instil discipline where it is least useful, to impose a rigid order on the lives of those least capable of coping with today's world, and elevating the goal of enforcing blind compliance over a genuine concern to improve the well-being of those at the lowest levels of British society.[45]

Contempt for disabled people is evident in the government's failure to properly assess many of the impacts of the vast array of punitive policies they have relentlessly driven through since 2010. This is something the WPC has repeatedly challenged the government on and that has been consistently ignored. With regard to the removal of the disability premiums under UC, the WPC found that it 'risks disabled people living more isolated lives, relying more on unpaid care (including from their own young children), or simply being unable to gain support to complete basic daily tasks', and yet the DWP had 'carried out no analysis of its own to assess the effect of removing the premia'.[46]

The truth is that the Tories simply don't care what the impacts are. Endless reports and statistics evidencing the destruction wreaked by their numerous policy changes have been presented to them, so they can be in no doubt as to what is happening. The only conclusion to be drawn from this is that their mistreatment of disabled people is entirely deliberate. They have no intention of stopping a direction of travel that has caused disabled people to be 'routinely driven into destitution, pushed from the workplace and stripped of the right to live in their own homes'.[47] Without an official assessment by government of the damage done, the

Conservatives will simply continue to deny the evidence and push on, causing further pain.

The outlook for the future is frightening. Philip Alston has warned that '[b]y emphasising work as a panacea for poverty against all available evidence and dismantling the community support, benefits and public services on which so many rely, the government has created a highly combustible situation that will have dire consequences'.[48] Growing social problems, soaring levels of anxiety and mental distress and increased strain on public services, including the NHS, are already at critical levels.

It is small comfort to know that, for as long as the Conservative Party stays in government, it will not be able to escape the fallout from its pernicious policies. Chapter 8 considers the political damage the Conservatives have incurred as a consequence of policies that deliberately and detrimentally target disabled people.

SEVEN | Re-segregating society

The experience of being disabled in Britain has been transformed as the direct result of government policy and rhetoric since 2010 as society is reshaped to more fully exclude us. This is the combined effect of funding cuts and policy in a number of different areas, including education, social care, mental health service provision, housing and social security, in addition to trends emanating from privatisation in areas including health, housing and transport.

Attitudinal barriers against disabled people have also increased as part of a deliberate and coordinated strategy within implementation of welfare reform. The narrative of 'benefit scroungers' used to justify welfare reform has enflamed hostility towards disabled people. In response to disadvantage caused by austerity and the growing need among disabled people to rely on charity to survive, pity images of disability have proliferated, which, while attempting to emphasise the brutality of the cuts, have reinforced an 'othering' of disabled people.

This all amounts to a significant reversal in trends towards greater inclusion of disabled people that occurred in Britain in the decades towards the end of the twentieth century. The current situation is grave, but resistance is not straightforward: effective re-segregation is the cumulative impact of decisions and policies driven forward by many different government agencies for the most part independent of each other. This helps obscure an appreciation of the wider social significance in terms of disabled people's place in the community for almost anyone beyond our disabled community. The individual human tragedies caused by austerity and welfare reform have received far greater attention.

This chapter looks at different areas of policy and practice that are limiting disabled people's ability to participate in society and are re-institutionalising large numbers of those with the highest support needs. It argues that we are experiencing a re-segregation of society as a direct consequence of Tory rule. It also considers the influence of political rhetoric, media coverage and socio-economic circumstances in shaping attitudes towards disability that encourage an othering of disabled people and are another significant element within growing social exclusion.

Reversing inclusion

A backwards impulse towards the re-segregation of disabled people is being exerted in multiple areas of policy and practice. It is only discernible as a stated policy aim in education. In their 2010 General Election campaign, the Tories pledged to 'end the bias' towards the inclusion of children with special needs in mainstream schools. Under pressure from campaigners, the Children and Families Act 2014 retained a 'presumption for inclusive education'. In practice, as a result of deliberate funding cuts to education and pressure on schools to reach attainment standards, disabled pupils have been pushed out of mainstream education while placements in 'special' schools have increased.

Segregated schooling is harmful for society in a number of ways. Disabled pupils in special schools are less likely to obtain the same educational opportunities or the life experience required to transition to adulthood, and this acts as a barrier to social inclusion in later life. Lack of exposure to disabled peers at school age fosters negative attitudes that beget discrimination, hatred and hostility towards disabled people.

Re-segregation may not be a stated aim but it has been a clear product of numerous other policy measures since 2010: the failure to invest in community support options and the closure of Assessment and Treatment Units, while allowing private companies to open new institutional 'hospitals', have left thousands of disabled people incarcerated in abusive and neglectful environments; the chronic shortage of accessible housing combined with investment in large 'supported housing' and 'extra care' complexes has the potential to ghettoise our communities; the closure of community support services for people living with mental distress alongside investment in more acute units represents a return to the asylum; the cost-capping of community care awards by local authorities and the NHS threatens disabled people's right to live in their own homes. At the same time, welfare reform is increasing financial exclusion.

Since 2010 we have seen the emergence in Britain of the phenomenon of disabled people becoming 're-institutionalised' in their own homes. In 2017, shortly after providing its Concluding Observations on the examination of the UK under the United Nations Convention on the Rights of Persons with Disabilities (UN CRPD), the UN Disability Committee published a General Comment on interpretation of Article 19: the right to independent living and being included in the community. Within this, the Committee clarifies that 'institutionalisation' is not 'just' about living in a particular building or setting, but is 'first and foremost, about losing personal choice and autonomy as a result of the imposition of certain life and living arrangements'. It goes on to specify that '[not] even individual homes can be called independent living arrangements if they have other defining elements of institutions or institutionalization'. A General Comment is intended for use within all state parties signed up to the UN CRPD; however, the Committee clearly had in mind the situation in the UK when drafting this one.

One of the biggest factors contributing to re-institutionalisation is the ever-diminishing lack of adequate social care support to enable disabled people to live in the community with the chance to participate on an equal basis with others. It is estimated that there are now 1 million disabled people living with unmet social care support needs. A survey by the Care and Support Alliance found that, due to a lack of social care, over a third of respondents could not leave their homes and over a quarter have been unable to maintain basics like washing, dressing and/or visiting the toilet. This absence of support is 'making people unwell, unsafe and unfed'.[1]

Inability to leave the house is a product of cuts and shortages in a number of areas in addition to social care. In 2018, the British Red Cross warned that a UK-wide shortage of wheelchairs was leaving as many as 4 million people a year housebound and isolated, some of whom were terminally ill and spending the last few months of their life trapped at home. Research by Disability Benefits Consortium in 2017 found that four in ten disabled people said that the transition to the Personal Independence Payment (PIP) had led them to become more isolated as a result of reduced awards. Over a quarter reported that they were no longer able to get to hospital appointments.[2]

Access to appropriate facilities and adequate support for toileting and keeping clean are priority components for the social inclusion of disabled people. Over a quarter of a million people with physical impairments need toilets accessible to the Changing Places toilets standard – larger sanitary accommodation for people with more complex support needs – to enable them to go out. A lack of these means that some people and their families are never able to travel more than a short distance from their homes.

Support with toileting and personal hygiene is a basic need for disabled people with many different impairments; this includes not just people with physical and mobility impairments, but also affects people with learning difficulties, those living with mental distress and people who are autistic. People who are able to leave their homes, use public transport and use community spaces but who do not have support to keep clean experience a different but equally real and unfair social exclusion. These are issues that receive less attention than they deserve due to social stigma. Among disabled people, they are more widely discussed. Incontinence pads became one of the props commonly used on protests against closure of the Independent Living Fund (ILF).

The sketch 'Parfum de Piss', written and performed by the great Sophie Partridge and Penny Pepper, conveyed their deep personal fears, shared by many of those in receipt of the ILF, about what the future held for them:

> We would like to announce to you advance notice of a new perfume range.
>
> 'Parfum de Piss' – the authentic aroma of the neglected disabled person, capturing the fragrance of the lavatoire, fresh from the soiled bed and chair. This scent is for those special enforced moments, hours, and days, when the care funding and independence is cut. Available to you now in several varieties.
>
> 'Damn-You Dew', the delightful smell of meaningless lives and empty existence.
>
> 'Non-Veggie', with the top note stench of the individual disabled person starved of fresh food.
>
> 'Bouquet de Minuit', an essence of frustration that encapsulates captivity – within your bed, your four walls, set against the happy aroma of folk living their lives.

'Desperation', the ultimate scent, full of the final inevitable pong of condemned worthlessness.

Available shortly from Ex-recipients of the Independent Living Fund.

Living in fear of surveillance

Surveillance of people on benefits discourages social participation. Fear of being accused of benefit fraud is stopping people from taking part in activities that could enhance their well-being and improve their quality of life. On a wider level, this has led to greater social exclusion of disabled people and more entrenched divisions within society.

After the 2012 Paralympics were hosted in London, various initiatives sought to establish a disability sport 'legacy' from the Games. In spite of the time, money and effort invested in these, sport and physical activity levels among disabled people have dropped. Figures published in December 2016 showed that 20,900 fewer disabled people played sport once a week than they had 12 months earlier. Sport England subsequently stopped collecting this data.

Research published in 2018 showed that fear of losing benefits is preventing disabled people from taking part in physical activity and accessing the associated health and social benefits. More than a third (34 per cent) of those surveyed reported that they or someone they know had benefits sanctioned or removed as a result of being physically active; almost half (47 per cent) were fearful of losing their benefits if they were seen to be more active; and more than half (55 per cent) said that they were likely to be more active if benefits weren't at risk of being taken away.[3]

Surveillance has become increasingly widespread, with more and more private companies asked to send in footage and with gym memberships, airport footage and surveillance videos from public buildings now used to build cases against claimants. Posts from social media are also used to suggest that people are lying about their impairments and the barriers they face. Collaboration with the Department for Work and Pensions (DWP) is a tactic now used by the police to target protestors. In one example of this, Lancashire Police admitted to *Disability News Service* to passing video footage and other information to the DWP about disabled protesters peacefully campaigning about the drilling activities of the energy company Cuadrilla near Preston New Road, on the edge of Blackpool. Lancashire Police were also accused of repeatedly targeting and assaulting the same disabled protestors. It is simply not true that the ability to participate in any of the activities where surveillance is used automatically translates to an ability to find employment and engage in the labour market.

Scroungers versus superhumans

The Tories have deliberately enflamed hostility against disabled people as an integral element within their strategy for pushing through welfare cuts. This tactic of demonising in order to scapegoat benefit claimants has heightened oppression and encouraged dehumanisation of disabled people. Many disabled people have been left afraid to leave their homes or to go online. A 2018 parliamentary inquiry into online abuse found a 'culture of fear' triggered by soaring levels of hatred targeted at disabled people both online and in person.

This is a direct consequence of public attitudes being affected by statements made by politicians about fraud in the disability benefits system that are then relentlessly amplified in the media. The inquiry report records that '[m]ultiple participants in our events spoke about a culture of "demonising" disabled people. The hostile language associated with benefits and using blue badges came up at all the events we ran.'[4] Testimonies given by disabled people to the inquiry describe how 'a fixation on disabled people as "benefit scroungers"' has created an environment of constant suspicion, hostility and resentment.[5]

A second contrasting, but no more realistic, representation of disability was introduced to the British public in 2012: the image of the 'superhuman' disabled athlete, originating with Channel 4's coverage of the Paralympic Games. Celebration of the achievements of disabled athletes was used cynically by the right wing in juxtaposition with the image of the 'benefit scrounger' to promote to the public a version of disability that fitted the Tory agenda. According to this, the acceptable disabled person is someone who looks disabled, conforms to society's preoccupation with individualism and works hard to overcome their 'adversity' rather than asking for support. A piece by Leo McKinstry that ran in the *Daily Express* illustrates the interconnection between the narratives of 'scrounger' and 'superhuman', contrasting the 'heroic Paralympics' with a view of the benefits system as 'a grim world of state-controlled victimhood'.[6]

Neither narrative conveys the reality of disabled people's experience. Paralympians need support with the extra costs of disability as much as anyone, without which they are unable to compete. Since 2012, numerous Paralympians have spoken out about the negative impact of welfare reform and austerity measures on their own sporting careers and those of future generations of disabled athletes. The impact of the 'two conflicting image sets' was, as artist-activist Liz Crow has written, that 'disabled people's real lives are rendered invisible, even as they feel the full force of the images'.[7]

With this duality created in the popular imagination, those who fail to fit the acceptable image of disability – as the vast majority of disabled people do – are then assumed to belong to the category of 'scrounger'. As a result, the Paralympics failed to deliver the dramatic improvement in attitudes towards disability that had been hoped for from the sell-out crowds and widespread public enthusiasm. A year after the Games, a poll by Scope showed that 81 per cent of disabled people had not noticed that attitudes towards them had improved since London 2012, while just over a fifth believed that matters had deteriorated. Eighty-four per cent said that they felt the language used in the debate about benefits and disabled people had caused a negative shift in public attitudes.

The public obsession with cheats and fraudsters fostered by the demonisation of benefit claimants has produced widespread harassment of disabled people. Public awareness about disability is low and filled with misconceptions. Levels of benefit fraud are also vastly exaggerated in the popular imagination. Focus groups held as part of a wider study into changing portrayals of disability in the media found that members of the public thought that levels of benefit fraud were as high as 70 per cent at a time when the true figure was no more than 0.5 per cent. The researchers concluded: 'There has been a significantly increased use of pejorative language to describe disabled people, including suggestions that life on incapacity benefit had become a "Lifestyle Choice" ... These changes reinforced the idea of disabled claimants as "undeserving".'[8]

Coronation Street actor Cherylee Houston spoke out after one incident which has become commonplace in the lives of disabled people in Britain. She told the *Daily Mirror* that a man came to her home and made accusations to her husband that she was a benefit cheat after having seen her walk a few steps to her wheelchair.

Public 'policing' of disability entitlements extends throughout disabled people's lives, affecting the use of blue badges for parking, bus passes, priority seating on public transport and toilets as well as social security payments. Crohn's and Colitis UK publicised the 'suffering and devastating consequences' for disabled people with invisible impairments caused by 'sincere' public intentions. A survey on behalf of the charity found that 93 per cent of people think that by challenging a 'healthy-looking person' for using the toilet, they are 'standing up for the rights of disabled people', or they are doing it because they believe it is 'not fair' on the rest of society; 12 per cent admitted they would directly confront someone who didn't show any visible signs of an impairment if they were using a disabled toilet.[9]

Demonisation of benefit claimants has unleashed expressions of hatred towards disabled people concerning the worth of our lives. In the online sphere, growth trends in cyberbullying and social media abuse have made this an even greater problem. Giving evidence to the parliamentary inquiry into online abuse, writer-activist Penny Pepper commented: 'At present, the zeitgeist of disabled people as scroungers and benefit cheats is almost permission to further this abuse.'

Research into disablist hate speech on the online comment forum Reddit found evidence of an inter-relationship with welfare rhetoric. Disablist comments that had been posted by ordinary members of the public included statements such as 'I hate retards', 'I believe that children with severe mental handicaps should be killed at birth' and 'All parasites should perish … You do NOT have ANY right to exist on the INVOLUNTARY backs of others.'[10]

Individual-level attitudes such as these link back to the tenet underlying capitalism – that no one owes disabled people a living.

Charity cases and passive victims

The idea of disability as personal tragedy has been strengthened through austerity and welfare reform, taking wider society further from the social model of disability and an understanding that people with impairments are not inevitably held back from life opportunities but that the barriers they face are socially created. Charitable giving has stepped in as state support has been cut, more firmly establishing the links between disability and charity that disabled campaigners fought to sever over generations. Meanwhile, the portrayal of disabled people as victims in anti-government rhetoric has tended to invoke pity imagery and contribute to a view of disabled people as 'other'.

Cuts have undermined years of fighting for disabled people to be seen as having equal value in society and to be given entitlements to support in place of charity. As state support has been pulled away, disabled people have had no choice but to turn to charity in order to continue with their lives. The growth of food banks is one example of this. Another is the use of crowdfunding sites to raise money for disability equipment by, effectively, begging from friends, colleagues, strangers – anyone who can spare something. Between 2015 and 2016, the amount of money raised for wheelchairs on the internet site JustGiving increased fourfold, from £365,000 to £1.8 million.

Many disabled people in desperate situations have thankfully received the help they needed in this way when there was nowhere else to turn, but it should not be necessary. The feelings of shame this can arouse were conveyed by one research participant interviewed by Daniel Edmiston. She explained:

> I needed a shed for my mobility scooter, because it was deemed a health and safety risk having it in my household. And I had to fundraise to get that money and I felt like quite soul-destroyed, I just like, I wanted a shed ... I didn't have that control and having to go out to friends and family – I felt like begging. Yes, if you're not earning your own money, you have to do that.[11]

Increased reliance on charitable giving is a regressive trend that affects the way in which disabled people are seen, reinforcing an unequal power dynamic between disabled people and the rest of society.

Disabled campaigners have persistently criticised the wider left for its use of negative portrayals of disabled people in railing against the impacts of austerity, in particular for the repeated use of the word 'vulnerable' to describe those worst hit by welfare reform. While wanting people to speak out firmly against cuts, campaigners have argued that it is possible to do this without resorting to language and imagery that contribute to an other-ing of disabled people. The word 'vulnerable' is not consistent with the social model in that it suggests that the disabled person is inherently and inevitably inferior. It is a use of language that locates the essential problem within the person with impairment, and, in so doing, removes attention from the role played by the socio-economic structures of the system we live under in putting disabled people in situations of risk.

A post on the Disabled People Against Cuts (DPAC) website from 2014 made a 'plea to the left' to stop using the 'V' word:

> Too often though over the past few years in the fight against the Tories, negative portrayals of disabled people have been pushed by people on our own side, including disabled people themselves, who have, consciously or otherwise, sacrificed principles of disability equality for the sake of lazy invective against the Condems.[12]

This is an issue that has been picked up within the disability sector from across the political spectrum. Some have used it to support their mistaken position that left-wing politics do not rep-resent the interests of disabled people. For example, disability consultant Neil Crowther commented in a blog post on rhetoric that 'speaks not of the consequential limitations on equality and participation, but of "cruelty" to the "most vulnerable members of our society'". He described this as 'language reminiscent of a pre-disability rights era where disabled people were regarded only as objects of charity or care'.[13]

Disabled campaigners with a better grasp of the situation, such as Professor Peter Beresford, call for the involvement of disabled people in the process of creating and sharing stories so they are helpful 'rather than just simply serving as a source of "sad stories" and passive accounts of disempowerment and marginalisation'.[14] He encourages the connection of individual experience with broader analyses that can point the way to change rather than just focusing on the failings of the current system. The same sentiment has been expressed by DPAC:

> Railing against Tory savagery is all very well if you are just looking for someone to hear you and come to the rescue. Increasingly however people are realising that rescue isn't an option, that if we want change, it is up to us to make it happen.[15]

The fight for equal life chances

'The gains that generations of disabled campaigners fought for have been rapidly rolled back,'[16] as Frances Ryan, among many others, has highlighted. Retrogression is terrifying for anyone acquainted with the levels of violence, abuse and neglect that characterised the lives of disabled people in previous generations.

Life under capitalism embeds a view of disability within social consciousness that sees the dehumanising treatment of disabled people as inevitable. This makes it immensely difficult to challenge discriminatory practices once they take hold. When disabled people lose access to places where we can challenge our own oppression, the odds become dramatically stacked against us. Any rolling back of progress therefore presents an enormous threat to social inclusion.

Patterns of re-segregation and the implications for inclusion on a societal level seem to be on the radar of no one except disabled campaigners ourselves. This is because disability is still predominantly viewed through a pity prism rather than understood to be an equalities issue. The amount of print space and airtime given over to accounts of the personal suffering inflicted by specific policy measures is vast. By contrast, opportunities to comment on the collective oppression of disabled people are rare. Formats used in the mainstream media prevent communication of a politicised understanding of disability. News features stick to a formula of individual case study and dispassionate analysis by professional experts. Politicised disabled campaigners are not what the media wants in either category. On disability topics, these experts are invariably representatives from non-user-led charities that do not promote the social model.

On the wider left, while there is always eagerness to find a stick with which to beat the Tories, understanding of the social model is also generally absent, except among campaigners and journalists who are themselves disabled. The greater tendency is to present a personal tragedy caused by Conservative policy, then move straight to a party political conclusion without putting what is happening into the wider context of disabled people's oppression. This can be immensely frustrating to campaigners who understand what is at stake but is reflective of the powerful material forces that maintain disabled people's marginalisation and present it as common sense.

EIGHT | Political fallout

A government does not attack its own citizens en masse without consequence. Government legislation and policy since 2010 is directly responsible for what the United Nations Special Rapporteur on Extreme Poverty and Human Rights has described as the 'systematic immiseration of a significant part of the British population'.[1] According to Iain Duncan Smith, the Tories calculated that '[disabled people] don't vote for us'[2] and that any fallout from their attacks would not affect their chances of re-election – especially if they managed to hide from their voter base the full picture of the harm they were causing. Lies, misinformation and scapegoating have been used to achieve this concealment.

In terms of retaining control of Westminster, the Tories were largely correct in their assumption and it was the opposition parties that initially had most to contend with: the Scottish National Party (SNP) benefited from adoption of a clear-cut anti-austerity and anti-welfare reform position while Labour's failure to do the same scuppered their chances at the 2015 General Election and the Liberal Democrats were almost wiped out in parliament as punishment for their collaboration in the cuts agenda.

The Tories have not escaped punishment. Zac Goldsmith's London mayoral election campaign was arguably damaged by disabled campaigners chasing him around London protesting about his vote in parliament in favour of cuts to Employment and Support Allowance (ESA). A local disability organisation also publicly asked him to resign as patron in response to his vote as MP for Richmond in favour of passing the Welfare Reform and Work Bill that introduced the cut to ESA.

What David Cameron miscalculated was the impact on the two big referendums he promised on Scottish independence and on leaving the European Union (EU), expecting to win and settle both debates for a generation. He narrowly won one and lost the other. His replacement as prime minister, Theresa May, consistently failed to get a Brexit deal past her own MPs. Ongoing civil war among the Conservatives over the question of Brexit was so intense that the party's own members feared its destruction. After the Tories' worst ever European election result in May 2019, Minister Jeremy Hunt admitted that there was an 'existential risk to our party unless we now come together and get Brexit done'.

Another foreseeable consequence that was clearly of no concern to David Cameron or George Osborne was the deep social division that their austerity policies would cause. These have led to political polarisation and have made Britain dangerously exposed to the global growth of the far right. Duncan Smith told *The Andrew Marr Show*:

> I think [the government] is in danger of drifting in a direction
> that divides society rather than unites it. And that I think is unfair
> … that unfairness is damaging to the Government, it's damaging
> to the party, and it's actually damaging to the public.[3]

He was correct about the wider damage inflicted on society by cuts that hurt the poor to benefit the well-off; he was wrong that the Tories were only drifting in that direction – it was an agenda that he was involved in enacting from when they first took power in 2010.

This chapter looks at the levels of anger and distrust aroused by austerity and welfare reform measures and argues that they have played a significant but overlooked role in the political upheaval of the current climate. It examines how the SNP recognised the impacts of austerity much earlier than Labour, which continues to be divided over the question of its approach to social security, and argues that clear pledges against welfare reform garnered support for both the SNP and Jeremy Corbyn as leader of the Labour Party. The chapter also considers the cynical exploitation of disability issues by UKIP in its attempts to build support and argues that factors other than racism accounted for their successes and for the vote to leave the EU. The chapter concludes with the argument that one of the reasons why political commentators keep getting their predictions wrong is that they are out of touch with issues affecting the daily realities of large numbers of the population.

Politicising the people

People become quickly politicised when their lived experience brings them to question the system they live under. Since 2010, austerity and welfare reform have directly interrupted millions of people's lives in unwelcome and often distressing ways. Journalist Mary O'Hara witnessed the 'mushrooming intensity of the financial and mental strain inflicted by austerity with each passing month' as she travelled around Britain back in 2013.[4] Conditions have worsened since then, affecting many more people.

Welfare reform is particularly adept at politicising large swathes of people. Experiences where individuals have their benefits stopped are obviously traumatic for those affected but all benefit claimants are now subject to an approach which is personally harrowing. All claimants are subject to processes of assessment and reassessment that assume they are guilty of claiming support they do not need until they can prove otherwise. This is upsetting for the vast majority of claimants who are not attempting to defraud the system. The entire system is riddled with unfairness as claimants are expected to jump through hoops with zero compassion for the strain and pain it causes them, while officialdom in the form of the benefit assessors and Department for Work and Pensions (DWP) make error after error.

This is happening on a considerable scale. In 2013, it was reported that tens of thousands of disabled people were going through reassessments for ESA every month. Through considerable effort and stress, many claimants do receive the correct award, but also many do not. Those who do not are in the comparative minority, but, as the Work and Pensions Committee (WPC) pointed out, this is a sizeable minority representing hundreds of thousands of disabled people. From 2013 to 2018, 290,000 claimants of the Personal Independence Payment (PIP) and ESA – 6 per cent of all those assessed – received the correct award only after going through the drawn-out and difficult process of challenging the DWP's initial decision. There are many others who give up or who are unable to overturn the decision.

The model of disability that underpins welfare reform, known as the biopsychosocial model of disability, assumes that many disabled people adopt a 'sick role' and are held back by negative ideas about what they can do – in other words, that they could do more if they were pushed to. It is an approach that invalidates disabled people's own judgements, and, as such, is deeply confrontational. By taking this approach, the DWP has effectively brought itself and the government it represents into direct conflict with millions of individual disabled people, as well as the friends, families, neighbours, acquaintances, doctors, disability support workers, welfare advisers, public lawyers and journalists who support their assessment of their own support needs.

The biopsychosocial model builds on practices developed by the insurance industry in the USA to deny disability claims (this is discussed in more detail in Chapter 9). The insurers' aims were to reduce high claims on a type of policy they regretted having sold when their profits began to fall. The amount they paid out in legal settlements was offset by the overall savings they made from adopting an aggressive approach towards disability claimants. The DWP's situation, as a department of government, involves different consequences. Anger incited by mistreatment at the hands of the DWP extends to the political party in charge and has wider political consequences beyond the issue of welfare.

There is now a 'chronic' lack of trust in the social security system. The WPC has highlighted its concerns about this development, commenting: 'Trust is fundamental to the overall running of a successful society. Likewise, trust in the assessment systems is essential to PIP and ESA functioning effectively.'[5] Research findings show that 'the public are more concerned about the unfair treatment of genuine claimants than the unfair claims of undeserving ones'.[6] More people participating in studies carried out by Ben Baumberg Geiger 'said they knew a deserving claimant who has struggled to get benefits than a claimant who is not genuinely disabled (28 per cent vs 19 per cent). And more people thought it was more important to support genuine claimants than to root out fraud (45 per cent vs 22 per cent).'[7]

According to research by the think tank Demos, only 20 per cent of the public think the DWP understands the concerns of disabled people. Their conclusion is that it is now impossible for the DWP 'to ever meaningfully engage with [disabled people] and provide successful employment support'. While I do not agree with their recommendation that DWP functions should instead be outsourced to the third sector – reversing welfare reform and changing policy direction is a better way to restore trust and does not further the erosion of our public services – the suggestion is a reflection of how destructive welfare reform is seen to have been.

The principle of a social safety net that is there for those in need is generally well supported within British society and assumed by many to exist. When people discover its limitations, for example when they find they need to pay for social care or are found ineligible for out-of-work benefits even though they are too ill to work, they are often shocked and upset. Many have been left in 'utter bewilderment' that a government in one of the richest nations on earth is 'eviscerating the social safety net for its poorest citizens'.[8] There is intense anger against politicians who either support the government's policies or who have not been seen to do enough to stop them.[9]

A topic currently under the media spotlight is the growing culture of hostility towards politicians, particularly on social media. This is a complex issue involving unacceptable sexist and racist abuse and the growth in confidence of the far right. In relation to government legislation and policy that deliberately and callously remove support from disabled people, it is naïve to think that those who are experiencing and/or witnessing daily desperation and suffering will not be angry towards those in positions of power who are involved either in their active implementation or in failing to oppose them adequately. There are aspects of this hostility that need to be understood for what they are: the communication of how unbearable life has become for so many people in Britain as a direct consequence of the decisions made by government. Simply condemning expressions of anger without looking into the causes will not change the underlying socio-economic factors that are creating divisions.

Trauma, confusion and anger can turn to demoralisation and distress, but they can also lead to politicisation and activism. Research into the impact of conditionality on disabled people by the University of Essex and Inclusion London found evidence that, in order to make sense of their situation, claimants came to think about their difficulties within the context of the political climate and Tory attacks on disabled people. Those who adopted an attitude of resistance towards the system and/or became politically engaged were better able to restore a sense of self-esteem that had been taken from them by their interactions with the DWP. The evidence supports an observation made by David Frayne, who writes: 'For every person turned towards blaming themselves for problems like unemployment or work stress, I strongly suspect there is another person who sees through the ruse, and another still who becomes so frustrated by the con that they link up with others and take action.'[10]

Lib Dem calamity

The Lib Dems were severely punished by voters for their role in facilitating austerity and welfare reform. Even now this is something they deny, continuing to justify their coalition with the Tories as providing a 'restraining' influence. They have grossly underestimated the levels of anger that are still directed their way as the legislative and policy measures they helped implement continue to wreak havoc on society.

The outcome of the 2015 General Election was, in the words of then Lib Dem leader and Deputy Prime Minister Nick Clegg, 'immeasurably more crushing' than he had feared. The fact that he failed to see this coming is evidence of a remarkable level of out-of-touchness with the electorate.

In the 2017 General Election, the Lib Dems regained another four seats although their vote share dropped another 0.5 per cent. It was a particularly celebrated moment for anti-austerity campaigners when Clegg, the man who had taken the Lib Dems into the Coalition government, lost his seat as MP for Sheffield Hallam after 12 years to a disabled candidate, Jared O'Mara, in one of the shock results of the election.

The two key grievances that disabled campaigners hold against the Lib Dems are, first, their support for welfare reform as it passed through parliament, and, second, their failure to halt escalating crises in either the social care or mental health systems. It was under their watch that such serious retrogression occurred as to pass the threshold of evidence for the UN to find grave and systematic violations of disabled people's rights.

The introduction of the Care Act 2014 was led by Lib Dem ministers. Assurances that the Care Act would protect disabled people were entirely empty and its passage created a dangerous distraction that effectively provided cover for the savage cuts to social care going through at local authority level. A succession of Lib Dems held the position of Care Services Minister within the Coalition government. They arrogantly dismissed disabled people's concerns about the closure of the Independent Living Fund (ILF) and the growing social care crisis and sided with the Tories in voting down an amendment that could have introduced the wording of Article 19 of the UN Convention on the Rights of Persons with Disabilities (UN CRPD) to the Care Act.

Before the legislation was passed, nine out of 10 councils warned that a lack of adequate government funding could jeopardise implementation of the Act – and this is what came to pass. The supposed benefits of the Care Act in legislating for more personalised support have never been realised in a context where budget savings are the only targets on the agenda. It was estimated that the establishment of a national minimum eligibility threshold by the Care Act would remove support from around 340,000 disabled people.

Benefit claimants were aghast to discover that their welfare had been traded by the Lib Dems in exchange for a 5p charge on plastic bags. In 2018, Polly Mackenzie, former Director of Policy for the Deputy Prime Minister from 2010 to 2015, brashly revealed on Twitter how:

> Four years ago Lib Dem Ministers started agitating for a 5p charge on plastic bags. It took us months to persuade Cameron and Osborne.
>
> We finally got the policy in an eve-of-conference trade, in return for tightening benefit sanctions.

This was OK, though, because:

> PS the benefit sanction turned out to be illegal and never went ahead. Ha Ha.

Even dyed-in-the-wool Lib Dems were outraged. Caron Lindsay, editor of *Liberal Democrat Voice*, blogged in response:

> This was not ok. Sanctions were implemented and tightened by the Coalition Government and caused untold hardship. Our MPs voted for it. The fact that such a brutal policy was traded in such a blasé fashion probably isn't news either. It shouldn't happen again though ... in no universe could increasing the hardship faced by the most vulnerable people in our society ever be in tune with [the preamble to the Lib Dem constitution].

Unlike the Lib Dem leadership, Lindsay seemed aware of the role austerity and welfare reform played in demolishing their electoral support. She added: 'And it would be helpful if those involved in making such deals didn't boast about them on Twitter. It really, really doesn't help.'

This is not a lesson learned by Jo Swinson, Lib Dem leader during the 2019 General Election. She told *Channel 4 News* that she 'had no regrets about the coalition', stating that it was the right move 'to get our country back on track'. She named the bedroom tax as a specific measure that, in her view, should not have been let through, but she 'remained unrepentant on a whole host of others'.[11] She lost her own seat in the election and the Lib Dems went down from 21 MPs, including the nine defectors who had joined from other parties, to just 11.

SNP victories

The SNP capitalised on Labour's failure to present the kind of opposition that victims of austerity and welfare reform were calling out for. Scottish independence was only narrowly defeated in the referendum held in 2014. The following year the SNP won a historic landslide victory in the 2015 General Election, winning 56 out of 59 seats as Labour lost 40 seats and the Lib Dems lost 10. At the Scottish government elections in 2016, Labour came third place for the first time in 98 years, behind the SNP and the Tories. The result fulfilled a prediction by SNP MP Hannah Bardell in 2015 that Labour's failure in Westminster to vote against Tory plans to cut £12 billion from the welfare budget through the introduction of the Welfare Reform and Work Bill would 'haunt' them in the next Holyrood election.

In building support for the 'Yes' campaign as well as electoral support, the SNP not only made policy pledges that disabled campaigners wanted to hear, they even acknowledged the existence of disabled people in a way that mainstream politicians had never done before. Leading SNP politicians made explicit references to key issues facing disabled people in mainstream political debates. A clear difference in approach was noticeable in a BBC televised referendum debate between Alex Salmond, then leader of the SNP, and Labour's Alistair Darling, representing the 'Better Together' campaign. Within the debate, Darling referred only once to 'people with disabilities' (not the preferred terminology), and then only because he was asked a question specifically about disability benefits, while managing to focus most of his response on the need to have a strong economy. Salmond, by contrast, deliberately mentioned 'disabled people' eight times, referring to them as victims of austerity.

In the run-up to the 2015 General Election, a number of disabled people contacted Disabled People Against Cuts (DPAC) to ask if the SNP could stand in England. On both sides of the border, disabled campaigners were interested in the policy pledges the SNP was prepared to commit to that Labour continued to shun. One key example of this was the ILF, a source of support for disabled people with high support needs enabling them to live in the community when the alternative was residential care. Whereas Labour maintained its position 'not to keep the ILF' if elected, the SNP committed not only to ring-fence funding for existing ILF recipients but to establish a new Scottish ILF open to new applicants.

Once in Westminster, the new SNP MPs set about providing the opposition to Tory cuts, speaking for disabled people and anti-austerity campaigners across the UK. Mhairi Black used her maiden speech in July 2015 to attack Tory cruelty and hypocrisy but also to pour shame on Labour's failure – failure to stand up for the victims of legislation passed in Westminster and failure to understand the political realities behind support for the SNP:

> I have heard multiple speeches from Labour benches standing to talk about the worrying rise of nationalism in Scotland, when in actual fact all these speeches have served to do is to demonstrate how deep the lack of understanding about Scotland is within the Labour party ... The SNP did not triumph on a wave of nationalism; in fact nationalism has nothing to do with what's happened in Scotland. We triumphed on a wave of hope, hope that there was something different, something better to the Thatcherite neo-liberal policies that are produced from this chamber. Hope that representatives genuinely could give a voice to those who don't have one.

She concluded by offering an olive branch to Labour, saying: 'Ultimately people are needing a voice, people are needing help, let's give them it.'

A week later the SNP voted firmly against the government's Welfare Reform and Work Bill. Labour were whipped by acting leader Harriet Harman to abstain. Forty-eight Labour rebels defied the whip to vote against the bill, with John McDonnell famously stating in the House of Commons Chamber that he would 'swim through vomit to vote against' it.[12] Less than two months later, Jeremy Corbyn, another key rebel and close ally of McDonnell's, was elected leader of the Labour Party in a landslide victory.

While pushing through their own cuts in Scotland, the SNP continued to capitalise on their opposition to austerity and welfare reform. Despite frustration from disabled campaigners at delays on measures such as ending the outsourcing of benefit assessments to private contractors under the Scottish government's devolved powers, the SNP took its electoral advantage even further in the 2019 General Election, gaining another 13 MPs in Westminster.

The dangerous rise of UKIP

Prior to Corbyn's election as leader of the Labour Party in 2015, disabled people and others hit by austerity and welfare reform had no mainstream political party in England defending their interests. That handed an opportunity to UKIP as they went about building support for their politics of hate that scapegoated migrants and refugees for the cuts. The Green Party made a number of key pledges important to disabled campaigners, including retention of the ILF, and worked closely with DPAC, but its position in favour of assisted suicide, where a person unable to commit suicide due to illness or impairment is supported to terminate their life, contravenes the staunch anti-legalisation standpoint taken by the Disabled People's Movement. However, the Green Party was never considered to pose a serious electoral threat to the Tories. Voters being crushed by Tory cuts were in urgent need of an alternative. UKIP enjoyed some success in local elections while constant media attention focusing on their leader Nigel Farage contributed to an impression that they had the ability to shake up the establishment.

As UKIP looked to build their support base ahead of the 2015 General Election and when pushing for a referendum on leaving the EU, they spotted the opportunity presented by swathes of voters let down by the main opposition parties and desperate for change. UKIP's 2010 welfare policy statement, which described benefit claimants as a 'parasitic underclass of scroungers', disappeared from their website. Policies aimed at slashing benefits were replaced with positions echoing demands by campaign groups such as DPAC to scrap the Work Capability Assessment (WCA) and save the ILF. A disabled woman, Star Etheridge, who had herself gone through the WCA, was appointed as disability spokesperson and attempted to distance UKIP from their 2010 manifesto.

A web post reposted several times on the DPAC website expressed sympathy with frustration against the main political parties but argued that support for UKIP was not in the interests of disabled people:

> Many disabled people feel that none of the main political
> parties represent us … As things become ever more desperate
> for disabled people pushed into poverty and destitution, with
> independent living under greater and greater threat, people
> are searching for a way to escape the onslaught. One thing
> that is certain in these uncertain times is that UKIP is not the
> answer. UKIP have undeniably rattled and inflicted defeats on
> the government. They have also succeeded in capturing the

imagination of substantial sections of the electorate, pulling
support away from the Tories. They are however nothing but
bad news for disabled people.

As UKIP supporters began noticeably infiltrating disability campaign groups on social media, bringing with them the message
that migrants were to blame for benefit cuts, DPAC orchestrated
a concerted intervention against UKIP's attempt to position
themselves as the party representing the interests of disabled
people. A motion passed at DPAC's national conference in 2014
against scapegoating of any kind empowered its National Steering
Group to terminate the membership of anyone supporting a party
that holds discriminatory policies. Disablist comments made by
UKIP representatives were collated and shared; these included
the statement by by-election candidate Geoffrey Clark that 'disabled children are a burden on the state and should be aborted
as a foetus'. DPAC's Andy Greene concluded: 'So not only do
UKIP not offer an alternative to the status quo, the attitudes their
representatives show towards disabled people are even worse
than anything anyone other than the most out of touch Tory
councillor would dare publicly express.'

UKIP's readiness to counter the DPAC intervention was confirmation that they were cynically targeting the disabled vote.
An attempt by Russell Brand on BBC *Question Time* to voice
DPAC's view that UKIP were bad news for disabled people was
met with an immediate angry response by a disabled man, ready
and waiting in the audience, who was later exposed as the brother
of a UKIP MEP.

Sadly, many disabled people were convinced by the hope that
Farage appeared to offer them – not because all of them were racist, but because UKIP presented both an accessible explanation
for the bewildering situation they faced – that migrants were to

blame – and a clear solution – to exit the EU. Meanwhile, neither the Tories, the Lib Dems nor Labour considered disabled people's vote worth any serious interest.

From Labour's betrayal to Corbyn's election

Throughout the pain of the Coalition government years, Labour offered little that was different in spite of mounting evidence of the harm being inflicted by Coalition government policies. As disabled campaigners were all too aware, a punitive approach to welfare was just a continuation of New Labour policy. In his 2011 Labour Party conference speech, then Shadow Secretary of State for Work and Pensions, Liam Byrne, stated his view that Labour needed to be tough on welfare in order to get re-elected. Using language aligned with Tory rhetoric demonising benefit claimants, he said: '[M]any people on the door step at the last election felt that too often we were for shirkers not workers.' Throughout his tenure as Shadow Minister, Byrne supported the overall direction of Tory policy in cutting benefits, just disagreeing on details of implementation. For example, Labour did not object to the principle of introducing a benefit cap but favoured regional caps over one national one. Byrne stated that Labour would make cuts to the welfare budget if elected in 2015.

Pledges to reverse the damage of welfare reform have had to be squeezed out of Labour. Concerns about electability override principles of social justice, and so demands are adopted as party policy only once the leadership is confident that a position already has wide popular support. It was not until after Corbyn became leader that Labour finally committed to scrap the WCA if elected. Their previous pledge was limited to removing the contract to administer the assessments from private company Atos. As it happened, campaigners chased Atos out of the contract to deliver the WCA without waiting for Labour. Only a handful of

Labour MPs, including Jeremy Corbyn, John McDonnell and Michael Meacher, stood with disabled campaigners at a memorial service for the victims of welfare reform in September 2013 under a banner calling for the abolition of the WCA, while Labour's 2015 disability mini-manifesto went no further than committing to 'overhaul' – but still retain – the disastrous assessment. In the run-up to the 2015 General Election, Labour's position on the ILF became farcical, with their own parliamentary candidates in utter confusion as Ed Miliband attempted to criticise the government for its decision to close the fund while insisting that Labour would not retain it if elected.

When Rachel Reeves was quoted in the *Guardian* just two months before the 2015 General Election as saying 'We are not the party of people on benefits. We don't want to be seen, and we're not, the party to represent those out of work', it was the final straw for many disabled voters. Reeves, who was then Shadow Minister for Work and Pensions, claimed that what she had said had been taken out of context, but to those living day to day at the sharp end of benefit cuts there was no context that could justify words with such a clear message of rejection. People out of work enduring rampant stigmatisation as benefit cheats and scroungers desperately wanted a party that would defend them. Here was a dismissal not only of their votes but also of their plight. One disabled campaigner wrote a resignation letter to his local constituency Labour Party. While stressing that 'every member' of his local party had afforded him 'nothing but friendship, respect and camaraderie', he explained: 'As someone who claims benefits only because they cannot work, I feel personally betrayed and insulted by that statement and I now feel that I am unwelcome within the UK Labour Party.'

Corbyn's election as leader of the Labour Party gave disabled people and those hit by Tory cuts hope that a better future was within reach. As Sean McGovern, a long-standing disabled campaigner and disability representative on the TUC General Council, told me: 'When Corbyn decided to run for the leadership of the Labour Party with John McDonnell at his side, disabled people knew they had a prospective leadership team who understood disabled people and their issues.' Corbyn and McDonnell's support for disabled people's resistance against the Tory attacks was referenced by Francesca Martinez in what has been praised by viewers as one of the 'best ever moments' on BBC's *Question Time*.[13] Martinez stated that politicians had 'blood on their hands' as a result of austerity but also explained that, consistently since 2010, no matter how small the protest, Corbyn and McDonnell had been at the side of disabled campaigners. Disability issues are rarely voiced on *Question Time* but the response on social media confirmed that this is not because they are of no interest to viewers.

Policies that protect the interests of disabled people are not only popular with disabled voters but with all those who care about social justice. The wider appeal of anti-austerity politics was in evidence as support for Labour climbed following clear opposition to Osborne's 2016 Spring Budget that promised tax breaks for the rich on the back of cuts to disability benefits. Standing at the dispatch box in the House of Commons chamber, Corbyn declared: 'This budget has unfairness at its very core, paid for by those who can least afford it. The Chancellor could not have made his priorities clearer. While half a million people with disabilities are losing over £1 billion in Personal Independence Payments, corporation tax is being cut and billions handed out in tax cuts to the very wealthy.'[14] That week Labour went ahead in the polls for the first time since Corbyn's election as leader. In the 2017 General Election, Corbyn defied expectations, winning more seats and the largest increase in the share of the vote by a

Labour leader since Clement Attlee in 1945. It was an election defeat, but in the context of constant attempts at sabotage from the right wing within his own party, it felt like success.

Labour remains divided over its position on welfare, regardless of Corbyn's personal commitment towards a society that provides an adequate social safety net for all who need it. During the London mayoral campaign in 2016, Sadiq Khan abstained in the Commons vote on passage of the Welfare Reform and Work Bill, despite being whipped to vote against it under Corbyn's leadership. This suggested that Khan was one of those in Labour who still believed they needed to be tough on welfare in order to win a General Election – a position articulated by Will Straw in a pamphlet published by the Fabian Society after the 2015 General Election. Straw argued that Ed Miliband's mistake was not adopting as 'the centrepiece of his entire campaign' the mantra that it is 'wrong to be idle on benefits when you can work'.[15]

Whereas politicians from across the Labour Party now talk against austerity, in particular bemoaning cuts to education and housing, it is noticeable how few will come out against welfare reform in general terms (as opposed to specific measures within the wider welfare reform programme). Cuts to social care that affect working-age disabled people virtually never get a mention. This is linked to the fact that, in many cases, it is Labour councils who are delivering the cuts on the ground.

Labour was very slow to move towards a 'stop and scrap' position on Universal Credit (UC), even after this approach was adopted by the TUC, Unite the Union and PCS, the union representing those who work delivering UC. Claimants on the ground, nearly 40 per cent of whom are in paid employment, detest UC. The new system had already gained a toxic reputation while only part way through roll-out, in spite of expensive

DWP public propaganda campaigns. The fact that Labour did not feel confident to come out fully against UC suggested that the leadership was listening to voices other than those of disabled people, claimants and workers on this matter. Corporate disability charities, with their concern invested in preserving the status quo and their own survival above the interests of the people they claim to represent, are undoubtedly among these voices.

Under Miliband, Labour made itself unelectable by aping the Tories and underestimating the importance of austerity and welfare reform. Greater numbers are now affected by the Tories' war on disabled people and the poor than in 2015. Those who have been brutalised by current government policy may not have loud voices in the media or a presence in the lobby halls of Westminster but their experiences are a dominant issue in deciding how they vote, even in elections that may not appear immediately relevant.

Brexit

Backlash is inevitable when politicians and the media ignore the issues that are of burning concern to the lived realities of masses of the population. Brexit is one example of this. The EU referendum was not a vote that the majority of the working class in Britain ever wanted. We were pulled into a fight between warring factions of the ruling class at a time when many people felt uninvested in the status quo, with little to lose and desperate for something different. It is wrong to characterise the referendum result as simply a product of racism, although a terrible outcome has been the growth in confidence of the far right and a rise in race hatred. It is difficult to quantify how far the 'Leave' vote was influenced by opposition to the EU's neoliberal agenda of privatisation and to the operations of 'Fortress Europe' in constructing detention camps such as those in Libya with appalling human rights records to keep out refugees – yet this was clearly a minority view, with Lexit (Left Exit) views denied any space in mainstream debate or media. What is certain is that, when politicians who were responsible for grave injustices affecting so many people's daily lives, such as Cameron and Osborne, told people to vote 'Remain', it undoubtedly had the opposite effect, including among disabled people.[16]

Brexit became an enormously divisive issue within a society pulled apart by growing social and economic divisions. Pro-Remain disabled campaigners expressed anger on social media about how actively non-disabled people were opposing Brexit when they had never shown more than a passing concern about the death and distress caused by welfare reform. There was a flicker of acknowledgement of the relationship between growing inequality and Brexit in Theresa May's announcement that a new government 'Office for Tackling Injustices' would be set up. This was part of her desperate attempt to build a legacy, having failed to deliver Brexit. Collecting data about injustice, which will be the primary function of the new office (if it ever comes into existence), is not going to stop injustice, of course. Ongoing cuts and welfare reform will instead embed it further within society. For as long as these continue, there will be an anger towards politicians who are viewed as part of the 'establishment' and thus associated with policies that have caused so much harm.

The outcome of the 2019 General Election, with a strong majority for the Conservatives, was devastating for disabled campaigners. Many venting their anger on social media took the vote to signify a lack of concern towards the victims of austerity and even an expression of public disdain for disabled people. Few of those who voted for the Conservatives will have been consciously motivated in this way. The reality is much more complex.

The Conservative vote share rose by only 1.2 percentage points from the 2017 result – far from a ringing endorsement of continued brutality. There is even anecdotal evidence that some of the traditional Labour supporters who went Conservative believed – however absurd this may seem to those actively involved in the struggles of the last decade – that they were voting for an improvement in living conditions for the working class, including disabled people. Although the Labour vote increased under Corbyn in the 2017 election, the 2019 picture was consistent with Labour's declining vote from 1997 onwards. The electorate in Labour heartlands appeared to be fed up with cuts from Labour-run councils and with their vote being taken for granted.

The 2019 General Election result was a clear expression of frustration over Brexit – over parliament's prolonged delays in delivering it and in the near complete dominance of Brexit in public debate since the EU referendum. Journalist Sadie Robinson warned in October 2019: 'Ruling class machinations over Brexit are driving some working class people and left wingers into the arms of the Tories – or worse ... People had many reasons for voting Leave. But one of them was a deep dissatisfaction with mainstream politics and a desire to give the establishment a kicking.'[17] The experience of feeling ignored and devalued by those in power that led to the Leave vote was replicated in the way in which parliament responded to Brexit. When the chance came for the electorate to have a say, a number of historical Labour heartlands fell to the Conservatives.

The voting power of disabled people
Predictions by political commentators in successive elections since 2010 have been wrong. What that tells us is that there are issues of considerable social and political importance to the masses of the population that are being misjudged by politicians

and ignored by the media. I would argue that one of those issues is the attacks on disabled people since 2010.

Issues affecting disabled people have the potential to cause far greater social upheaval than the public and political profile of disability suggests. Disabled people make up 22 per cent of the population, a figure that is often underestimated. We are geographically and generationally dispersed across the population, which means that we are present throughout society, and those issues which have an impact on us also have an impact on our friends, family and neighbours, as well as workers in a range of sectors who provide us with services. Lack of media representation does not mean that the issues affecting disabled people do not exist and are not widely felt within our communities; it only confirms to those experiencing them that their lives are not valued by those in power.

There tends to be a high level of politicisation among disabled people. This may not be obvious to those who only understand disability according to portrayals of disabled people as either benefit scroungers or the passive victims of the cuts. Our lived experience is one of continuously facing socially constructed barriers that expose the unfairness of the system we live under; the fact that we rely on state-funded support in order to have the same chances in life as other people means that our lives are very directly and immediately affected by who is in government and what their policies are. Whereas lower-income groups are traditionally less engaged in politics, this is not true for disabled people. A recent survey of Londoners found that 94 per cent of disabled respondents were registered to vote, compared with 89 per cent of non-disabled respondents.

Disabled campaigners have been fighting for survival by paying close attention to the details of the political decisions that affect us. What the 2019 General Election result tells us is that we cannot rely on the electorate as a whole to have the same clarity of understanding and immediate concern for the issues affecting disabled people when casting their vote. The lesson is that we cannot defer our fightback to the ballot box and the promise of a future change of government. We need to lead with grassroots resistance.

PART IV
UNDERSTANDING THE WELFARE WAR

Why disabled people are under attack

> We need a complete change of direction. I'm not just talking
> about changing one group of Ministers for another. Or one set
> of policies, plans and proposals for another. I'm talking about
> a whole new, never-been-done-before approach to the way this
> country is run ... The age of irresponsibility is giving way to the
> age of austerity.
>
> David Cameron[1]

The Conservatives came into power in 2010 with a clear plan of action to make cuts and reshape the social security system. Their 2010 election manifesto outlined a punitive approach to welfare reform, declaring that they would tackle the 'tidal wave of worklessness' and 'reduce benefit dependency'. Their policy commitments included harsh policies on benefit sanctions, pledging that 'people who refuse to accept reasonable job offers could forfeit their benefits for up to three years'. George Osborne's first budget as chancellor initiated a period of austerity with the worst ever spending cuts. A few months later, disabled people protested outside the Conservative Party conference: it was clear that this government meant very bad news for the poorest members of society.

It has been particularly important for the government to conceal its treatment of disabled people. This is because the idea that disabled people should not be harmed is still pervasive in British society, and, as such, disability is an area with the potential to cause unrest. The maxim that society is judged by how it treats its 'most vulnerable' or 'weakest' members is oft quoted. Although anything that holds back the attacks is welcome, this is not a notion that advances the fight against disabled people's oppression because it reconfirms capitalist social hierarchy in placing disabled people at the bottom of the pile. The assumption that a desire to protect the most disadvantaged in society is a universally shared world view is something the Tories have been able to exploit in order to evade notice of how their policies are actually targeted.

Without time and effort to understand what is happening to us and why, we cannot hope to formulate a successful strategy to halt, let alone stop or reverse, government-led attacks against disabled people. In September 2012, disabled activists met from around the country to discuss how to respond to the mounting government attacks. The conference was organised around Jenny Morris's paper *Rethinking Disability Policy*. The message of this was that the Disabled People's Movement needed to move out of the disability policy agenda and engage with broader political and economic debates and developments.[2]

Understanding political economy is not straightforward. Our rulers do not openly reveal their agenda and explain to the masses why they are exploiting us or how. If they did, they wouldn't remain in power for very long. Deceit and distraction are imperative for maintaining a system geared towards achieving profit for an elite, where the accumulation of misery is a necessary condition for the accumulation of wealth.

What they say to each other can be revealing. Speaking to members of the financial elite from a golden throne at the Lord Mayor's Banquet in November 2013, Cameron talked of forging 'a leaner, more efficient state'. He spoke of the 'need to do more with less. Not just now, but permanently.'[3] This was, as journalist Mary O'Hara has observed, a declaration of permanent austerity, representing 'the dream even Margaret Thatcher hadn't dared to dream'.[4] It was confirmation of what many had by then worked out: that the Conservatives had 'seized on the economic consequences of the financial crisis as a means to push policies they always desired but did not think possible in normal circumstances'.[5]

What the Tories lacked for their plans was majority backing by the British public. It was only by forming a coalition with the Lib

Dems that they achieved a majority in the House of Commons. With a vote share of 36.1 per cent, less than a quarter of the total electorate had voted for them. Once in government they set about a coordinated strategy to build support for their policies through a calculated combination of myth-making, misinformation and scapegoating. They were aided in their endeavours by the right-wing media faithfully repeating the stories fed to them and by charity partners willing to give them cover in return for funding and profile. A special mention must also be given to the Department for Work and Pensions (DWP) press office, which has gone above and beyond in its efforts to spin reality.

This part of the book attempts to understand key factors behind welfare reform, including ideological goals as well as the level of incompetence for which the DWP has become notorious. It also examines the role of charities and disability organisations in colluding with the government agenda and failing to provide a level of opposition needed to achieve effective resistance in the current climate.

NINE | A story of ideology and incompetence

If you take the government's stated aims at face value, their policies affecting disabled people since 2010 are confusing to say the least: they claim to be protecting 'the most vulnerable' while implementing policies that hit harder the more disabled you are; they endlessly stress the importance of supporting disabled people into employment and then implement policies that push us further from the labour market.

While those setting the policies could never be accused of having a good understanding of disability, the impacts are not accidental. To take the approach that these impacts stem from lack of awareness as opposed to conscious design is a mistake: it lets them off the hook while wasting effort and resources on education that will fail to lead to the substantial change needed.

The deliberate causation of harm to disabled people makes sense only by taking a wider political-economic view. In this way, it is possible to unpick the ideological priorities behind the agenda.

Legislative and policy changes in the UK from the Coalition government onwards have not happened in isolation. They represent a continuation, albeit an accelerated one, from the neoliberal policies of the New Labour government. They also follow similar approaches adopted in other countries that have restricted access to social security, placed greater burdens on claimants and provided profit-making opportunities to the private sector.

Writing on the development of welfare reform in the UK, disabled activist Bob Williams-Findlay observes that: 'Arguably the economic down-turn and financial crisis simply hastened the move away from the post-war Social Democratic welfarist policies and the changing relationships between the State and society.'[1] In other words, austerity merely provided an excuse for the Tories to move more quickly along the neoliberal course that New Labour had already set.

This chapter starts by looking at the role of welfare under capitalism in order to provide the wider political-economic context for changes since 2010, before considering the global and historical context. It then looks at the ideology driving welfare reform, identifying three defining, interrelated aims: the first being to slash welfare expenditure through permanently reducing claimant caseloads in line with the austerity agenda; the second, to effect privatisation, both by opening up areas of public finance to private companies and by facilitating a move towards an insurance model of social security. This aim serves the interests of profit but additionally benefits the government by enabling them to outsource and therefore distance themselves from the 'harm production' of welfare reform. The third is to embed punitive approaches across social security as a way of disciplining both unemployed labour and the existing workforce. This has the effect of helping reduce caseloads at the same time as serving the interests of 'business confidence'.

One aspect that is less straightforward to fathom is the role of incompetence within Tory welfare reform. This is where ineptitude seems to undermine their ideological goals, causing greater unnecessary expense and failing to cover the tracks of their lies and spin. Over the past 10 years, there have been many occasions when the scale of error within a department as major as the Department for Work and Pensions (DWP) has seemed almost unbelievable. This is also considered in this chapter.

Context

Welfare and capitalism

Policies and practice that act to deny disability status to those seeking it need to be understood within the overarching ambitions of capital to keep 'unproductive' welfare expenditure at the minimum possible and to open up new markets for private profit in the welfare sector. The human and societal costs of these endeavours as assessed in previous chapters are a price the Tories are willing to make the working class pay in order to advance their ideological agenda.

A historical materialist perspective based on Marx's analysis of capitalism is essential to understanding what has happened. As Rosa Morris explains: '[I]t is impossible to fully understand the current position of disabled people who are unable to engage in waged labour without considering their role and position in the capitalist mode of production.'[2]

The growth of the welfare state took place well after Marx's lifetime, as did developments in healthcare and technology that have altered both the demographics of disability and the possibilities for disability and employment. As Chris Harman notes: 'Public expenditures [on welfare] become a central focus for class struggle in a way in which they were not in Marx's time.'[3]

Nevertheless, Marx's grasp of the dynamics of capitalism was enough to prefigure the basis upon which the welfare state was developed: when considering the costs involved in supporting those who fitted into the category of 'pauperism', including 'the demoralised, the ragged, and those unable to work', he observed that 'capital usually knows how to transfer these from its own shoulders to those of the working class and the petty bourgeoisie.' The contribution principle of National Insurance that sits at the heart of the welfare state is exactly that: a cost for the maintenance of the working class borne by the working class rather than out of the profits they create.[4]

Marx's analysis is fundamental to understanding government policies affecting out-of-work benefits. It is not in capitalism's interest to get rid of unemployment benefits altogether for those 'able and willing to work'[5] because what Marx called the 'reserve army of labour' plays such an integral role in the functioning of capitalism. The existence of unemployed workers ready and on hand to step into jobs enables capital to expand, to reinvent the means of production so that workers with different skills are required, and to move operations geographically. Unemployment benefits maintain these workers' survival at times when they are not required, thus also enabling capital to contract at times of economic downturn in order to protect profits. Marx explained that unemployed workers form 'a disposable reserve army, which belongs to capital just as absolutely as if the latter had bred it at its own cost. Independently of the limits of the actual increase of population, it creates a mass of human material always ready for exploitation by capital in the interests of capital's own changing valorization requirements.'[6]

The other function of the reserve army – one that is just as important to capital – is to exert a downward pressure on wages. Its existence also gives employers a stronger hand in resisting workers' demands for better wages. Worsening pay and conditions can be imposed under threat of replacing existing employees with new workers willing to accept the terms offered.

Government welfare policies targeted at out-of-work benefits are concerned with disciplining the workforce and controlling the reserve army. The imposition of claimant commitments and work search requirements is directly linked to capital's need to push unemployed workers into jobs that have become less and less able to support an adequate standard of living. This explains politicians' obsession with what they label 'permissive' welfare, by which they mean social security payments that provide a level of income and security that enable unemployed workers to choose what work they accept.

A speech by David Cameron early in the Coalition government expressed the fear and vitriol that capital has for workers not under its direct control. Responding to the summer riots of 2011, Cameron proclaimed that welfare 'encourages the worst in people – [it] incites laziness ... excuses bad behaviour ... erodes self-discipline ... discourages hard work ... people thinking they can be as irresponsible as they like because the state will always bail them out'.[7] It was a warning of the determination with which the Tories were about to attack the social security system.

Just as a Marxist analysis enables us to understand that disabled people have been hit by offensives aimed at disciplining the workforce, we also need to understand the lack of concern shown towards the brutal and disproportionate adverse impacts of austerity and welfare reform measures on disabled people. Here, it is important to understand that support for disabled people does not flow from capitalism in the same way that it does for other areas of the welfare state, such as education and healthcare.

Support for disabled people who have never been and will never be part of the labour force is one aspect of welfare expenditure that capital 'would love to be able to do without and does its utmost to minimise'.[8] At times of economic recession, it is the first thing to go. Harman explains that, at such points in time, there is a pressure on states to restructure and reorganise their operations: 'On the one side this means trying to impose work measurement and payment schemes on welfare sector employees similar to those within the most competitive industrial firms. On the other side it means cuts in welfare provision so as to restrict it as much as possible to servicing labour power that is necessary for [profit].'[9]

This analysis explains the ideological approach behind New Labour's intention to 'release resources from social security in order to spend more on health and education'.[10] A leaked document quoted in the *Guardian* on 13 December 1997 revealed how it was 'likely that a high proportion of the necessary savings will have to come from benefits paid to sick and disabled people'.[11] These proposals met with a backlash that included disabled campaigners from Direct Action Network throwing red paint at Downing Street. Researchers Linda Piggott and Chris Grover formulated the view that learning from this setback led to construction of a 'scroungerphobia' narrative to demonise benefit claimants. Welfare reform measures through which the Work Capability Assessment was developed were then successfully implemented later in the New Labour administration.[12]

The global and historical context

A significant paper published by the Organisation for Economic Co-operation and Development (OECD) in 2003 outlined the policies to be adopted towards support for disabled people by neoliberal governments across the world.[13] As Stewart explains:

> Essentially, neoliberalism and austerity fiscal management are espoused and embedded in OECD policies which influence social policies in the 36 member countries ... The negative human impact of neoliberal politics has swept the world and the reduction of state funding for disabled people, using a flawed assessment, is not unique to the UK. Similar processes have been ongoing in Canada, New Zealand, Australia and in other OECD countries.[14]

The approach promoted by the OECD was one that prioritised reduction of 'benefit dependency', challenged the use of state funding to support disabled people and made recommendations to limit spending on disability benefits; it advocated moving towards stricter eligibility criteria, greater expectation on work-less disabled people to get into employment, and the redefinition of who counts as disabled.

Before the Coalition government initiated its programme of welfare reform, other governments were well ahead with the process of 'collectively sanction[ing] disability income'.[15] Major examples of this can be seen in the US under the Clinton administration and through the German Hartz IV programme.

Policies introduced by Democrat President Bill Clinton in the US during the mid-1990s savagely cut costs by restricting eligibility to decrease numbers of benefit claimants, creating caps on how long and how much a person could receive in support, and instituting harsher punishments for recipients who did not comply with the new requirements. The 1996 law that created the Temporary Assistance for Needy Families, or TANF, programme changed the financing and benefit structure of cash assistance. TANF added work requirements for aid, reducing the number of adults who could qualify for benefits. Studies have shown that it now 'barely reaches the poorest Americans and has all but ceased doing the work of lifting people out of poverty. "Welfare reform" didn't fix welfare so much as destroy it.'[16] In Indiana, for example, more than 60 per cent of the families in poverty were in receipt of cash assistance before Clinton's reforms but by 2016 that figure had shrunk to 7 per cent.

In the US under Trump, free health insurance for those out of work is now linked to work search requirements, while the amount of bureaucracy and related obstacles for those who wish to remain covered have pushed many out of the system altogether.[17] The private company Maximus has made millions administrating welfare-to-work programmes that 'churn people through the system' without actually helping them. In a contract to deliver work programmes for the state of Indiana, Maximus estimates it will see 93,000 clients and earn about $9.1 million each year, but expects that 'fewer than 200 people annually will find and keep jobs for at least six months'.[18]

The Hartz IV programme introduced in Germany in 2003 is notorious for its strict conditionality rules. The new element that brought the most profound change was the contract, drawn up between the jobseeker and the jobcentre, coupled with sanctions for failure to meet the contract commitment. Hartz IV has been attributed with helping 'to accelerate inequality in Germany'.[19] While unemployment has unarguably dropped in Germany since 2003, critics say that this is because the regime forces jobless people to accept the next job they can find regardless of pay or hours, which means that they are still dependent on some sort of state welfare. The backlash against Hartz IV has led to significant support for the idea of a Universal Basic Income in Germany.

There are also historical precedents from before the founding of the welfare state and the post-Second World War consensus for a number of the measures introduced under welfare reform, such as sanctions, surveillance and cuts introduced during the Great Depression of the 1930s.[20] The historical impacts of these measures included mass destitution, as well as deaths and suicides resulting from the removal of out-of-work benefits. This human cost is referenced within the seminal monograph *Ten Lean Years* written by Wal Hannington in 1940. This 'examination of the record of the national government in the field of unemployment', which covers the decade from 1930 to 1940, includes individual case studies taken from national and regional print news stories which are markedly similar to present-day welfare reform case studies.

One example is taken from the *Morning Post* a few days before Christmas 1931. It tells of a man, William Castle, who returned home after 'vainly searching for work all day' to be handed a letter that had arrived that day for him. It was: 'AN INTIMATION THAT HIS BENEFITS HAD CEASED.' Hannington records:

> At 5 a.m. he got up and wrote a farewell letter. At 6 a.m. he took his wife a cup of tea and kissed her tenderly. Then abruptly left the room. His wife heard a strange noise downstairs. She found him on the floor. He had cut his throat. The doctor came, but too late. WILLIAM CASTLE was dead. He had passed through the horror of war, and now he had the horror of a hungry wife, three hungry children and an empty cupboard and Christmas was near. It was too much for him to bear.[21]

Another story from the *Birmingham Gazette* on 8 December 1931 reports a suicide. The coroner is recorded as saying at the inquest that out-of-work benefit changes[22] 'provided the last push sufficient to make him temporarily insane and in that state throw himself into the canal'.[23] Hannington described this suicide as 'typical of many others'.[24]

There are striking similarities between measures affecting unemployment benefits introduced in Britain during the Great Depression and what Daniel Edmiston terms 'welfare austerity'[25] implemented by the Tories since 2010, as well as between the social harms they respectively caused. What is new in this current era is the existence of out-of-work benefits targeted specifically at disabled people, legal protections afforded to people who fall under the definition of being disabled and dominant social attitudes towards disability that support the idea of a societal obligation to protect those affected.

These are the outcomes of progress achieved in times of greater economic prosperity, when the capitalist state could afford to make concessions in the interests of maintaining civil content. They are factors that have made it more complex and difficult to roll back state provision while blaming those out of work for their own predicament. It is no surprise that Tory public spending cuts since 2010 have been targeted at disabled people. Failure to reach their goals, for example of reducing the budget for Disability Living Allowance/Personal Independence Payment (DLA/PIP) by 20 per cent, as examined below, has not been for want of trying but is rather a mark of the resistance they have faced.

Driven by ideology

Although welfare reform has been motivated by a prerogative to remove 'the psychological security of the UK's financial safety net, as provided by the welfare state',[26] the goal has not been to get rid of it entirely. The ideological goals have rather been to drastically cut, limit and privatise.

A core aim of welfare reform has been to slash expenditure. Welfare spending was one of the key areas targeted by George Osborne at the start of the Coalition government for budget savings he said were necessary in order to reduce the fiscal deficit. In his autumn 2010 spending review he announced a further £7 billion of welfare cuts on top of the £11 billion announced the preceding spring. He used these additional cuts to justify lower reductions in government departmental budgets than those planned by the previous government, which he set at 19 per cent rather than the 20 per cent previously proposed. This was represented in the media as him 'turning the tables on Labour'. Osborne told MPs that 'today is the day that Britain steps back from the brink', as he outlined the long-awaited Comprehensive Spending Review, which he said would achieve a balanced budget and falling national debt by 2014–15 while putting public services and the welfare system 'on a sustainable, long-term footing'.[27]

The manifesto on which the Tories were re-elected in 2015 then pledged to 'find [a further] £12 billion from welfare savings'. This was said to be 'on top of the £21 billion of savings delivered in this Parliament'. As the fact-checking charity Full Fact points out, £21 billion was a Treasury estimate of the savings amount legislated for by government. Using more up-to-date figures, the Institute for Fiscal Studies estimated that the actual amount saved by welfare policy changes was £17 billion – £17 billion being the difference between actual spending on benefits and tax credits in 2015–16 and the amount the government would have spent if no policy changes had been made. In real terms, spending on those items was expected to be roughly the same in 2015–16 as it was in 2009–10.

Reducing incapacity numbers

The Work Capability Assessment (WCA) was not a Tory invention but 'a culmination of ideas that were developed over a long period of time and which also influenced previous forms of assessment for out-of-work disability benefits'.[28] The manifestation of these ideas in the form of the WCA originated under New Labour. Its stated aim was to identify recipients of Incapacity Benefit (IB) who were capable of work, thereby reducing the caseload and cutting welfare expenditure. The test was to be delivered by private companies, opening up public finance to for-profit interests.

Consecutive governments from John Major onwards set targets to substantially reduce the numbers of people claiming out-of-work disability benefits. Rather than stemming the tide of a rising caseload, claimant numbers continued to climb under IB. By 2006 they were up to 2.7 million. There was a startling lack of evidence base for policies targeted at getting disabled people off out-of-work benefits and into employment. At the time when New Labour announced its aim to get 1 million off IB, there were only 500,000 job vacancies. James Purnell, David Freud's former boss as Work and Pensions Secretary, told writer Owen Jones:

'I mean, that was a figure that David Freud just kind of plucked out of the air.'[29]

Concerted effort went not into understanding the issues and developing evidence-based policy but into a media campaign purposefully demonising benefit claimants in order to build support for measures that had proven unpopular in the past. Tony Blair 'warned the unemployed, single parents and those on incapacity benefit' that they could 'no longer expect "a lifetime" on benefit' as the government released proposals to get 1 million people off IB and into work.[30]

Welfare reform policy is divorced not only from the daily realities of living with different impairments, but also from the material conditions of the workplace. Although the enormous diversity of impairment makes it difficult to generalise, there are numerous ways in which the modern workplace can broadly be seen to have become less accessible and more discriminatory towards disabled workers. Disability employment trends are understudied but what evidence there is suggests that it is actually more difficult for disabled people to be in employment now than previously. The extent to which a disabled person was less likely to have a job than a non-disabled person increased from 17 per cent in 1987 to 28 per cent in 2000.[31] Baumberg Geiger found that, in 2006, one-sixth fewer people would have moved out of work onto IB had there not been a deterioration in job control – a person's ability to influence what happens in his or her work environment.[32]

A view of history widely accepted on the left is that Thatcher's government pushed victims of industry closure onto invalidity benefits in order to massage the unemployment figures, effectively trapping them in 'dependency'. This is an argument that has proved dangerous for disabled people, justifying policy formation aimed at forcibly pushing those who are unable to earn a living off out-of-work benefits. It was claimed that incapacity was masking hidden unemployment and that welfare reform was needed to identify and 'free' those able to work.

When disability employment trends are analysed, it appears, conversely, that the actual situation is that it is impairment and ill health among people in employment which are hidden and unacknowledged.[33] These become evident when a worker loses his or her job and act as a barrier to finding alternative employment.

Successive governments have avoided looking too closely at the realities of disabled people's lives and factors behind barriers to work. The overriding concern has been an ideological one to reduce the numbers of people who are supported by the state to remain out of work, regardless of the consequences for individuals adversely impacted by this drive. Empirical evidence has been eschewed in favour of myths that seek to hold the individual responsible for their own disadvantage. In both the US and the UK, the government's approach to welfare has increasingly been 'one of dependency which the faulty individual on welfare must overcome, not as the structural outcome of an exclusionary labour market'.[34]

Privatisation and the denial of disability

A key characteristic of welfare reform developed under New Labour and escalated by the Tories was the opening up of public finance to private companies. In March 2007, *Reducing Dependency, Increasing Opportunity* was published. This was a review of the future for out-of-work benefits commissioned by New Labour from former banker David Freud. In it he stated: 'The scale of the potential market is large ... Based on the analysis in this report, I have no doubt that this will be an annual multi-billion market. Such scale would attract commitment from a wide range of private service providers and voluntary groups.'[35]

The core of his proposal was that government targets could be achieved by bringing in the private sector on long-term outcome-based contracts. Writing in 2007, researcher Jonathan Rutherford concluded that 'New Labour's politics of welfare reform has sub-ordinated concern for the sick and disabled to the creation of a new kind of market state'.[36]

The experiment in contracting out benefit assessments has proved that the private sector is neither more efficient nor provides better value for money than the public sector. Outsourcing is wasteful and leads to worse customer service from companies whose only real interest is profit. The histories of fraud and disability discrimination by firms engaged in delivering welfare reform such as Unum and Maximus indicate that they are perfectly prepared to damage the lives of disabled people to achieve their financial goals.

Private companies have been given substantial government contracts to deliver services linked to welfare reform, including benefit assessments for Employment and Support Allowance (ESA) and Personal Independence Payment (PIP) and the Work Programme, now replaced by the Work and Health Programme. Figures published in 2018 showed the DWP to have awarded £4.7 billion in outsourced contracts across all areas of its work since 2012.[37]

As an experiment in public service delivery, it has failed in multiple ways: the government has experienced unmet target after unmet target while the cost of the assessments has risen, and it has been unable to develop greater market interest; private companies involved in welfare reform have experienced both reputational damage and hits to their profits; the notoriety that the providers have gained for cruelty towards disabled people has aroused public discomfort towards the principle of private companies profiting from removing essential support from disabled people.

In 2018, the Work and Pensions Committee (WPC) concluded: 'The Department will need to consider whether the market is capable of delivering assessments at the required level and of rebuilding claimant trust. If it cannot – as already floundering market interest may suggest – the Department may well conclude assessments are better delivered in house.'[38] This represented a notable shift from the previous cross-party consensus concerning private-sector involvement in public delivery of welfare services. The government response did not agree.

Later in the year, the government announced that it was handing two-year extensions to Capita and Atos to continue delivering PIP assessments without going to tender. At the same time, the Minister for Disabled People, Sarah Newton, said that they would be 'developing a DWP owned IT system'. This wasn't about bringing assessments in-house but rather about helping the market by enabling 'more providers to deliver PIP'. It showed that, even if the government wanted to, at that time it didn't own the infrastructure needed. This would have to be developed, presumably over a number of years and at considerable cost. Meanwhile, the government is 'chained' to a handful of companies. This situation is indicative of a misplaced confidence in the ability of the private sector to deliver welfare services.

Under devolved powers, the Scottish government is taking over responsibility for PIP assessments in 2020 and has promised to end the practice of using private-sector organisations to carry them out. Campaigners will be watching with interest to see if this makes any difference to claimants' experiences of the assessment process or to the outcomes. However, it is unlikely the Tories will follow suit without considerable pressure.

What the government has achieved through outsourcing is the ability to cloud transparency and pass the buck. 'Commercial sensitivity' prevents disclosure of the content of current contracts and this enables the DWP to withhold information from the public domain more easily than if the activities were carried out in-house. Outsourcing also allows politicians to conveniently blame providers for individual cases that come to light of wrongful assessment decisions. Researcher Lewis Elward describes this as the deliberate establishment of proxy measures by the state to 'outsource harm production to distance themselves from potential ramifications'.[39]

There is nothing new about the government cutting benefits and punishing the poor. One factor with which the Tories have had to contend – and that didn't apply to the governments of the 1930s – is the existence of disability as a legally protected characteristic and a majority of the public opposed to consciously harming disabled people. In light of this, the approach taken over successive governments has therefore been to attempt to restrict numbers within the population who can claim that status by redefining who is and who is not disabled.

In 1992, Peter Lilley, then Secretary of State for Social Security, pointed the finger both at claimants and at the way in which illnesses are diagnosed as justification for an overhaul of out-of-work benefits. According to Lilley, sickness and invalidity benefits were originally intended for those people who 'by reason of some specific disease or bodily or mental disablement were unable to undertake work'. He said that now 'social or psychological causes' had been taken into account, 'the rules have been progressively widened and complicated' and the definition of 'incapacity' had become 'fuzzy'. Similar rhetoric was utilised by New Labour to justify their assault on out-of-work benefits.[40]

There is a clear and direct link between aggressive claims management practices adopted within the US insurance industry to deny payouts and protect profits and welfare reform policy in the UK. Both are underpinned by an approach to disability known as the biopsychosocial (BPS) model, developed by scientists Gordon Waddell and Mansel Aylward and derived from an earlier BPS version originating with George Engel in 1977. Waddell and Aylward's careers are heavily linked to both the DWP and Unum.

Crucially for understanding the major, serious flaws with welfare reform and the extensive harm it has caused, Waddell and Aylward's work treated IB trends as a social and cultural phenomenon rather than a health problem. Key to the BPS model is the idea that it is the negative attitudes of many ESA recipients that prevent them from working, rather than their impairment or health condition.

As Shakespeare, Watson and Alghaib demonstrate in their excellent demolition of the scientific credibility of Waddell and Aylward's work, it is an approach that 'can only blame victims for their plight'.[41] While acknowledging the social and cultural dimensions of illness, the model fails to consider that these and other structural and economic forces might be 'the dynamic causes of genuine ill health'. Instead, 'the problem of illness is located in the individual, whose beliefs and behaviour then become the focus of moral judgement and action'.[42]

The WCA is the outcome of the practical application of the BPS model to managing incapacity claims. It is a functional assessment carried out by a generalised healthcare professional using a computerised evaluation called a Logic Integrated Medical Assessment (LiMA) system. Failure to take into account medical evidence and assessors' lack of specialist knowledge appear to be deliberate design functions that are fundamental to a BPS analysis. Within this, the opinions of medical professionals to whom the claimants are known, as well as the evidence presented by the claimants themselves, are doubted, held to be infected by obstructively negative ideas of the expectations that can reasonably be placed on claimants. Rosa Morris describes this as a 'downgrading' of diagnosis.[43] It explains the high level of assessment decisions overturned at appeal stage, where a tribunal considers all evidence. It also explains wrongful decisions that have led to tragedies.

Much of the anger and opprobrium against the WCA has been directed at the private contractors that carry it out. Neither Atos nor Maximus could be described as a friend of disabled people as they continue to profit from causing misery and disadvantage, and campaigners continue to press for an end to the wasteful and opaque system of outsourcing. It is also important to recognise that the harms caused by the WCA are the outcome of deep-seated aspects of its design. These flaws cannot be fixed by tweaking; the fundamental approach to disability on which it is based must be overhauled.

Stewart is undoubtedly correct that the neoliberal agenda to replace state-funded social security with a model of private insurance protection has not gone away. The government command paper *Improving Lives* stresses: 'We also want to ensure that any options taken forward ... consider the services that employers can already access to support employees, such as occupational health and Group Income Protection insurance products.'[44]

At the same time, we should recognise that this agenda has not progressed as far as was intended, as is evident from the fact that Unum was forced to pull the plug on its 2011 TV advertising campaign.[45] Grassroots resistance, including Stewart's considerable efforts to draw attention to the issue, has been a significant factor within this.

Punishment and discipline
Accessing social security has been made increasingly difficult. The bureaucracy is now more onerous while the adoption of punitive attitudes towards claimants has made the experience less and less bearable. This is now true across the social security

system, from disability-specific benefits to Jobseeker's Allowance (JSA), and is an approach that sits firmly at the heart of Universal Credit (UC). Penalties for failing – or being judged to have failed – to comply with benefit conditions have become progressively harsher: in 1986, sanctions involving benefit loss had a maximum duration of six weeks; by 2012 this had escalated to three years.[46]

The rationale given by the DWP to justify conditionality and sanctioning is made to sound reasonable. In their view: 'Conditionality and sanctions are an important part of the welfare system, motivating claimants to engage with the support on offer to look for work while ensuring the system is fair to the taxpayer.' As we have seen in previous chapters, there is nothing rational nor reasonable about the regime, with mounting evidence of both unjustifiable harm combined with an absence of evidence to prove the efficacy of the approach for supporting people into employment.

The entrenchment of punitive approaches throughout the social security system has a dual ideological purpose: first, to discourage benefit claims, thus driving down claimant numbers and reducing welfare expenditure; and second, to ensure that being out of work is a less tolerable experience than being in employment, however bad the working conditions or however low the pay. Punishing those who are out of work is a way of disciplining those in work so that they will accept lower wages, longer hours and worse conditions. Throughout the history of welfare provision under capitalism, the principle of 'less eligibility' had been applied so that 'getting the benefit must still leave the recipients worse off than the worst paid work'.[47]

At times of economic recession, the imposition of greater punishment and discipline on those who are out of work helps ensure a ready supply of workers willing to take on bad jobs for no pay because there are no other options available. Thus, welfare reform measures enable businesses to keep generating profits.

In the current period, the workplace has become increasingly insufferable through the rise of insecure work and underemployment, the intensification of labour and heightened pressures. Shortly after the Coalition government took office in 2010, the number of people on zero hours contracts (where the employer is not obliged to provide any minimum working hours) rose significantly. It reached a peak of around 900,000 at the end of 2016 and in 2017, before falling back slightly to around 850,000 at the end of 2018. Earnings have stagnated if not fallen in real terms since 2010. According to the charity Full Fact, in June 2019 they remained below their 2008 peak. This is because the growth in earnings has failed to exceed inflation.[48]

Incidences of work-related depression and anxiety have 'shown signs of increasing in recent years'.[49] The total number of cases of work-related stress, depression or anxiety in 2017–18 was 595,000 and accounted for 57 per cent of all working days lost due to ill health. Stress, depression or anxiety is more prevalent in public service industries, such as education, health and social care, and in public administration and defence.

Another negative trend is the growth in workplace surveillance through which heightened pressure can be exerted on workers. Advances in technology have expanded the capacity to track workers' every movement. James Bloodworth spent six months working in an Amazon warehouse and recounts the company's use of devices through which workers are 'sent admonishments … saying you need to get your productivity up'. He told the *Guardian*: 'You're constantly tracked and rated. I found you couldn't keep up with the productivity targets without running – yet you were also told you weren't allowed to run, and if you did, you'd get a disciplinary. But if you fell behind in productivity, you'd get a disciplinary for that as well.' '[G]oing to the loo' was described by bosses as 'idle time' and he once found a bottle of urine on one of the shelves.[50] Such pressured and perverse conditions are becoming increasingly commonplace across largely low-paid and insecure employment.

As the workplace has become less bearable, the experience of claiming out-of-work benefits has had to become harsher to prevent it becoming a way out of intolerable jobs for overstressed workers. It is no longer enough that unemployed workers receive too little in out-of-work support to provide an adequate income, because rising numbers of those in work are living in poverty: 60 per cent of those living in poverty are now in a family where someone works. Those who are unemployed must also now endure harassment and fear on top of impoverishment. That disabled people are discriminated against within this regime is apparently of too little concern to warrant a reconsideration of approach.

While sanctions have limited outcomes in terms of getting people into sustainable employment, their success lies in pushing claimants into more exploitative jobs. Research has shown how 'sanctions can, particularly in slack regional labour markets, allow employers to increase the rate of exploitation over their workforce by prohibiting refusal and forcing unemployed individuals to accept atypical working conditions facilitated through temporary work agencies'.[51]

It is no coincidence that the relationship between work coach and claimant has been reconfigured into an unequal power dynamic that mirrors the types of pressures and belittlement that workers experience in low-control jobs. In this way, they are being prepared for workplace compliance. One of Daniel Edmiston's research participants, 'Ashley', speaks to the experiences of many claimants when she says: 'You could apply for ten jobs ... and they're like "Is that all you've done?" ... like they talk down to you kind of thing. Like you've never done enough.'[52]

One of the big concerns for the ruling class in the current period is low productivity growth. In 2018, the *Financial Times* declared that 'Britain's productivity crisis should be keeping the country's politicians and civil servants awake at night'. The 'slump in productivity growth since the financial crisis' was showing 'no sign of coming to an end', with a slowdown 'more acute than any other western country'. The *Financial Times* explained: 'It matters because achieving higher growth in productivity – or output per hour worked – is the way nations become richer, living standards rise and governments have the resources to improve public services or cut taxes.'[53]

It is the aim of growing 'business confidence' in order to restore productivity that researcher Jamie Redman links to what he describes as the 'weaponising' of sanctions against the unemployed. Given that these 'have been found as overwhelmingly ineffective in enabling claimants to make positive, rewarding choices in the labour market', Redman concludes that 'such phenomena can be interpreted as part of a wider strategy to ensure "business confidence"'.[54]

He explains that this is achieved on the one hand by 'directly benefit[ing] capital, [by] subordinating claimants to exploitative employment relationships', while, on the other, by 'reduc[ing] aggregate caseloads' and 'by, in part at least, ostracising claimants for behaviours (e.g. poor time keeping) which did not reflect the discipline often required to perform wage labour'.[55]

The DWP claims that mandated work activity is teaching claimants the skills and discipline they need to gain and keep employment. The reality as experienced by disabled claimants is that they are being punished for the skills and capacities they lack and cannot acquire for impairment-related reasons. Sanctions have been shown to discriminate against disabled people. Following Redman's logic, we can impute that rather than this being an entirely unintended outcome, it flows from the very purpose of conditionality, which is to weed out those who are 'unable to demonstrate the necessary behaviours and competences (e.g. good time keeping/basic reading and writing skills) commonly required to participate in the labour market'.[56] Disabled people are disproportionately more likely to fall into this category.

The incompetence factor

There are too many examples of momentous error and ineptitude from the DWP since 2010 to overlook the issue of incompetence within welfare reform implementation. It would be wrong to see each of these as part of a consciously orchestrated conspiracy to deprive and punish benefit claimants; it is also a mistake to view this incompetence factor as entirely unrelated to ideology.

Poor management, under-resourcing and lack of attention are all the result of choices, whether the consequences to which they lead are deliberate or otherwise. When significant errors have been made by the DWP, it is disabled people and the poorest in society who have suffered.

Sizeable DWP errors include both under- and overpayments of benefits. In both cases, claimants have suffered. When it emerged that disabled people had been underpaid when they moved from IB to ESA, the DWP attempted to limit back payments to 2014. It was only through legal action from the Child Poverty Action Group that back payments were guaranteed for up to 70,000 disabled people from the date that they moved to ESA.

DWP staff shortages led to thousands of carers being overpaid benefits. In 2018–19, the DWP detected 93,000 overpayments of Carer's Allowance, compared with an average of 41,000 a year in the previous five years. The National Audit Office (NAO) said that the DWP was detecting 'significantly more' overpayments because it had recently put in place more people and new systems that meant the errors came to light. In some cases, carers faced repaying more than £20,000 they had received in error, a task that could take 34 years.

On numerous occasions, the DWP has been forced to undertake major reviews of benefit caseloads at considerable cost and requiring intensive staff input. In January 2018, the Minister for Disabled People, Sarah Newton, announced that the government would need to review 1.6 million PIP claims as a result of a legal judgement at a cost of £3.7 billion. It was expected that around 220,000 disabled people would be owed backdated payments but that it could take until 2023 to finish the review.

These costly exercises, requiring disabled people to wait years in some cases for important income, could all have been avoided. One way to do this was through choosing to better resource the DWP, another was by listening to disability organisations and campaigners when they urged the government not to tighten benefit eligibility in ways that break the law.

On issues such as changing PIP regulations around making or planning a journey, the government appears to have taken a calculated gamble on the likelihood of legal action being taken within the time frame for launching judicial reviews. In this case, they were caught out, but in other areas of policy they have been able to get away with implementing measures that can reasonably be viewed as discriminatory because no legal challenge was taken. The way in which they have so determinedly fought those challenges that have been taken confirms their total lack of regard both towards the welfare of claimants and for principles of equality and non-discrimination.

The scale and multitude of errors made by the DWP throughout the execution of welfare reform are suggestive of gross incompetence. At the same time, it cannot be ignored how this incompetence has served the purposes of an aim of discouraging benefit claims.

Leading a parliamentary debate on the WCA, Labour MP Laura Pidcock declared that people are dying because of 'institutionalised bullying and harassment of sick and disabled people' by the government. She said: 'I have no doubt that administrative ineptitude is part of it, but on this scale, there can be no other conclusion.' The response from Minister Justin Tomlinson was unconvincing, claiming: 'There have been times when you think "how on earth could this have happened".'[57]

It simply isn't credible for Tomlinson, who has twice held the appointment of Minister for Disabled People, to effect surprise or confusion about the impacts of a policy that has been in place under the Tories for a decade and subject to five independent reviews. By now the government must either be happy with the way in which the WCA is working, including the harm it is causing, or in denial about its deadly outcomes. Both are inexcusable.

A lack of concern for the poorest in society is clearly discernible in the choices that led to the wasting of funds intended to alleviate child poverty and homelessness. A House of Lords committee wrote to the government in 2019 about its failure to spend more than £3.5 million, saying it was 'extraordinary' that the EU funding has not been used. They warned that some of the cash has already been forfeited and were worried about the rest being handed back. At a time of cuts to public spending, with dramatically escalating child poverty and homelessness, it is difficult to fathom how these funds could have been ignored. It is a clear demonstration of Tory values and where their priorities do not lie.

A final point to consider are the contradictions that exist between different aspects of welfare reform. One of the most obvious is the conflict between the scale of what Iain Duncan

Smith set out to achieve with the introduction of UC, requiring huge investment if it could have a hope of succeeding, and the major cuts to the DWP budget demanded by George Osborne. Conditionality sits at the heart of UC, requiring constant contact between claimants and work coaches employed by the DWP. Since 2015, 10 per cent of Jobcentres have been closed; since UC roll-out began, DWP staff have been cut by 21 per cent, amounting to a loss of one in five employees. This has led to a rise in staffing errors that leave claimants 'cleaning out their savings to survive'.[58]

A 'digital by default' approach is intended to square the circle of increased claimant contact with decreased resources. For disabled people, there are major issues concerning access; 'digital by default' effectively shuts out a substantial proportion of disabled people. How many we do not know, because this is not something the DWP ever considered looking into before closing centres, laying off staff and putting everything online. The human cost of what is proving to be a failed experiment in a 'digital by default' approach is the outcome of the terrible combination of incompetence and ideology – where those making the decisions have such a poor understanding of the lives they hold in their hands but also have no interest in improving that understanding.

Resisting neoliberal attacks

The array of legislation, policy and practice that make up welfare reform has been driven by fierce ideology. What it has lacked is a coherent framework. This can be observed in conflicting agendas between key players such as Duncan Smith and Osborne, as well as in the error and ineptitude of their delivery.

The lack of a coherent framework can be attributed to the wider picture of mainstream neoliberal political crisis. Austerity was supposed to fix the crisis of profitability triggered by the financial crash of 2008. With many firms now regarded as too big to be allowed to fail, state intervention has increasingly attempted to manage the crises that are inherent in the workings of capitalism. The 'creative destruction' that occurs through the cycle of boom and bust that capitalism naturally follows enables the system to reset itself and so begin a new period of growth. As economist Joseph Choonara explains: 'The more our rulers seek to defer crises, the more the result is sluggish, miserable growth along with new forms of instability.'[59]

The alternative plan to letting the 'too big to fail' fail was austerity, squeezing workers' wages, and quantitative easing. It was a plan that failed, meanwhile creating a political backlash that has shaken the neoliberal consensus. There are now warnings of a new global recession just about due and the ruling class has no coherent ideas on where to turn next.

The Tories will keep pushing their agenda to cut and limit social security, 'claiming to address the future' while in effect 'turning the clock back, to [a] time ... when the cost of sickness was born by the individual and the family',[60] for as long as they remain in power.

We should not be fooled by very minor concessions on UC or the 'fresh approach' announced by Amber Rudd to make the system 'fairer'.[61] Campaigners would be wise to assume that the £36 million pledged in 2019 'to ensure DWP decision-making is accurate and the application processes are straightforward and accessible, as well as improving safeguarding by creating a new independent Serious Case Panel' will be largely spent on merging assessments for ESA and PIP. This will bring PIP into UC; a core aim is undoubtedly to try through this approach to achieve the missed savings targets for reducing the PIP caseload and expenditure.

We must fight further attacks alongside coordinated campaigns to reverse the damages already done. There is no good reason why, as has been suggested, we should have 'to accept that there will be little if any out of work disability benefits by the mid 2020s'.[62] To concede to neoliberalism would be to give in to the inevitability of disabled people's oppression. Change is far from easy but it is possible through unity, resistance and strategy.

TEN | Collaborators

In the years before he died, influential disabled academic Mike Oliver came out of retirement to 'deliver [a] stinging rebuke to "parasite" charities'. Oliver was heavily critical of 'the big disability charities', which he said had 'proved predictably useless at defending the living standards and lifestyles of disabled people' from the government's 'vicious attacks, while continuing to do very well for themselves'. He referred to the phrase 'parasite people', once used by the disabled activist Paul Hunt to describe those 'who furthered their own careers on the backs of the struggles of disabled people to lead ordinary lives'. Included in his criticism was Disability Rights UK (DRUK), which, although user-led, has promoted soft approaches to challenging the government such as writing 'letters to our MPs and government' in place of radical 'political activism'.[1]

National charities have considerable resources at their disposal as well as public profiles and reach. Instead of utilising these to build a movement against the social murder being committed by government, they have continued with their traditional practices of lobbying through research and polite meetings with ministers. Charity-commissioned research reports demonstrating the impacts of cuts and benefit changes provide useful data but it has been clear for many years that these alone are an ineffective way of influencing a government notorious for denying evidence.

At the same time, they have consistently undermined the efforts of more radical campaigns by presenting themselves as 'defenders of disability rights',[2] co-opting our ideas and language to disguise their corporate agendas. In a web post for Disabled People Against Cuts (DPAC), Debbie Jolly wrote: 'They stole our words, our lives, our campaigning terms ... a wolf in sheep's clothing.'[3]

While doing too little in the face of the onslaught against disabled people, the charities have taken media attention away from the efforts of campaigners. This creates a false impression regarding the relative merits of different techniques for influencing change. DPAC responded angrily to media coverage of the legal challenge taken by two disabled campaigners from Mental Health Resistance Network (MHRN) against the discriminatory nature of the Work Capability Assessment. They noted that 'the big Disability charities have, as usual, chosen to take the credit for this success'.[4]

Charities 'usually present themselves as the nation's conscience'. People give them money on the assumption that they are 'supporting the disadvantaged'. But, asks Peter Beresford, as they pursue their own corporate agendas, who then 'is speaking up for disempowered and marginalised people, including the young, disabled and unemployed?'[5] Public trust in the charity sector has been rocked over recent years by the scandal involving the use of sex workers by Oxfam staff and complaints over the high salary of charity bosses. Awareness is growing that they may not be all they seem. However, as long as they claim to speak for disabled people, occupying positions at the table with government and in the media, they have the ability to keep undermining disabled people's interests.

This chapter examines issues of vested interests as well as the limitations of third-sector lobbying approaches. It considers two specific examples – the Time to Change anti-stigma campaign and purple pound initiative – which have provided cover to the government and thus facilitated its attacks on disabled people.

Vested interests

National disability charities are major concerns whose interests are firmly rooted in maintaining the status quo. They prioritise their corporatised agendas over and above the real interests of disabled people. As Beresford explains: '[M]any charities have lost sight of their traditional value-base, and become indistinguishable from the state and private sectors. They have become permeated by their personnel, ways of working and ethics.'[6]

In 2017–18, the combined annual turnovers of the charities Mencap, Leonard Cheshire, Scope and Mind amounted to almost £500 million. Their top executives are rewarded well for their services. According to a charity rich list from 2013, the salary bands for the CEOs of Mencap, Leonard Cheshire and Scope were between £130,000 and £180,000 per year. Key sources of income require that their charitable activities are not too challenging of government. For 2017–18, the largest part of Mencap's income (£171.3 million) was made up of receipts for the provision of direct service delivery and included income from central and local government contracts. They raised £13.1 million through fundraising and attributed improved performance against objectives in part to an increase in legacy income. Donors come from across the political spectrum.

Outspoken criticism of the government is avoided in favour of opportunities to work in partnership. An independent advocacy role 'tends not to sit comfortably with securing public service contracts, especially when the state is the main commissioner … But as grants have dried up, it is largely through providing services that charities seek to achieve financial security.'[7] This has tied them into delivery of the large work programmes associated with welfare reform and hence compromised their ability to challenge the government over the most pressing issues of the day.

Many disabled people have felt let down by the charities for failing to present the level of opposition to welfare reform that the situation requires. In 2016, when a number of disability organisations sacked as patrons MPs who had voted in favour of the £30 per week cut to Employment and Support Allowance (ESA) claimants in the Work-Related Activity Group (WRAG), the big national charities and their local branches refused to do the same. Instead, a number of charities including Scope, Leonard Cheshire, RNIB and the National Autistic Society agreed to join a 'task force' announced by Employment Minister Priti Patel to advise on how money saved through the cut could be spent on employment support for those affected. In this way, the national charities effectively let the government know they could get away with the cruellest cuts and there would be no backlash from them. Jolly railed: 'How could any group, charity or even user-led organisation even agree to this travesty? ... [S]o whose side are they on? It isn't ours.'[8]

Citizens Advice was heavily criticised by campaigners for failing to speak out against the deaths of benefit claimants just hours after Work and Pensions Secretary Esther McVey announced contracts worth £51 million to support the roll-out of Universal Credit (UC). Citizens Advice's Head of Policy on Families, Welfare and Work, Kayley Hignell, failed to raise concerns or call for action when asked about Department for Work and Pensions (DWP) reviews into four claimant deaths at a panel meeting at the Conservative Party conference. Linda Burnip, co-founder of DPAC, commented on Twitter: '[Citizens Advice] selling out to DWP for £51 million. No wonder we don't trust charities.'

The DWP was nevertheless sufficiently concerned about public criticism to insert clauses into its work and health contracts banning organisations from criticising or harming the reputation of McVey. At least 22 organisations were required to sign gagging clauses as part of their involvement with programmes aimed at supporting UC claimants to get back to work. The contracts, worth a total of £1.8 billion, state that groups receiving the money must 'pay the utmost regard to the standing and reputation' of the Work and Pensions Secretary.

There was an outcry among disabled campaigners when 11 charities refused to support a petition started by families of welfare reform victims calling for ministers and senior civil servants to face justice over the deaths of benefit claimants. *Disability News Service* (DNS) revealed that at least two of those charities – RNIB and Leonard Cheshire – had signed the gagging clauses. Another, the National Autistic Society, not only refused to support the petition or answer any questions about its demands but instead praised the DWP for apologising for its failings in the Jodey Whiting case. While being unwilling to add their names in calling for the DWP to make the safety of benefit claimants a priority, Scope and Sense were meanwhile happy to publicly praise measures announced as part of Theresa May's legacy that amounted to nothing more than a few token scraps, described by campaigners as 'cynical leftovers'.

Within the disability sector, there now exist user-led disability organisations with a similar set of priorities to the big national charities and operating at local, regional and national levels. This is for reasons to do with increasing funding pressures as well as the political views of their leadership. For these organisations, strong public criticism of government is considered too risky when weighed against overriding concerns over income security and face-to-face contact with respective levels of government, which are prioritised over proper representation of the issues and experiences of disabled people on the ground.

Complicity by cover and the limits of third-sector lobbying

While speaking against the impacts of individual policy measures and lobbying for specific mitigations, the charities and other disability organisations have continued to engage with government and thereby have lent legitimacy to the overall programmes of welfare reform and social care cuts. This has undermined the attempts of more radical disabled people's organisations and campaign groups to expose the unprecedented nature of the situation we are in.

The Tories have consistently invoked involvement with the charities to legitimise their policy direction. This acts to placate their own backbenchers and members of the public who are less familiar with the issues. Priti Patel's above-mentioned 'advisory task force' helped quiet rebel Tories during passage of the ESA WRAG cut. In another example of this tactic, Esther McVey reassured parliament that she was 'working with Mind' on how to go forwards in the aftermath of the High Court ruling that changes to the regulations for the Personal Independence Payment (PIP) were 'blatantly discriminatory'.[9] McVey told parliament that she had 'decided' not to appeal, but in reality she had no choice: the legal judgement was so damning that it left no room for appeal.

Time and again, charities that engage with government have been cited by the government as supporting controversial measures with which they in fact disagree. In 2017, two senior civil servants claimed that the Health and Work Conversation (HWC) was co-designed with 'health charities, front-line staff, disabled people's organisations and occupational health professionals'.[10] When DNS obtained the names of those Deaf and Disabled People's Organisations (DDPOs) and charities through a Freedom of Information request, they denied any such endorsement of the HWC.

In 2018, Mind was forced to take to Twitter to issue a public clarification of its position on the managed migration regulations consultation after it was misrepresented by McVey in parliament. Her comments to MPs suggested that the charity supported the government's response to the consultation that rejected automatic transfer – ignoring recommendations from the Social Security Advisory Committee in doing so. Mind clarified: 'Yesterday the Secretary of State for Work and Pensions @EstherMcVey1 mentioned us in a list of organisations who had recognised and welcomed changes to #UniversalCredit. We thought it was important to set the record straight.'

Lobbying wisdom encourages organisations to identify shared values and common ground with those they are seeking to influence as the basis for creating positive change. This assumes some form of mutually occupied centre ground. But what happens when there isn't one? What happens when you are faced with a government wholeheartedly intent on effecting negative change, thereby adversely impacting the people you represent – a government fully committed to its policy direction but prepared to lie and spin to conceal it? In such a situation where engagement achieves little but is meanwhile used to legitimise a wider regressive policy agenda, can that engagement be justified or does it represent a betrayal of all those suffering as victims of that agenda?

Strategies for influencing change encourage a focus on measurable and 'realistic' targets. This approach has led to concessions, such as the reduction in waiting times for first benefit payments under UC from six to five weeks, which have undoubtedly helped significant numbers of people. At the same time, the overall direction of policy remains unchanged and grave injustices continue. Speaking at a parliamentary inquiry into the impacts of the Welfare Reform and Work Bill, a former policy and campaigns manager from Mind explained that had he still been working for the charity, he would have still been involved in work that aims at achieving 'incremental change'. Now he had left and could be 'more political' he was able to express his view that conditionality must be removed as an absolute priority.[11]

The Tories have made it clear that they disagree with some of the fundamental premises on which disability charities are based: for example, the idea that disabled people should have equal socio-economic rights. Speaking at the launch of a report by the Equality and Human Rights Commission about 'economic, social and cultural rights', a junior justice minister whose responsibilities included human rights suggested that 'the realities of the world' make it unfeasible for the government to do more. Dominic Raab, a key player in the Johnson administration, has publicly stated that he does not support 'economic or social rights'.

By continuing to engage with a government whose overall agenda is so clearly at odds with the interests of the people the charities claim to represent, those charities are, at best, wasting their not insignificant resources at a time when they are needed more than ever. At worst, they are complicit in implementation of policies that are harming disabled people.

Time to Change

Anti-stigma campaigns are an easy win – for charities wanting to show that they are working with politicians across the political spectrum and for politicians wanting to show a caring side without making any commitments. It is unquestionably positive to raise disability awareness and encourage more openness about issues associated with stigma for reasons outlined in Chapter 2. It is less helpful, and in some ways counterproductive, when this is achieved by giving a platform to politicians – one that enables them to obscure their role in supporting regressive policies that damage the lives of disabled people. As Vic Finkelstein observed: 'When we argue about attitudes before real problems, then we are being "conned".'[12]

An example of this in practice is the Time to Change mental health campaign set up by charities Mind and Rethink, with the objective of reducing mental health-related stigma and discrimination. Launched in 2007, it ran throughout the years of the Coalition government, funded by grants of over £20 million from the Big Lottery Fund and Comic Relief for its first four years. A central emphasis of the campaign was on funding local groups to recruit volunteers with personal experience of mental distress to go out into their local communities to talk about mental health. Another is End the Awkward, a campaign run by the charity Scope to help people feel more comfortable about disability that 'uses humour to get people thinking differently'.

Time to Change missed its initial target of a 5 per cent positive shift in attitudes towards mental health problems by 2012, although by 2014 it had achieved a measured improvement of 6 per cent with the help of celebrity endorsement, most famously comedian Ruby Wax. Any positive shift in public attitudes is, of course, to be welcomed. What was disappointing was its failure to make any significant change in the proportion of members of the public agreeing with the statements 'People with mental illness are a burden on society' and 'As soon as a person shows signs of mental disturbance he should be hospitalised'. This is especially disappointing given the millions of pounds and hours of staff and volunteer time invested in a programme that in its first three years alone was estimated to have reached 34 million people.

Time to Change did not achieve the level of change it aimed for, but it did succeed in providing cover for politicians making savage cuts to mental health services. David Cameron, Nick Clegg and 110 MPs pledged their support to the campaign. One who did this very publicly with a feature in a local newspaper for his constituency was MP Jason McCartney. Like the overwhelming majority of Tory MPs, McCartney voted through legislation removing £30 per week from people with mental distress in the WRAG of ESA.

Material deprivations and the removal of life-saving support are priority concerns for people with mental distress in the current climate. Anti-stigma campaigns allow politicians to adopt a caring façade that arguably makes it easier for them to get away with regressive policy.

The problem with anti-stigma campaigns is not only the cover they provide, but also that they focus the narrative on attitudinal barriers to the exclusion of material conditions. This reduces the pressure on politicians pushing through cuts and chimes perfectly with a neoliberal ideology that blames disadvantage on individual deficiencies while denying the role of structural inequalities.

The fiction of the purple pound

One concept that has emerged in a desperate attempt to find common ground between capitalist ideology and disability equality is that of the 'purple pound', a term coined to represent the combined spending power of disabled people. This was the focus of the Conservative Party annual disability colloquium in 2018, which was attended by a number of charity representatives and at which the Head of Policy for DRUK spoke.

An amount of £212 billion, said to represent the value of the purple pound, was calculated and mentioned in a press release by the DWP in 2014. This figure (which has now risen to £249 billion) has become the basis for numerous campaigns and initiatives targeted at business. The user-led organisation Purple (formerly Essex Coalition of Disabled People) held the first ever 'accessible shopping day' in 2018, supported by the Office for Disability Issues and the Minister for Disabled People. Its aim was to '[highlight] the business benefits of welcoming the "Purple Pound" into inclusive and accessible shops, restaurants, pubs and clubs', and the day was presented as 'an opportunity for retailers to improve customer service for disabled people'.

There is a sizeable discrepancy between how the value of the purple pound has been calculated and what the figure is often said to represent. According to a presentation given by Scope's Extra Costs Commission and written up by DRUK: 'Altogether disabled people spend £212 billion a year, known as the "purple pound".'[13] This statement is misleading.

As the 2014 DWP press release explained: 'The data for the £212 billion calculation was sourced from the Family Resources Survey (FRS) and Households Below Average Income (HBAI) … Annual net (disposable) income has been summed across all households containing an adult or child who is disabled, as classified under the FRS definition of disability.'

The £212 billion figure therefore represents the total disposable income of all *households* including a disabled person, not the disposable income of just disabled people ourselves. This amount represents the *disposable income* of those households. Technically, disposable income, which is net income after tax, is distinct from *discretionary income*, which is the amount that households have left to spend after tax, housing costs and other necessities such as bills. The significance of discretionary income is that households have greater freedom to choose how they spend it.

The term 'disposable income' is often commonly used to refer to discretionary income. However, it is the value of the discretionary rather than the disposable spending power of older people and members of the LGBT community that have made the 'grey' and the 'pink' pounds so appealing to business.

The combination of lower incomes, excessively high additional unavoidable costs and higher levels of debt carried by disabled people tell us that the discretionary spending power of disabled people is not going to make the purple pound as attractive to the kind of businesses that have targeted its grey and pink equivalents. There are, however, plenty of businesses that needed no help from charities to realise the value in taking access and inclusion issues seriously. As unpalatable as it might perhaps be to aspirant disabled people such as Mike Adams, the CEO of Purple, the majority of disabled people are poor.

This is a fact of which the burgeoning 'poverty industry' is well aware: by far the most accessible premises on the high street are those belonging to businesses targeted at people on low incomes such as pound shops and chains such as Wetherspoon. Many betting shops can boast textbook accessibility that they have undertaken through their own initiative without the incentive of a 'purple shopping day'. They would seem to understand the disability demographic far better than disability organisations frantic to prove that there is a valued place for disabled people within capitalism.

Failed by those believed to represent us
At the time of writing, the disability charities are selling out disabled people over government proposals to merge the assessments for ESA and PIP. Both assessments have been designed for the purpose of pushing disabled people off benefits. There is a high risk for anyone going through them of being stripped of essential income.

The idea of merging two assessments that are each failing disabled people into one test on which all of a person's income will depend is terrifying. The charity Scope's response? To welcome the process as having 'the potential to be positive news'. They say it will be beneficial for those who are asked the same information at different assessments, while qualifying that 'the Government must streamline the proposal to ensure minimal impact for when assessments go wrong'.[14] In this way, they have legitimised plans that are likely to increase the levels of distress and impoverishment to which disabled people are subjected and to lead to further harm and avoidable deaths and suicides.

As the public face of disability, the charities can easily eclipse the voices of disabled people ourselves. When they push messages that are not in our interests, it makes the job of campaigners even harder: not only do we have to contend with the government and the right-wing media but we also have to battle against a sector that is widely considered to represent us.

There is a prevailing idea within wider society that the big charities would somehow alert the public to a government that had crossed a line. When it comes to red lines, the present government has gone well beyond the point at which it would have been reasonable to draw one.

The fact that charities continue to work with the government encourages a belief that everything is essentially OK. This is based on a failure to appreciate that the bottom line for these charities is not to do with the treatment of disabled people but their own organisational interests. It is useful to understand that the reaction by charitable institutions towards the mass extermination of disabled people's lives by the Nazis was to negotiate over saving individual lives and lobbying for exemptions for, for example, disabled clergy. Around half of the victims of the murder programme were taken from church-run institutions. Historian Michael Burleigh concludes that 'the Church's failure was to prefer high-level private talks to open confrontation with … government'.[15]

The resources, profile and reach that the charities possess mean that they are able to place pressure on government that can win valuable concessions. These have helped mitigate the worst harms for significant numbers of people and are to be welcomed. At the same time, we must remember that they have the power to do a lot more. They choose not to, and in that they are guilty of actively facilitating the Tories' war on disabled people.

Ultimately, corporatised charities are invested in maintaining the status quo as opposed to the full transformation of society that is required to free disabled people from oppression. Their continued existence 'demands that disabled people are oppressed, vilified and subjugated'.[16] On a wider level, they operate as part of a civil society that upholds and strengthens the capitalist system.

PART V
FIGHTING BACK

The rise of resistance

> Disabled people have a proud history of resistance and fighting
> back which goes back many years.
>
> Paula Peters[1]

There is a long tradition of disabled people fighting against the system. As a group of people defined by the experience of social and economic oppression, there has been plenty to challenge.

Progress towards greater inclusion and equality for disabled people was hard won through sustained collective action. Mike Oliver recorded:

> Disabled people began to take to the streets when our concerns
> and wishes were either ignored or derided; notably in support
> of fully accessible public transport and against disabling media
> images ... All this forced both government and disability
> charities to take notice ... so much so that, in 1995, after many
> false starts the Disability Discrimination Act became law.[2]

These were the achievements of the Disabled People's Movement (DPM) in Britain but there are many other historical and global examples of disabled people's resistance. Disabled people were 'a significant contributing factor to the upheaval' that resulted in the 1917 Russian Revolution. Keith Rosenthal emphasises how 'people with disabilities everywhere were involved in, helped shape, and played a leading role in all of the changes and upheavals taking place'.[3]

Much of disabled people's resistance has taken an anti-charity stance, demanding equality of opportunity alongside non-disabled people. The march of the National League of the Blind and Disabled in 1920 provided the template for the later, more famous, Jarrow March and secured passage of the Blind Persons Act 1920. It involved 171 blind workers who marched from Newport, Leeds and Manchester to Trafalgar Square in London behind a banner that read 'Justice Not Charity'. In 1939, blind workers in Derry, Ireland, marched from their workplace to the town hall with a banner reading 'Blind, but not to the hard facts of life' in protest against low pay and poor employment conditions. This is described by Blackmore and Hodgkins as evidence of the emergence of a 'militant positioning' within the self-organisation of disabled people.[4]

The category of disability, created as a way of identifying and removing 'unproductive' elements from society, provides a basis for a shared identity that can be galvanised into collective action. The practices of disability denial implemented through welfare reform and analysed in this part of the book represent not only an attack on disabled people's living standards but also on our platform for resistance.

Visible protest by disabled people can be powerful. Constructs of 'deserving' and 'undeserving' that date back to the Poor Law of 1834 still hold sway today, providing a similar function in limiting numbers entitled to support. Physically disabled people fit the popular notion of what counts as 'deserving'. If this group of people are seen to be sufficiently unhappy to take radical action, it can bring into question the fundamental decency of whoever is the cause. This is something any government laying claim to compassionate attitudes or liberalism would rather avoid.

In the US, what has become known as the 'Capitol Crawl' occurred in 1990 when disabled people gathered in Washington DC from 30 states to demand immediate action on rights legislation. At the close of the rally dozens left their wheelchairs to crawl up the steps to the Capitol entrance. The visual spectacle of disabled people pulling themselves up by their elbows secured mass media attention. When proposed Medicare cuts were considered under Clinton's administration a few years later, he is reputed to have told his adviser, 'Ah hell, I don't want to wake up and see a whole bunch of cripples in wheelchairs chained to my front gate.'[5]

Chapter 11 examines the development of disability activism over the past nine years, including points of continuity with the DPM and new approaches. Campaigners have won significant victories while succeeding in pushing disability issues onto the mainstream agenda in a way that is unprecedented. Despite these efforts, the direction of government policy is further regression of disabled people's living standards. One of the impacts of this is that it is becoming harder for disabled people to mobilise resistance.

The final chapter attempts to present some thoughts about the way forward for disabled campaigners after nearly 10 years of Tory rule with more to come, covering both the practice and theory of resistance and the importance of unity between the two.

ELEVEN | Forefront of the fightback

In 2012, a backbench opposition MP named John McDonnell told the House of Commons chamber: 'We now have a disability movement in this country of which we have not seen the equal before. Black Triangle occupied Atos offices in Scotland; members of DPAC – Disabled People Against Cuts – chained themselves in Trafalgar Square. These people are not going to go away. They will be in our face – and rightly so. I will support them.'[1]

Just as welfare reform has been a defining policy programme of Tory rule since 2010, so the rise of disabled people's resistance has been a key feature within the anti-austerity movement. In typically valiant fashion, DPAC co-founder Linda Burnip states: 'Disabled people have refused to capitulate to the ongoing onslaught of their rights by the very nasty parties in power – they have joined together to fight back and will continue to fight back until they win.'[2]

That those at the sharp end of neoliberal ideology would play a leading role in the fightback was far from a given. Disabled people's lives have become dramatically more difficult to a point that few if any of us could have imagined prior to 2010. Space, time and resources have had to be carved out for activism on top of attempting to navigate the ever more wearing daily grind.

On the other hand, the one thing disabled people are familiar with, by the very definition of being disabled, is struggle.

In many ways, we are a group of people better prepared than most to understand that reality is never as it is presented by those in positions of power; to be able to see behind the empty words and rhetoric and to embark on campaigns when the odds seem to be overwhelmingly stacked against us. As DPAC explained in a 2014 publication: 'Despite everything they throw at us, if the government thought disabled people would be an easy target, they were wrong ... For many of us our whole lives have been spent fighting against continuing discrimination, stigma and prejudice.'[3]

Whereas other anti-cuts groups have come and gone, and levels of struggle have wavered across the years from 2010, disabled campaigners have ploughed consistently on. This is because the stakes facing disabled people have been too high to do otherwise. We are the first in the firing line when public services and the welfare state start to be dismantled. The 'fallout' as explained by disabled activist Andy Greene, is that 'people's lives shrink or people die'.[4]

The determination and consistency with which disabled people have taken the fight back to the government have earned respect from across the wider left and have given a new profile to disability issues. What it hasn't achieved is the level of change needed to sufficiently halt – let alone reverse – the cuts that continue to destroy lives and take disabled people's standard of living back decades.

This chapter examines disabled people's resistance since 2010. It analyses the key characteristics of this 'new' activism, assessing those that represent principles and practice developed within the Disabled People's Movement (DPM) and those that signalled a new direction. It also considers what can be regarded as tangible campaigning 'wins' achieved within this period and argues that collective action was pivotal to these. The chapter concludes by acknowledging that, while what we have achieved is immense, we are still, at the time of writing, in a situation where living standards are continuing to regress and the self-organisation of disabled people is becoming more difficult.

The growth of 'new' activism

Coordinated opposition to government policy among disabled people from 2010 onwards represented a new wave of activism. Much of the impetus behind this came from individuals personally affected by welfare reform who had become politicised by their experiences but without necessarily having links to the DPM or an understanding of the social model of disability politics.

These new campaigners were shocked and traumatised by a system that was denying them essential support and income. Facing severe disadvantage and without an analytical framework to draw a distinction between experiences of impairment and of social and economic oppression, anti-welfare reform initiatives grew up that tapped into a personal tragedy model of disability.

Not all 'new' activism was reactive in nature or disconnected from a DPM heritage. DPAC was established in 2010 to respond to the political-economic situation, but to do so according to a fundamental set of principles in line with the tenets of the DPM; these included the social model and opposition to charity models of disability. It has thus been described by activist-academic Steve Graby as 'straddling' old and new activism.[5]

Co-founder Debbie Jolly explained:

> DPAC believes that the lack of power in many different forms is the reason why disabled people remain at the margins of society. The creation of DPAC wasn't a spur of a moment thing; a knee-jerk reaction to what the Coalition was doing. The roots of DPAC were firmly within the politics of the social movement we often refer to as the Disabled People's Movement.[6]

The new activism is largely situated within a socialist analysis. This represents a linking back to the historical materialist perspectives of the early days of the DPM, as evident in the analyses of disabled people's oppression developed by the Union of the Physically Impaired Against Segregation (UPIAS), Vic Finkelstein, Mike Oliver and Colin Barnes. It also represents a shift away from the identity politics approach which came to dominate the DPM from the 1990s until 2010.

'Crip Culture'

There are nevertheless a number of characteristics of the new activism that represent a continuation of campaigning styles developed throughout the life of the DPM and that reflect what is referred to as 'Crip Culture'. The term 'crip', as an example of reclaimed language, itself reflects the legacy of an identity politics approach. Its meaning has developed along with the growing inclusiveness of the movement to refer to any disabled person, not only those with physical impairments.

Campaigning tactics developed in earlier periods also provide practical solutions for organising within the context of the varied and multiple material barriers that disabled people face in everyday life. These include incorporation of a sense of disability/mad pride, the relationship between disability art and protest, and the use of direct action tactics. Across both 'old' and 'new' activism, the weight of fallen activists who have died or had to give up activity has been felt.

Disability pride represents a break from the dominant negative view of disability forced on disabled people by the prevailing conditions of exclusion – a break which brings people into conflict with the idea that they should accept those conditions and that can provide a vital impetus towards active resistance. It is particularly important in the current context of increasing stigma and hostility towards disabled people whipped up by right-wing politicians and media to justify cuts. It turns upside down negative attitudes that are not just held by bigots but are also pervasive among those closest to us – friends, family, neighbours and colleagues who essentially view disability as tragedy according to the dominant ideas about disability examined in Chapter 2. Experiencing one's disabled identity as a positive is powerful and can be life-changing. It gives disabled people the confidence and emotional strength to defy the everyday barriers we face in order to join the struggle.

Within the age of austerity, disability pride has manifested in a way that is directly linked to disabled people's resistance. DPAC national steering group member Bob Ellard commented:

> Disabled people are enduring a vicious assault of cuts and hate propaganda from the austerity zealots in the Coalition government who've been targeting disabled people, who they perceived as being the weakest in society. They were wrong. DPAC was formed to show them and everyone else that disabled people can and will fight back against oppression and will continue to do so as long as that oppression exists.[7]

The articulation of resistance through creative expression has a strong tradition within the DPM. The founder of Disabled People's Direct Action Network (DAN) was singer-songwriter Johnny Crescendo (real name Alan Holdsworth) and artist-activists have always played an important role in the movement.

The use of creative elements within campaigning serves a number of different purposes. It aids accessibility and inclusion of disabled people with different communication support needs. Attention-grabbing stunts also help with awareness raising, since they provide an alternative to resorting to the pity porn narratives that media coverage otherwise depends on.

There is also a long history of artist-activists using their creative talents to draw attention to issues of disabled people's oppression.

Exhibitions and performances can be a powerful method for awareness raising that reaches audiences who are not necessarily politically engaged. Artist-activists such as Vince Laws, Liz Crow and Gill Crawshaw, among many others, have worked tirelessly since 2010 to use their work to highlight the impacts of welfare reform on disabled people.

One initiative neatly embodying a synthesis between art and activism was a 'disobedient' guerrilla exhibition organised by DPAC and the culture sector of the Public and Commercial Services Union in 2016. This saw 'activists invade the Tate Modern in London and produce an unscheduled "pop-up gallery" of artworks highlighting the experiences of disabled people dealing with the welfare system'.[8]

The use of direct action tactics is another element with a strong tradition within the DPM. This is partly about disabled people almost literally throwing off the role of passive victim that society commonly envisages us as inhabiting. It is also a campaigning strategy that can compensate for our inability to turn out en masse.

DPAC is arguably best known for our direct actions. Williams-Findlay writes: 'DPAC's high-profile civil disobedience actions have earned it a great deal of admiration. The first one that caught the public's attention and imagination was in January 2012, when DPAC, along with UK Uncut, blockaded Regent Street in London. This was followed up three months later with a blockade of Trafalgar Square.'[9]

Actions in subsequent years included delivery of an 'eviction' notice to Iain Duncan Smith's mansion in Buckinghamshire in protest against the introduction of the bedroom tax. In 2014, there was a failed attempt to set up an accessible protest camp in the grounds of Westminster Abbey to draw attention to the plans to close the Independent Living Fund (ILF). This involved a 17-tonne truck of camp equipment that was sadly never erected due to an immediate and heavy police presence. The attempt ended after a stand-off for around five hours between a group of about 50 activists and hundreds of police.

An ILF campaign action the following year was more successful in getting media attention. This was played out in front of a live BBC news camera in the lobby of the House of Commons as noisy protesters attempted – and very nearly managed – to storm the chamber during Prime Minister's Questions.

Greene commented: 'What's been great is the way disabled people have constantly escalated our tactics. From demos outside buildings to blocking roads, to taking the fight to government members' front doorsteps and then onto occupying their departments, to assembling a camp under the shadow of parliament. We've fought the battle on our terms every time.'[10]

Many of the actions over the years have taken an attitude that is deliberately cheeky and disrespectful towards politicians responsible for implementing policies of harm. In July 2015, campaigners dropped a massive banner from the river wall opposite parliament as George Osborne announced his budget inside. The banner, made for DPAC by the Banner Collective, said in large letters 'Balls to the Budget'. This was the first budget of the new Tory government and it proposed wiping another £12 billion off welfare expenditure. Disabled people around the country were terrified of what was to come and in desperate need of something to smile about.

DPAC's tactics are often rubbished as 'thuggish' by campaigners who prefer more genteel activity, under an illusion that this will make them more likely to be listened to. The aim of DPAC's style of campaigning and the message of defiance it sends is to give all-important hope and confidence to people, disabled and non-disabled alike, suffering under the very real and debilitating impacts of austerity and welfare reform.

The findings of research published in 2020 show the importance of involvement in campaigning for coping with life under welfare reform. Anger towards the government was expressed by half of the research participants. Their comments illustrate how, in contrast to experiences of welfare conditionality that are characterised by feelings of powerlessness under a perverse and punitive system, an attitude of resistance to that system provides a way to form connections with others, make sense of the world and regain a more positive sense of self.[11]

The current wave of activism has not escaped the problem of early deaths and burnout identified by Oliver and Barnes in 2012. They wrote:

> Another factor in the decline of the disabled people's movement
> is the very real toll that impairment takes on both the leadership
> and other activists within the movement. Through untimely
> deaths and emotional burn-out, the movement has been robbed
> of many important members long before their contributions have
> been completed. Of course, all political movements suffer from
> this, but we would argue not to anything like the same extent.[12]

Disabled campaigners rarely get to retire, often dying at the height of their activism. Reasons for shorter lifespans can be impairment-related but also include lack of equal access to healthcare, poverty and disadvantage. For campaigners, there is also the question of the additional strain that comes with a determination to be active despite disabling barriers.

New directions

There are a number of ways in which new activism differs markedly from former incarnations of the DPM. For one, the idea of a single movement representing the voices of all disabled people has been largely put aside. The Reclaiming Our Futures Alliance

(ROFA) is a network of grassroots disabled people and disabled people-led organisations and campaigns across England. It was set up following the *Rethinking Disability Policy* conference in 2012 with the aim of coordinating resistance to austerity. It therefore took a specific political position that would always exclude those disabled people and their organisations coming from a different standpoint.

'New' activism is inclusive of people with impairments that historically were not well represented within the DPM. For all that the Disability Discrimination Act can be criticised as a watered-down version of the civil rights legislation disabled people campaigned for, its definition of disability, now enshrined in the Equality Act 2010, has led to more people self-identifying as disabled. People with impairments who do not fit society's idea of disabled people as wheelchair users now feel that this is an identity to which they can legitimately lay claim.

Those first hit by welfare reform tended to be people in 'impairment categories [that] were not necessarily well-recognised at the time of UPIAS and LNPD [Liberation Network of People with Disabilities]'.[13] Graby explains that 'the "newer" activists/groups largely consist of those most severely affected by the recent cuts and punitive policies, which to a large extent has been people with so-called "invisible" impairments, neurodiversity, mental health issues (who may or may not be the same people who identify as "Mad" or "survivors"), or chronic pain/fatigue conditions'.[14]

This led to older campaigners with physical impairments accusing 'new' activists of being 'fake disableds'. The hostility was linked to the idea that opposing welfare reform feeds into negative perceptions of disabled people and should be avoided in preference to campaigns focused on inclusive employment.

One of the key characteristics of new activism is its use of information and communications technology (ICT) within campaigning. Social media has transformed campaigning for everyone – with online networks now used to coordinate protests and citizen journalism playing an increasing role in sharing information. For disabled people, online technology has a particular significance due to its potential to bring into activism those who are otherwise disconnected from political engagement for impairment- or disability-related reasons. This includes people from impairment categories that were not historically well represented within the DPM, such as those living with mental distress or energy-limiting chronic illness. People with physical impairment are also increasingly reliant on technology to engage with the outside world as support packages are cut back.

The now prominent role of ICT within disability activism represents a response to the demand to be more inclusive and more widely accessible. It also reflects the fact that disabled people, on our own initiative, have made use of new possibilities now open to us to get involved and be active. As a result, campaigning is richer and more diverse, and social media is now an everyday part of campaign events from meetings and conferences to protests and demonstrations.

New campaigns such as DPAC and Mental Health Resistance Network (MHRN) were set up with a strategic aim of making known the impacts of neoliberal government policy on disabled people beyond the disability sector. Williams-Findlay outlined the co-founders' analysis: 'This is a life or death struggle and disabled people must force their issues onto the public agenda by engaging in mainstream politics as collective groups of disabled people.'[15]

Some disabled activists have been unhappy with the association with the labour and trade union movement, seeing this as a move away from the traditional framework of disability politics. Nevertheless, the approach of situating disabled people's struggle within wider anti-neoliberal politics has contributed to an unprecedented awareness of disability issues among potential allies on the left.

The agenda was not just to raise disability issues within the mainstream, but to go further than that in working alongside progressive campaigns and to influence the mainstream resistance agenda. This signalled 'a political dynamic that was without precedent in the traditional Disabled People's Movement'.[16]

Solidarity with other campaigns and actions that shared an anti-austerity stance became an integral part of DPAC's day-to-day activity. Jamie Kelsey-Fry, a long-time ally of DPAC through the Occupy London movement, commented in 2016: 'DPAC are the only direct action group in the UK who come out to physically support a very wide range of other anti-cuts and anti-neoliberal grassroots groups. From trade unions to Sisters Uncut, Fuel Poverty Action to Reclaim the Power, you will find DPAC there on the ground supporting.'[17]

The principle of solidarity is based on the idea that we are stronger together. The concept of one united DPM, however, is neither obtainable nor desirable, as recognised by DPAC co-founders at the campaign's inception. Jolly commented: '[T]here is a certain political naivety within the community of disabled people which still believes "we all want the same thing" – a political analysis of the last twenty years of disability politics, we would argue, shows that this might not be the case.'[18]

The emergence of 'new' activism provoked a significant split within the DPM between campaigners and organisations situated within an anti-capitalist analysis and those who seek acceptance for disabled people within the neoliberal status quo.

The 'new' activism represented a return to grassroots campaigning, led by activists without salaried positions in largely unfunded networks that lack bureaucratic infrastructure. This contrasted sharply with more established disabled campaigners and Deaf and Disabled People's Organisations (DDPOs) that had grown dangerously out of touch with the reality on the ground. It was ILF recipients themselves who initiated the campaign to save the ILF, since they were all too familiar with the limitations of the mainstream adult social care system. A number of the DDPOs that were involved alongside DPAC in ROFA, such as Inclusion London, came on board and provided invaluable capacity.

The single issue that drew the deepest line in the sand was the closure of the Remploy factories. This divided disabled campaigners and organisations invested in promoting an idea of disabled people that conforms to neoliberal ideals from those whose interest was in fighting to protect material living standards.

The closure of the factories was recommended in a report by disabled consultant and CEO of the newly formed Disability Rights UK, Liz Sayce.[19] Her position reflected a long-held principle of the DPM that promoted inclusion over segregation and she recommended that the money saved be invested instead in the government's Access to Work (AtW) disability employment programme. Those within the disability sector who believed money released by the closures would actually end up with AtW had clearly failed to grasp the nature of the government that had come into power. An inquiry into AtW by the Work and Pensions Committee in 2014 commented on the Department for Work and Pensions' (DWP's) failure to provide 'a satisfactory explanation of how the money saved from the closure or sale of Remploy factories has been used'.

DPAC initially agreed with Sayce's recommendations, but, following contact from Remploy shop steward, Les Woodward, and with other disabled trade unionists working within the factories, was persuaded that the situation was more nuanced, especially given the political-economic context.

There was a considerable amount wrong with the Remploy set-up. The workers, however, preferred to be there than out of work. There was little hope of future employment once the factories closed. A survey by the GMB trade union of disabled workers made redundant in 2008 revealed that 74 per cent were left on out-of-work benefits; of the 26 per cent who had found alternative work, only 5 per cent of those had found work on equal or better terms. From the previous round of Remploy closures in the 1980s, 85 per cent of disabled ex-employees remained unemployed, and that was in a better economic climate than following the financial crash of 2008.

Throughout the process there was too little engagement with the workers themselves. Sayce was described as scuttling in and out of a handful of factories without speaking to the workers themselves while compiling the report that destroyed their futures. Workers were calling for investment in turning the factories into independent, worker-led co-operatives, but this was never on the table of those making the decisions.

In 2013, 54 Remploy sites were shut with the loss of 1,800 jobs. In 2018, it was reported that most ex-employees did not go on to find work, or they found only very short-term work; figures from 2017 showed that about 75 per cent were still out of work.[20] Outcomes for the workers were similar to those from the previous rounds of closures: deterioration of both physical and mental health and, for some, premature death or suicide.

The delight with which certain disabled campaigners and their organisations celebrated the factory closures sparked anger among those whose position was to support the workers. Southampton Centre for Independent Living (since renamed Spectrum) praised then Minister for Disabled People Maria Miller for implementing Sayce's recommendation to close the factories. An article in their newsletter for March 2012 said: 'Good on you Maria Miller.'

Activists hit back, arguing that the position in favour of factory closures was anything but progressive. On the DPAC website, Jolly wrote:

> It is dangerous, misguided and completely ludicrous to claim that all disability organisations and the disability movement have decided that a new perverse way of supporting disabled people is to make them unemployed and subject to the ravages that disabled people must endure under this government, as the Sayce report suggests.[21]

Wins

Perhaps the biggest achievement since 2010 has been to shift the narrative. It is now much more widely accepted that, far from being a necessity, austerity was a political choice. As we have seen, the misperception of welfare reform as being about fixing a broken system has also been replaced with wider recognition that it instead represents a deliberate attack on the poorest and most disadvantaged members of society in order to afford tax breaks for the rich.

A British social attitudes survey in 2017 showed 48 per cent supporting higher tax and more spending, up from 32 per cent at the start of austerity in 2010. Notably, there was a surge in support for spending on disabled people, with 67 per cent supporting funding for disability benefits compared with 53 per cent in 2010. There was also a significant softening in attitudes towards benefit claimants, with the proportion of people believing that claimants are 'fiddling' the system dropping between 2015 and 2017 from 35 to 22 per cent – the lowest level in 30 years.

Frances Ryan writes: 'While immediately after the global crash, the narrative that austerity in Britain is both necessary and – even – morally right was widely accepted (a narrative the Labour Party crucially failed to challenge), recent years have seen this dogma start to lose its clout.'[22]

It is frustrating for campaigners fighting since 2010 that we have not got further – that government policy is driven by the same ideological agenda that underpinned the Coalition, that living standards continue to be driven backwards, and that even worse is in store through the roll-out of Universal Credit and the social care funding crisis.

At the same time, it is important to recognise how much has been achieved in spite of having the odds stacked against us. When the determination and complexity of the spin and scapegoating used to conceal what was happening are considered, the achievement in shifting that narrative is really quite remarkable. Getting around the distortions and distractions presented by the mainstream media to build support for an alternative perspective has been no small feat.

Individual battles have also been won along the way. The government was compelled to provide £675 million to local authorities over four years for the 'Former Independent Living Fund (ILF) Recipient Grant' in response to pressure. A multi-pronged campaign led by disabled activists used every resource and opportunity at their disposal including legal challenges, lobbying, and a protest inside parliament. Chancellor George Osborne was caught out by ILF recipient Helen Johnson in a BBC *Look North* interview piece that saw him promising funding would be transferred 'pound for pound' to local authorities.[23] That was never the government's plan for what would happen post-closure. The four-year grant was un-ring-fenced and tapered but would never have been forthcoming without the campaign.

It is arguable that the ILF itself could have been saved had activists been sufficiently bold to try a stunt like the direct action inside parliament earlier. This is one example of a lesson learned too late – the lesson being not to look to people in positions of power to come down from on high and correct an injustice but to understand the power of collective agency.

Another example is the faith the Remploy workers put in their trade union leaders instead of taking their own action to occupy the factories – a strategy members of the Socialist Workers Party argued for in a series of easy-read leaflets distributed to disabled workers picketing the factories on strike days. The height of the campaign against the factory closures was right before the London 2012 Paralympic Games when media attention was tuned into disability issues. Bold action by disabled workers, especially at the Barking factory, so close to the Olympic Village, could have shamed the government in front of the world's media and forced a climbdown. The workers ultimately lacked confidence to act for themselves, trusting that someone would provide a rescue line before it was too late. That never came. As the Remploy fight faded, disabled activists who had been supporting the workers turned their attentions to using the Games to expose sponsors Atos and their role in delivering the Work Capability Assessment (WCA).

Where significant wins have been achieved, it has been as the result of collective action led from below. Three strong examples of this are the United Nations Disability Committee's damning findings against the UK government, Atos's flight from the WCA contract and the victory over workfare (the practice of forcing jobseekers to work in return for benefits). Additionally, the fact that the government has failed to make its projected savings through replacement of Disability Living Allowance (DLA) with PIP is not a sign of any developing compassion towards disabled people. It means they met with barriers and resistance they had not anticipated.

UN findings

The UN findings were in no way binding upon government and led to no immediate policy changes. What they did was to validate the experiences of disabled people since 2010. Issues raised by disabled people through the CRPD (Convention on the Rights of Persons with Disabilities) inquiry and examination processes influenced the subsequent work of the Equality and Human Rights Commission (EHRC) and opposition party policies. Labour, the Liberal Democrats and the Scottish National Party (SNP) have all now pledged to enshrine the UN CRPD in domestic legislation.

The DPAC research team triggered the special inquiry that took place in 2015 but the process involved a large number and range of disabled people, our allies and organisations. The Disability Committee that visited the UK interviewed more than 200 people including not only disabled people but also lawyers, journalists, the families of welfare reform victims and DDPO representatives across all the devolved administrations. The Committee read thousands of pages of written evidence submitted by both individuals and organisations. They also spoke to government. Their unprecedented conclusion was that the threshold of evidence had been crossed for a finding of grave and systematic violations of disabled people's rights, due to welfare reform and austerity.

The UK government clearly intended to claw back a more favourable verdict from the Committee through the routine examination of the UK under the CRPD scheduled for 2017. In this, they were thwarted by a collective effort from DDPOs and disabled campaigners across the four nations. The key here was coordination – what the Committee needs to hear is one shared message from civil society. With so many different organisations and individuals wanting to contribute to the process, this was a tall order. Disability Rights UK's position – that the subject of benefit deaths should be avoided due to an unsubstantial evidence base – was a particular source of controversy.

For the UK-wide civil society response required by the Committee before the August public examination sessions in

Geneva, ROFA took over the task of collation and editing. A 20-strong delegation of disabled representatives from the four nations went in person to Geneva. Coordination went smoothly, with Tracey Lazard, CEO of the DDPO Inclusion London, chairing many of the civil society preparation and debriefing sessions.

In addition to those physically present in Geneva, we additionally had campaigners at home following proceedings. They used their knowledge of specific policy areas to communicate important pieces of information and statistics to those of us in Geneva. This contributed to the process of briefing the UN Disability Committee members in order to assist them to see past the smoke and mirrors put up by the large government delegation. The value of this work was seen when, in August 2017, the UN Disability Committee publicly declared that they were more worried about the UK than any other country in the history of the Committee.

Atos

Forcing Atos, a global corporation with a revenue measured in billions, out of its contract to deliver the WCA was another significant victory for campaigners.

As the WCA began to roll out, disability and benefit claimant networks soon became aware of its dangers. These were communicated through the wider anti-austerity movement, and individual stories of wrongful benefit decisions and the human misery they were causing started to appear in the left-wing media. Protests against Atos organised by groups such as DPAC and Boycott Workfare failed to permeate into the mainstream. With a benefit fraud narrative dominating the media and political rhetoric, it was an issue that was not readily accepted as part of the public agenda. That was until Atos's sponsorship of the London 2012 Paralympic Games handed campaigners a golden opportunity. We knew we had done our job when Cameron and Osborne were greeted by booing crowds as they attempted to hand out medals to the disabled athletes.

To coincide with the Paralympics, DPAC and UK Uncut planned a week of action entitled the 'Anti Atos Games'. This was supported by a wide range of anti-austerity campaigns, DDPOs and trade unions. The activities commenced with our own opening ceremony, which was a parody of the assessment process. Over the week there was a day of protests outside local Atos assessment centres, a memorial protest to commemorate those who had died and suffered at the hands of the WCA, which appeared on *Newsnight*, and social media activities targeting Atos and the DWP. Two separate investigative documentaries on the WCA aired in the same week.

The final event was a mass protest outside Atos's headquarters on 31 August 2012 attended by around 450–500 people. At the same time, in a parallel action, disabled activists and allies acting as 'buddies' for those needing personal assistance occupied the lobby of the DWP's headquarters, Caxton House. The Atos protest journeyed across London to join them and a celebratory atmosphere took hold, inspired by this simple act of defiance. The mood turned to one of determination when inappropriate tactics on the part of the Metropolitan Police in separating the two groups at the entrance of the government department resulted in one wheelchair user having his shoulder dislocated and an occupier becoming DPAC's first member to be arrested. The remaining occupiers held out and footage of them emerging to the cheering crowd waiting outside made the primetime news that evening. By the end of that week, Atos had become a household name.

Anti-Atos protests became so popular that DPAC no longer needed to organise them. This was an indication of how many lives the WCA was now affecting negatively, as well as how far the issue had caught the popular imagination. There was some disagreement among campaigners as to what was an appropriate attitude to adopt towards individual assessors and Jobcentre workers responsible for carrying out government policy. DPAC promoted a line of disruption and aggression towards the policy but not the people. The assessment experience feels very personal, especially when assessors' reports are grossly misrepresentative, so this was at times a very difficult line to argue.

Awareness raising achieved through protests and support from the wider anti-austerity movement secured important solidarity from the student movement. Their efforts in chasing Atos recruiters off university campuses played a significant role in the company's decision to leave the WCA contract early, when, among other difficulties, they found themselves unable to attract staff. A policy adopted by the Students' Union at the University of Nottingham is evidence of this valuable student contribution. The policy states:

- That the Student Union shall boycott ATOS with immediate effect and shall not allow them to recruit or advertise themselves in or around Student Union Buildings or designated areas.
- The Student Union shall work with Careers and Employability to stop ATOS from recruiting on campus or operating in any way on campus.
- The Union shall lobby the University to cut all ties with ATOS and implement a boycott.[24]

Atos's failings became a popular media topic even among the right-wing media in favour of welfare reform. Outlets competed at national, regional and local levels to find the most extreme examples of bizarre and clearly wrongful 'fit for work' decisions.

In March 2014, the Minister for Disabled People, Mike Penning, announced that Atos would quit the WCA before its contract ended. Although Atos themselves claimed they were prompted by unacceptable abuse experienced by their staff, journalist Amelia Gentleman pointed to the reputational damage that stopped them being able to recruit as a more motivating factor: 'The decision to leave the contract does not appear to have been a hard one ... Atos's global reputation took a savaging from its association with the fitness-for-work programme.'[25] This was a significant victory for campaigners.

Although the WCA carried on, delivered instead by an arguably even more ruthless firm, Maximus, the win against Atos was nevertheless strategically very important. It demonstrated to campaigners what could be achieved when they united their resistance. Media and politicians who were firmly behind the government's welfare reform agenda were willing to scapegoat Atos in the face of adverse publicity. This helped open a door in the public consciousness to a wider questioning of the policy behind the WCA and those responsible. It contributed to shifting the narrative, although the hateful tests remained.

Campaigns targeted at the companies responsible for delivering welfare reform have succeeded in undermining Lord Freud's big vision of privatisation and outsourcing of DWP functions. His dream of a vibrant market in the sector never materialised.

Mainstream opposition parties have now pledged not only to overhaul the WCA but to end outsourcing. This would aid transparency while stopping the abhorrent practice of companies making profits from pushing the poor further into destitution. Under Scotland's devolved social security powers, the SNP confirmed 'that there will be no contracting with the private sector in our assessment model'.[26] In 2019, Labour announced: 'Private companies will be banned by a Labour government from running services that deal with vulnerable people and their rights, under a far-reaching plan to restrict outsourcing.'[27]

Workfare

Attempts to place additional burdens on claimants at the same time as effectively subsidising business through the 'workfare' programme were eventually scuppered as a result of sustained resistance. This repeated the success achieved by the National Unemployed Workers' Movement (NUWM) in the 1930s in their offensive against the workfare equivalent of 'test and task work'. Introduced as 'a deterrent to the receipt of relief', this was mandatory manual labour that unemployed workers were compelled to undertake in return for out-of-work benefits.

Arguments against the Tories' introduction of what opponents labelled 'workfare' were similar to those voiced by the NUWM in its day. Related schemes consisted of Community Work Placements, involving six months' forced full-time work for the long-term unemployed, Mandatory Work Activity, which compelled claimants to work without pay for 30 hours a week for four weeks, and the so-called Work Experience Scheme, involving eight-week placements mainly in the private sector. The former was expanded to 70,000 placements a year despite DWP research showing that it had 'zero effect' on people's chances of finding work, while the government expected there to be around 350,000 Work Experience places in total from January 2011 to March 2015, with around 100,000 a year for the three years 2012–13 to 2014–15.[28]

Workfare allowed businesses to benefit from free labour, but it did nothing to improve claimants' prospects of finding work, enabling businesses to profit from the hardship of the unemployed, and putting at risk the jobs of paid workers who could be replaced. Stores such as Argos, Asda, Superdrug and Shoe Zone made use of the government's workfare schemes to meet their seasonal demand, instead of hiring extra staff or offering overtime.

A series of legal challenges initiated by Cait Reilly, a geology graduate, and Jamieson Wilson, an unemployed driver, put the spotlight on DWP workfare practices. In August 2012, the High Court ruled that the government had acted unlawfully by not giving unemployed people enough information about the penalties they faced if they refused to work unpaid, in some cases for hundreds of hours. In response to this defeat, the Coalition government, with the support of the Labour Party, subsequently rushed emergency legislation through parliament to retrospectively correct the flaws in the original employment scheme. This was again challenged and again found unlawful. This judgement was then upheld by the Court of Appeal in February 2013, which rejected the government's argument that the legislative change was justified on the grounds that sanctioned claimants did not deserve a benefit repayments 'windfall' paid for by the taxpayer. The legal ruling stated: 'The rule of law endures for the benefit of the undeserving as well as the deserving.'[29]

Coordinated resistance by campaigns including Right to Work and Boycott Workfare, supported by DPAC and other anti-austerity groups, led to the abandonment of workfare schemes. In 2014, the DWP quietly announced that private-sector contracts to run Community Work Placements and Mandatory Work Activity would not be renewed. This was the result of high street stores and charities either pulling out of or boycotting both schemes in response to 'furious campaigning'.[30] Days of action took place across the UK involving activity 'from cheeky post-it notes left throughout stores to occupations and pickets of key offenders', complemented by an ongoing social media assault.[31]

Targeting the work placement providers was, as right-wing commentator Matthew d'Ancona remarked, a 'deft strategy' that played on fears of reputational damage.[32] In February 2012, Tesco announced it would immediately offer a wage to all benefits claimants working unpaid in its stores following an occupation by protestors of one of its stores. Several other big chains, including Argos, Superdrug, NHS, Waterstone's, Sainsbury's, TK Maxx, Maplin, Matalan, HMV and Oxfam, reported that they were suspending involvement or withdrawing altogether. A 2013 DWP report noted 'a sharp reduction in placements since charities have been persuaded by the campaign to withdraw'. Long before the Coalition government came to an end, their workfare scheme was in tatters, leading to its eventual abandonment.

Missed DLA/PIP savings

A sizeable problem experienced by the Tories since 2015 has been with trying to realise the projected savings from replacing DLA with PIP.

In December 2012, the government predicted that moving to PIP would save £2.9 billion a year by 2017–18 and that introducing PIP would see a reduction in the number of claimants of 28 per cent by May 2018 (compared with what this number would have been under DLA). The transition to PIP was intended to save 20 per cent compared with DLA remaining in place, but it appears to have cost around 15 to 20 per cent more. Those estimated savings have since been revised to an overspend of £1.5 billion to £2 billion, leaving an estimated £4.2 billion gap, and the Office for Budget Responsibility (OBR) calculates that it would have proved cheaper to retain DLA.

Reasons for the unexpected rise in costs identified by the OBR include the growing number of appeals. Figures for July to September 2019 on rates of PIP and ESA assessments overturned at appeal are 76 per cent and 77 per cent respectively.[33] The system has also come under pressure from an increase in claimants, especially of working-age adults, a group that was due to see a large fall, and from information sharing between 'claimants (and their advisors) learning how to navigate the system better – a factor accentuated by the rise of the internet and social media'.[34]

Another factor to which the OBR attributes the government's failure to realise its projected savings are 'legal challenges'. Its claim that these 'widened the benefit's scope' is not strictly accurate. The legal rulings to which the OBR refers found that changes brought in by government were contrary to the original intentions of PIP as outlined by the government itself at the time of introduction. Rhetorical justifications for replacing DLA that were designed to dispel resistance included the argument that it was insufficiently accessible to certain impairment groups, in particular people with mental distress. When the cost implications of the more equitable scheme came to be realised, the government sought ways to limit eligibility. The courts did not change the scope of the scheme; rather, they stopped the government from restricting it in contravention of its stated aims when introducing PIP.

A briefing by DPAC from February 2012 stated:

> Ms Mordaunt [then Minister for Disabled People] is keen to give the impression that she wants to 'restore' the original intention, when it would be better to say she is trying to restore DWP's plans to limit PIP mobility extra-legally that were devised in 2014 without consultation or a proper process. As the Upper Tribunal did not allow this, they now need to pass law, but cannot afford scrutiny. They are pretending that it is the Upper Tribunal who broadened the criteria, when it was actually DWP who tried unsuccessfully to limit them.

Another factor responsible for the failure to realise the intended budget cut has been high levels of resistance against government attempts to limit eligibility. In March 2016, Osborne was told by MPs that his budget was in 'absolute chaos' after campaigning pressure and the resignation of Iain Duncan Smith forced him to do a U-turn on proposed cuts of £4.4 billion to the DLA/PIP budget.

The government had planned to halve the number of points a person gets in the assessment for having to use specially adapted aids and appliances. The Disability Benefits Consortium estimated that the changes would affect around 630,000 disabled people. With the disability charities firmly against the proposals and Tory backbenchers threatening to rebel, protestors from DPAC forced Osborne to cancel a photo shoot with then mayoral hopeful Zac Goldsmith by shouting 'blood on your hands'. The next day Iain Duncan Smith resigned as Secretary of State for Work and Pensions, claiming that the cuts planned were a 'compromise too far'.

It is not surprising that the Tories have wanted to restrict any extra costs of disability benefits. What is arguably more surprising is the Tories' failure to achieve the cuts they set out to make when they have been so determined to do so. This is perhaps one area where their failure to properly understand welfare and disability has worked to the advantage of disabled people. Ministers now frequently cite the increased spending on PIP in response to any criticism of their record on disability.

Progress and pitfalls

Disability now has an unprecedented public and political profile. This is an important, tangible outcome achieved by hard-fought resistance since 2010, resistance that we must now build on.

Some of that attention is firmly grounded in a pity model of disability, as reflected by the popular refrain 'the most vulnerable in society', but there has also been a marked shift in attitudes as a positive outcome of non-disabled people's experience of engaging in struggle alongside disabled people since 2010. This, I would argue, is a more powerful way of questioning negative ideas of disability than through call-out culture, formal training sessions or information handouts.

The backdrop to this increased profile is a continuing regression of disabled people's material living standards. It is becoming increasingly difficult for disabled people to actively engage in resistance. Reasons include ever increasing cuts to living support and the growing barriers to daily life that disabled people are experiencing in the neoliberal age. Fear of surveillance terrorises many in receipt of disability benefits from participating in any activities that could be twisted into evidence against their claims. While I am confident that disabled people will continue to fight injustice through whatever means are available to them, the reality is that coordinated self-organisation is becoming more difficult. The danger then is that we end up being spoken *for* and *about* and according to the oppressive views of disability that dominate society.

TWELVE | Concluding thoughts

Where do we go from here?

Disability is an issue that powerfully exposes the true nature of capitalism as a cruel system based on exploitation and greed. It therefore isn't surprising that the dominant ideas in society around disability are full of misperceptions and act to conceal an understanding of the true relationship between disability and capitalism.

The United Nations (UN) finding was that the UK government is responsible for grave and systematic violations of disabled people's rights. This is little known. Disability is an issue that affects a significant proportion of the population and yet another significant proportion of people have no knowledge or understanding of it. For many people in this category, even if they do hear about the UN finding, they simply don't believe there is any validity to it. This is because it jars with what they think they know about the treatment of disabled people in Britain today.

There are also those who know only too well what has been happening, but who view it as a terrible aberration in policy direction. Some believe the problem to be that the government is simply too out of touch and unaware of the impacts of its policies – we just need to crack how to communicate the information to politicians so they understand; at that point, they will of course change direction. Others are aware that it is all part of a deliberate strategy and put it down to the cruelty of the Conservative Party.

Of course, while in government, the Tories have been responsible for carrying out policies causing mass misery, destitution and additional deaths. The announcement in October 2019 by the National Audit Office (NAO) that it is to investigate suicide monitoring of benefit claimants in response to the continued refusal of ministers to publish data will shed more light on how callous they are.

But the situation we have experienced since 2010 is part of a bigger picture involving the relationship between disability and capitalism. Policies that ignore or make life more difficult for disabled people are not unique to the Tories. The roots of welfare reform date back to successive governments, both Conservative and New Labour; the Liberal Democrats had no qualms about going along with austerity and benefit cuts while in the Coalition government. The Scottish National Party (SNP) talks loudly in opposition in Westminster but has yet to deliver on many of its key pledges affecting disabled people – for example, on devolution of disability benefits. Labour under Jeremy Corbyn was painfully slow to adopt a position against Universal Credit, in spite of clear evidence that the system is rotten to its core, and shut out disabled activists from involvement in setting its social care policy.

There is a material basis behind this treatment of disabled people. The mainstream parliamentary parties are invested in maintaining capitalism. It is not inevitable that people with impairments should be excluded and discriminated against, but it is inevitable that policies under a capitalist state will tend to treat less favourably those who are unable to be as productive in the workforce.

Gains can be won through collective action – more easily at times of economic growth – and progressive parties will implement what reforms they can. There were many policy commitments within the 2015 and 2017 Labour manifestos that would have been ground-breaking for disabled people. But as long as we live under capitalism, there will always be the threat of cuts and regressions and a need for struggle. As Mike Oliver and Colin Barnes remarked: 'The chances of transcending [the] forces, conditions and relations [that cause disablement] are therefore intrinsically bound up with the possibilities of capitalism being transcended.'[1]

It is frustrating for politicised disabled people when disability issues are largely unseen within the wider anti-capitalist movement or when engagement with them goes no deeper than surface level – using disability cuts as a crude stick with which to beat the Tories rather than engaging with the theory of disabled people's oppression.

Probably the majority of people on the left (and the right) hold ideas about disability that align with an ideology of individualism as opposed to a social model approach to disability. However frustrating this can be, it is not surprising, given that the 'ideas of the ruling class are in every epoch the ruling ideas',[2] and this situation has a material basis that it is important to understand.

A true understanding of the nature of disabled people's oppression is deliberately obscured from view so that what is really interesting about it is hidden. Instead of understanding disability as the deliberate exclusion of people who can't serve the interests of profit, the dominant idea of disability in society is that it is somehow inevitable that people with impairments will experience disadvantage. Disability is a historical, socially created category, and yet the way in which it is commonly understood is as an individual problem.

As life becomes harder for all of us in the working class, the chances become much less likely that people who do not already live with disability will have the time or opportunity to step outside of their day-to-day routine and notice disability issues. This must not be seen as a moral failing but understood as a facet of current conditions that we need to address. As Frances Ryan observes: 'It is difficult to focus your energy on what is happening in a care home to a disabled stranger when you're struggling to pay the bills, or your children can't find affordable housing.'[3]

People do not automatically change their ideas. As the Italian philosopher Antonio Gramsci identified, 'popular consciousness contains all sorts of modern and progressive ideas together with some terrible throwbacks'.[4] It requires input and development for people to separate out which ideas they hold are 'common sense' – that is, which are the ideas of the ruling class that they have accepted uncritically – and which are 'good sense' – that is, an understanding that reflects the best interests of the working class.

Vic Finkelstein advocated '[m]eeting people, putting forward a point of view that they probably have never seriously considered'.[5] This is most effectively achieved by engaging in active struggle alongside non-disabled people. It presents opportunities to make new alliances and to push a social model understanding of disability onto the mainstream agenda.

Solidarity with other groups provides support in our campaigns to halt and reverse disability cuts. On a more fundamental level, it is also about being involved in building a wider movement that is strong in order to win a society that is free from all oppressions. Disability has an important role to play in this.

Because disability is so bound up with capitalism, the struggle to challenge society's dominant ideas on it can play an important role in undermining ruling-class control. Evidence of the ways in which welfare reform was having an impact on disabled people played a key role in shifting the narrative of austerity from one of necessity to one of political choice and to the election in 2015 of Jeremy Corbyn as the most left-wing leader of the Labour Party in its history.

Following the re-election of the Conservatives in December 2019 with an increased majority, disabled campaigners involved in the fight for a better society need to bring our political analysis to bear and intervene to drive the struggle forward. We have no choice. The stakes have become too high to do otherwise.

At this point, after 10 years of intense resistance, we are hit by burnout. At the same time, support cuts are pushing people out of political activity. We need to reconsolidate, assess our position and agree a strategy for moving forwards.

When Disabled People Against Cuts (DPAC) was set up, its co-founders identified three specific sites of struggle: 1) the erosion of the rights of disabled people; 2) the accommodation of the disability movement to the service sector from the 1990s and a return to grassroots self-organisation since the imposition of austerity in 2010; and 3) the necessity for disabled people to reclaim, at a political and ideological level, the social model of disability, the language and concepts developed by the Disabled People's Movement (DPM) that have been hijacked and transformed by neoliberal social policies.[6]

I want conclude with my views on the same broad areas that I characterise as: responding to the immediate situation facing disabled people; thoughts on organising; and finally, the need for a reinvigoration of the social model of disability.

Responding to the immediate situation

DPAC co-founders identified a need to fight against the erosion of disabled people's rights as a specific site of struggle following the election of the Coalition government in 2010. It should be noted that those co-founders were under no illusion about the limitations of overly focusing on a legislative rights agenda. What they recognised was the need to oppose regression.

In terms of anti-disability discrimination legislation, the Conservatives have not as yet made any retrogressive changes to what is written in statute. New Labour had already watered down the Disability Discrimination Act through the Equality Act 2010. Additional barriers to justice for disabled people have instead been created by changes to legal aid and cuts to legal advice services. As found by a Parliamentary Select Committee in 2016, the Equality Act is virtually unenforceable and there are no plans to enforce the socio-economic duty outlined in Section 1. The Care Act 2014 contains progressive sentiments but the social care funding crisis and cuts to local authority budgets mean that it has never been properly implemented. Disabled people negatively impacted by breaches to the Care Act effectively have no recourse to justice to challenge those breaches.

A stronger Tory government will undoubtedly want to come after rights legislation. The Human Rights Act will be in their sights, as will withdrawal from the European Convention on Human Rights (which is not affected by withdrawal from the European Union).

Where dramatic retrogression has occurred since 2010 is in disabled people's living standards, incomes and support. In this way, disabled people's rights to inclusion and equal life chances have been taken backwards.

Disability activism over this period has prioritised resisting that retrogression. This has been criticised from less radical political quarters as lacking forward-looking vision.[7] This is ironic given that the more radical activists understand the need for a total transformation of society. It is also unthinkable to countenance letting disabled people have their safety nets pulled from under them on such a scale without a fightback. An injury to one is an injury to all. This is a principle integral to working-class organisation and collective action.

Whether we are resisting cuts or fighting for reforms, our analysis must be grounded in an understanding of wider political economy and how disability fits in. This is necessary to prevent isolated campaigners inadvertently undermining their own interests, as happened with the personalisation agenda. Here, support from the DPM led the way to the disastrous marketisation of social care.[8] In the current context, the involvement of Deaf and Disabled People's Organisations (DDPOs) with the government's Work and Health Programme lends weight to the policy approach of disability denial.

Activity should focus on improving the material conditions of disabled people's lives. It is far more convenient for charities and organisations wishing to avoid overly political activity to concentrate on an attitudinal level – 'platitudes about attitudes', as Oliver called it. As he explained, this approach assumes a direct causal relationship between attitudes and behaviour, yet 'social scientists have known, at least since the 1930s, that there is no simple relationship between the two'. Thus, he concludes: 'Persuasion has then inevitably been a bankrupt approach to policy implementation.'[9]

Campaign issues that affect other groups and can thus build wider alliances should be identified as 'the only viable long-term political strategy for disabled people [which] is to be part of a far wider struggle to create a better society for all.'[10] The roll-out of Universal Credit had the potential to build a mass movement on a national level. When fully rolled out, it is due to affect nearly 7 million people, including low-paid and part-time workers, lone parents and disabled people, among many others. However, instead of focusing on this potential, campaigning energies were pulled out of the anti-austerity movement into the Labour Party, which became inward-looking due to internal divisions. The toxicity of Universal Credit is increasingly evident and yet the Tories are still pushing on with it. Local campaigns such as Norfolk Against Universal Credit – initiated by Norfolk DPAC – have been popular.

The priority must be to prevent further cuts and regressions in disabled people's support and income. Going forward, we need to fight for a reversal of the cuts and negative changes that have already been made. Through the age of austerity and welfare reform, campaigning of necessity became reactive, with attention diverted from ongoing struggles that we had yet to win. These struggles involve full de-institutionalisation, reducing the dominance of the medical model within the mental health system and securing access to support for people living with mental distress that aligns with independent living philosophy, and achieving a fully inclusive education system – to name only a few.

A robust political-economic analysis based on a historical materialist perspective can make us more effective in securing the improvements we need in the here and now. It also raises awareness of the limitations for any possible progress under existing conditions. As Rosa Morris comments with regard to the Work Capability Assessment (WCA), even if a new assessment were genuinely co-produced with disabled people, 'it would still operate within a system where individuals' worth to society is based on their participation in wage labour'.[11]

At the heart of our activism must be an understanding that people with impairments are not inevitably excluded from society. Rather, as Finkelstein wrote, 'the real reason for our oppression (as for all other oppressed groups) is in the way society is organised (the socio-political causes)'.[12] We must engage in struggle to secure the support disabled people need to be included and participate within society now. At the same time, we must raise awareness that an alternative is possible – one with different forms of human relationships, personal development and interdependency that we cannot even imagine from the constraints of our current position.

In relation to the controversy over whether organising against benefit cuts undermines a positive image of disabled people, Graby argues that:

> 'disability pride' does not need to be based on disabled people portraying themselves as capable of succeeding on the same terms as non-disabled people. Instead, disabled people's self-valorization can consist in the assertion that 'dependence' is neither shameful, nor incompatible with personal autonomy, and indeed that 'independence' in the sense of self-sufficiency is neither possible nor desirable.[13]

In other words, disabled people's inability to fit within the norms of capitalist society should not be a source of shame for us but rather the impetus to fight for something better.

There are powerful forces at work in the world today with the rise of the far right. Humankind's very existence is under threat from climate change. Disabled people are usually hit first and worst by any disaster or adverse changes. Our ultimate aim should not be fitting disabled people into existing society but contributing to the building of a movement capable of creating a new society, one that is fit not just for us but for all.[14]

Thoughts on organising

Disabled activists require some level of self-organisation where we can build campaigns on disability-related issues. While working with allies, disabled people's voices and experiences must be at the forefront. This is because disability is so hidden that, in the words of Mike Oliver, when non-disabled people do things for us, they 'get it wrong'.[15]

While it is also important for disabled people to be involved in political activity and with political parties, at present there exist significant accessibility barriers to doing so. These need to be challenged and alternative forms of activity developed. There are many disabled campaigners whose talents and drive for social change are wasted without appropriately inclusive and accessibly resourced activity.

Spaces for self-organisation led by disabled people offer much-needed peer support to continue the slog of breaking down barriers in mainstream political engagement. They also enable disabled campaigners to focus our energies on political issues rather than simply on the access issues that need to be overcome before we can get involved.

The most dynamic and radical campaigning led by disabled people since 2010 has been at a grassroots level. A handful of DDPOs involved with the Reclaiming Our Futures Alliance (ROFA) have been brave enough to take a principled stance in speaking out against the government. These organisations have prioritised the representation of Deaf and disabled people's needs, interests and experiences over and above their standing with government and their 'place at the table'.

As identified by DPAC co-founders, DDPOs became subsumed by service delivery and contract culture over the New Labour years. They lost their radical edge and became afraid of campaigning, instead taking on the role of 'critical friend' to government at national, regional and local levels in return for funding. Displays belonging more to the 'critical' than the 'friend' aspect of this role could be punished, with loss of income resulting in loss of jobs for disabled staff and loss of service provision. A number of braver DDPOs found this out to their cost. For example, Merton Council withdrew funding for Merton Centre for Independent Living's advice service just months after it published a critical report about social care provision in the borough.

Reduced funding and a more competitive tendering environment have led to the closure of many user-led organisations and

DDPOs. In 2019, the National Survivor User Network (NSUN) estimated that about 50 user-led organisations that were previously NSUN members had been forced to close in the previous year, following a loss of more than 150 member groups the year before that. Smaller organisations have been hit hardest. Those that remain tend to operate on a much larger scale that is bureaucratically incompatible with the flexibility needed to respond to the current political climate.

Larger user-led organisations and DDPOs are chiefly constituted as charities. This restricts their activities from anything deemed too political. With a government that isn't listening, the most effective approaches for influencing change since 2010 have been 'outsider' campaigning, which charitable trusts rarely fund. The only way to properly understand the attacks on disabled people is by taking a political analysis. This exposes the relationship between capitalism and disability and the invalidity of the idea that disability issues sit in a bubble that is politically neither right nor left. With the stakes as high as they are for disabled people at the moment, activity that attempts to ignore the very heavily political aspect of what we are dealing with is not worth the energy or resources, and it lacks credibility among those at the sharp end.

The imposition of austerity marked a return to grassroots self-organisation among disabled activists. This has enabled quicker and bolder action to be taken to keep up with and respond to the fast-changing political environment compared with what is possible through formal DDPO structures. Disparate groups and individual campaigners with shared values and goals have built up loose networks to coordinate activity. DPAC, Black Triangle, Mental Health Resistance Network, WinVisible, Recovery in the Bin (RITB) and Shaping Our Lives work in constant collaboration and have overlapping memberships.

The benefits of looser, more organic organisational structures have included adaptability towards the inclusion of people with diverse impairments and support needs. For example, there are individuals who are unable to leave their house fulfilling centrally important leadership roles within DPAC. Individuals participate in activity according to whatever contribution they are able to make and are valued for this. Having members with diverse skills and abilities who face diverse barriers requires a collective effort that is refreshingly interdependent within an increasingly individualistic society.

With action prioritised over building and maintaining organisational structures, this approach is open to the criticism of lacking democratic accountability and transparency. Another limitation is the lack of capacity infrastructure to more widely debate political strategy, develop ideas and educate members. The social model of disability and independent living philosophy are fundamental principles on which DPAC was founded, yet it is likely that a majority of DPAC's formal membership – those who are officially signed up as members – are unfamiliar with these concepts.

These are areas worth addressing as we go forward. As Finkelstein advocated: 'We need to constantly try and help turn the unconscious into conscious struggles.'[16] To realise this ambition we could use additional organisational capacity to focus on building greater unity between our theory and practice as activists. Within DPAC, at a leadership level all political strategies and actions are debated, and, when consensus cannot be reached, a majority view is taken. Involvement in this collaborative development of ideas informed by and informing our activism can feel extremely exciting and powerful. What are now needed are ways to engage more campaigners and allies within that process; we need to identify structures and resources with which political development and education can be disseminated through our everyday activity.

One key message to convey is the power of people's own agency and what can be achieved through collective resistance. Disabled people's experiences since 2010 have taught us that looking to those in power to make everything better only ends in disappointment; to guarantee the changes we need, it is up to us to take action and demand those changes.

Within our organising, we need to renew active links between activism and academia. The academic discipline of disability studies originally developed with an intention to intervene in the real world and to inform application in practice. The growing dominance of post-modernism/post-structuralism weakened the link, with output becoming less accessible to disabled people and less relevant to our lives.[17]

As the impacts of austerity and welfare reform reached mainstream attention, academia responded with studies providing a valuable evidence base to record what was happening. A good example of this is the research into impacts of conditionality on disabled people in the Employment and Support Allowance (ESA) Work-Related Activity Group undertaken at the University of Essex in co-production with the DDPO Inclusion London.[18]

Such studies have contributed usefully to awareness raising and political lobbying. Many analyses, emanating in particular from the field of disability studies, are nevertheless frustratingly abstract and inaccessible. Time spent discussing whether government attacks fit an interpretation of violent proletarianisation or institutional violence could arguably be better spent actively campaigning to stop them.

Overall, those who have been engaged in resistance since 2010 should be proud of what we have managed to accomplish. There is further still to go. To quote Marta Russell, 'disabled people must go beyond ramps, with a piercing gaze that can see through the agents of oppression into those economic and undemocratic dynamics that have created inequities'.[19] By building on and disseminating our past learning from disabled people's resistance, continuing to develop our ideas and growing our solidarity networks, there is much more we can and will do.

Reinvigorating the social model

The development of the social model of disability was earth-shatteringly ground-breaking. Without denying the pain or distress that are part of the lived experience of certain impairments, it provides a tool for explaining that, far from being an individual problem, disability is a form of oppression: if we want to end the oppression and ill treatment of disabled people, we don't need to 'cure' people with impairments, we need to fundamentally change the way in which society is organised.

The social model is still relevant today, but over the years it has been undermined by constant criticism on the one hand, and, on the other, it became entrenched in dogmatic interpretations that served to shut people off from it. A reinvigorated social model could bring it back to life and more fully realise the potential that its original interpretation from a historical materialist perspective offered. As a guide to action rather than rigid doctrine, it can play a fundamental role in taking forward disabled people's resistance.

Even critics of the social model testify to its considerable impact in fighting disabled people's oppression since its development. A. J. Withers writes about 'a plethora of positive changes in disabled people's lives' that have resulted. 'Without them,' they explain, 'many disabled people would not have been able to access education, housing, transportation, the electoral system or communities.'[20]

Another critic, Tom Shakespeare, acknowledges: 'The benefits of the social model approach are that it shifts attention from individuals.'[21] He writes: 'This unprecedented move to turn traditional views of disability upside down appears, several decades later, to be one of the bravest and most transformative moves in the history of political thought.'[22]

For disabled people, the social model can be extremely powerful on a personal level: 'It enables them to think afresh about themselves and their lives. Instead of having to feel guilty or inadequate as a result of their impairment or their need for additional support, it transforms their understanding of their relationship with society, giving them new confidence and a sense of equality.'[23]

The social model represents a direct challenge to the ideology of individualism on which neoliberalism rests. The power of the threat it poses is reflected in the way in which government has gone to such lengths to co-opt, subvert and ultimately circumvent it through development of the biopsychosocial model.

For all its impact, the social model has been subject to endless criticism. In 2013, Oliver complained that 'all we now seem to do is talk about it'.[24] Sensationalist claims, such as that 'the social model is wrong',[25] were made without putting anything in its place. Such undermining smoothed the way for the development and implementation of an alternative model, the biopsychosocial, which was better suited to a neoliberal agenda.

This was the context into which DPAC was set up. The need to defend and promote the social model was a core aim of the campaign from its founding. Uncritical defence of the social model fails to acknowledge issues of contention that even its originators had identified. Finkelstein raised the problem of how many had come to see the model 'in a rather sterile, formulistic way'.[26]To borrow a phrase from Engels, it had become 'a *credo* and not a guide to action'.[27] Oliver and Williams-Findlay have both suggested that a fresh historical materialist approach is overdue.[28]

A social model approach provides a basis for shared identity across impairment groups. Nevertheless, certain impairment-specific groups do not consider it to adequately cover their situation. This is true within self-organisation by mental health survivors, people who are neurodivergent, people living with chronic illness and Deaf BSL users. This can and does cause division that weakens the collective effort. For example, debate over whether the coalition of organisations involved in monitoring the UN Convention on the Rights of Persons with Disabilities set up in 2017 should be called a coalition of Disabled People's Organisations or of Deaf and Disabled People's Organisations was a point that led certain organisations to pull out. Such division plays into the neoliberal agenda, which actively wants to restrict access to disability status and thus to benefit entitlements.

DPAC itself manages to be inclusive of campaigners from all of these impairment groups while steadfastly adhering to a social model approach. Members are united by the struggle against austerity and welfare reform. In practice, we have developed an approach to the social model that facilitates this. I would argue that this has the potential to form the basis for a reinvigorated social model. Three themes are suggested below as a starting point:

- a social versus an individual model;
- a social model of impairment; and
- a tool for social change.

Crucially, though, any attempts to review and refresh the social model must be developed as a collaborative effort between grassroots campaigners, informed by the activism that it will underpin – not dreamed up by an individual in an ivory tower looking to make their name. This is how the social model originally developed, out of an analysis of disabled people's oppression developed by activists involved in the Union of the Physically Impaired Against Segregation (UPIAS) in the 1970s.

A social versus an individual model

Within the DPM, it is commonly taught that the social model was developed in opposition to both the medical and charity models of disability. Mike Oliver, however, was clear that, for him, there were only ever two models of disability: the individual and the social.[29] He maintained that 'there is no such thing as the medical model of disability, there is instead an individual model of disability of which medicalization is one significant component'.[30]

Oliver's analysis was that a core ideology of individualism promoted within capitalist society dominates the way in which disability is understood. This is served at different times by different peripheral ideologies. Medicalisation underpinned by personal tragedy theory is one. Under welfare reform, Oliver and Barnes noted that 'recently peripheral ideologies have shifted away from the ideologies of personal tragedy and towards disability as dependency'.[31]

From a historical angle, the DPM's focus on the medical model makes sense. This was a source of immediate oppression for people with physical impairments through whose self-organisation the DPM was founded. At that time, a medical model approach dominated their lives. In just one example of this, the activist Michelle Daley was made to spend hours of her schooling upright in an inflatable 'space suit'. The suit was funded by charitable donations from Magpie. Her school was keen that she should experience a 'normal' standing position; despite the fact that she would never stand or walk unaided, this was judged to be a more important use of her time than learning. It was only after she left a school environment dominated by the medical model that she could engage in proper education.

The problem with a focus on opposition to a medical model is that people with different impairments are primarily oppressed by different peripheral ideologies. People with energy-limiting chronic illness are desperate for medical validation in order to combat the daily oppression they face whereby their impairment experiences are dismissed. The origins of the Waddell and Aylward biopsychosocial model are closely linked to the development of approaches for 'treating' chronic fatigue syndrome (CFS) that deny its medical validity and have caused harm to patients on the receiving end.

The core ideology of individualism is enforced via different peripheral ideologies at different times. In the current period, disabled people's relationship with medicalisation has shifted. Medical opinion has assumed enormous importance in proving eligibility for the social security payments that many disabled people need in order to survive. Frayne writes: 'The function of a diagnosis is even more vital in the context of austerity ... In this context, it is important for people who need support to be able to say "I have a medical condition".'[32]

More recent, professionally led approaches to disability reinforce the ideology of individualism. Beresford identifies both the recovery model and normalisation within this category.[33] Both have been sold as progressive. For some service users, the attraction of the recovery model is as an apparent alternative to a medical model approach, in that it appears 'to reject conventional ideas of writing them off as permanently damaged, pathologized or deviant'. It is entirely consistent with the individual model. One of its core aims is the removal of support from those deemed to be 'recovered'. It insufficiently acknowledges the reality that, for many living with mental distress, this may never be helpful.[34]

The primary concern of normalisation is with integrating disabled people into existing society rather than changing it. As Beresford highlights, it 'fails to locate disabled people's experiences within a political framework', aiming to 'secure higher status through association with roles, people and activities that are conventionally valued'.[35]

For those of us focused on wanting to change existing society rather than find ways for disabled people to fit into it, an understanding of how the individual model operates is essential.

Taking a position that is clearly anti-individualism as opposed to anti-medical or charity model is a more expressly anti-capitalist stance to adopt. This may not be convenient for disability organisations that are registered charities and receive funding that limits their politicism, and it is no wonder that the historical materialist origins of the social model became watered down in its interpretation by DDPOs. A statement from Greater London Action on Disability (GLAD) in 2000 on how to 'rectify the social model' was criticised by Oliver as 'generalized enough to cover all human social behaviour and is quite useless as a "disability" model – a real "shopping basket" approach which enables people to pick and choose an interpretation that happens to suit their personal ambitions: and it perfectly matches the privatisation programme of New Labour for a free market in health and social services'.[36]

The social model was also co-opted by government. In that form it not only lost its power but became dangerous. The government now argues that the WCA and its determined efforts to push disabled people off benefits is in line with the social model. Its 2018 report back to the UN Disability Committee stated: 'The WCA aligns with the social model of disability as it is based on the understanding that the barriers to work are societal; therefore, those with functional capability above a certain threshold can, with the correct support and opportunities, work.'[37]

'New' activists lacking a link with the heritage of the DPM under-standably view the social model with suspicion. Reclaiming the anti-capitalist nature of the social model would improve its repu-tation at grassroots level.

A social model of impairment

Two of the key criticisms levelled at the social model are, first, that it denies the experience of impairment and, second, that the definition of impairment is inappropriate for certain groups of people who experience disabling oppression.

The first criticism is older and associated with arguments made by disabled feminist activists. Jenny Morris wrote:

> Such a perspective is a crucial part of our demand for our needs to be treated as a civil right. However, there is a tendency within the social model of disability to deny the experience of our own bodies, insisting that our physical differences and restrictions are entirely socially created. While environmental barriers and social attitudes are a crucial part of our experience of disability – and do indeed disable us – to suggest that this is all there is to it is to deny the personal experience of physical or intellectual restrictions, of illness, of the fear of dying.[38]

This issue has more recently been taken up by groups including those living with mental distress and those with chronic illnesses, for whom experiences of distress and pain are everyday conse-quences of lived impairment.

The second point represents a rejection of the notion that there is anything 'wrong' or 'broken' with the minds of people officially classified as disabled, including people who are neuro-divergent and people living with mental distress. Autism is, for example, a different rather than a wrong wiring of the brain; men-tal distress is a natural reaction of the brain to the experience of trauma rather than a 'deviance'. The neurodiversity movement rejects that autism is a disorder and fights for the right to be autistic. Activists – including both survivors and psychologists – have argued for the wholesale abolition of the term 'personality disorders', the symptoms of which are more to do with trauma and society than a medical diagnosis.

In response to the first criticism, I would argue that the social model in and of itself does not deny and never has denied the lived experience of our minds, bodies, pain or distress. Oliver writes that the idea that the social model denies impairment represents 'a conceptual misunderstanding because the social model is not about the personal experience of impairment but the collective experience of disablement'.[39] He himself wrote about male experiences with spinal cord injury.

The social model is a basis for collective identity, for identifying shared priority issues for campaigns and for framing political strategy. It does not deal with the lived experiences of impairment, but by no means does it follow that according to the social model there is no place for approaches that do. Indeed, Oliver called for development of the social model of impairment to sit alongside the social model of disability.[40] Writing in 2012, Oliver and Barnes were clear that their use of the term disablement 'refers to the economic and social processes that ultimately create both impairment and disability'.[41]

Unfortunately, this was not how it was always interpreted within the DPM. In 2006, Shakespeare wrote: 'Many disability rights campaigners concede that behind closed doors they talk about aches and pains and urinary tract infections, even while they deny any relevance of the body while they are out campaigning.'[42]

I have personal experience of the approach described by Shakespeare but would argue that it was, again, a product of its time. In the period when UPIAS was organising, disabled people were segregated into services with professionals constantly picking over the details of their impairments. Finkelstein recorded how '[t]here is a constant pressure on physically impaired people to talk about their feelings, their personal experiences, and their innermost thoughts', and how anything unsatisfactory in their lives was attributed to their impairment rather than their environment or socio-economic situation.[43] Within this context, the social model was immensely liberating. It is hardly surprising that it was embraced so enthusiastically.

Within DPAC's daily activist practice, a social model analysis is taken to the political struggle in which we are engaged, but there is also room for impairment. This can be attributed to the presence of new campaigners, previously not in contact with the DPM, as well as wide representation of impairment groups. Strong peer support is exchanged between campaigners on the basis of both the disabling barriers we face in society and our lived experiences of impairment. On this point, it is not so much a case of developing a new approach as of owning and articulating what I believe is already working.

On the second point, I would argue that there is a need to develop a social model of impairment that can address the fact that people can be disabled without possessing a difference that itself necessarily represents a physical or mental deficit or dysfunction. This would encompass the understanding that not all impairments are static, but many fluctuate depending on environmental factors. It could enable people to identify as disabled who rightly see their difference as a quality with value and could support the building of stronger alliances between disabled campaigners and groups that, like the neuro-diverse and Deaf BSL movements, view themselves primarily as minorities.

One way of approaching this could be through developing an understanding of impairment as a material rather than a mental or physical deficit. This material deficit could be experienced as pain or distress but equally as a lack of income or autonomy resulting from discrimination against people with mental or physical differences. For example, Silicon Valley is famously the site of tech workplaces that highly value possession of neuro-diverse characteristics. Autistic employees there may not experience their neurodiversity as a material deficit. There are, however, many employers across the world who do discriminate against autistic people, and autistic people are further disadvantaged by barriers to accessing social security. Many autistic people experience a material deficit as the result of having to live in a neurotypical-dominated world.

A social model of impairment could embrace the positive attributes of characteristics that do not fit socially imposed standards and 'norms'. Qualities that do not fit the standard workplace, such as heightened sensitivity and attention to detail, have many benefits. Withers writes: 'We are rarely recognized for the contributions we make *because of our disabilities*. For instance, when I am having a hard time walking, I walk very slowly and I notice a lot of what is around me. Because I experience the world differently than many of the people around me, I have a unique and useful perspective.'[44] This perspective shines a light on how current socio-economic structures deny the diverse talents and potential of so many people, instead limiting us to identities that are defined by what we cannot do.

Writing in 1996, Oliver argued that the DPM did not have the time, energy or resources to reclaim the social model. This was in response to co-option of the model by governments, charities and quangos. He said that putting efforts into such an attempt 'would reduce disability activism to the kind of intellectual masturbation in which academics sometimes engage. Instead, we need to work out and promote political strategies that are in line with the principles of the social model.'[45]

He was writing before the advent of Waddell and Aylward's biopsychosocial model and before developments in the self-organisation of groups fitting the legal definition of disability but objecting to an identification as 'impaired'.

In the current era, the primary focus of disabled campaigners must be on political activism, but although disagreements over the social model cause division, an attempt to reinvigorate it is worth considering. Part of the brilliance of the social model was that it 'became a vehicle for developing a collective disability consciousness'.[46] A social model of impairment to sit alongside a social model of disability could help build a still wider collective consciousness. The formulation of this must be done as a collaborative effort with the aim not of creating a 'perfect' theory, but rather of establishing a working definition that is good enough to enable groups to unite their resistance.

A tool for social change

The single most important feature of the social model is its role as a tool for social change. Those involved in its development were clear from the outset that it was never intended 'to be equivalent to a theory of disability'.[47] Its purpose was to provide a basis for collective action – both between disabled people with different impairment experiences and between disabled people and other oppressed groups. This was ground-breaking at a time when disabled people's lives were dominated by the type of impairment they had. This determined which institutions they were segregated into, how they were treated and what opportunities were restricted from them.

Over the years, use of the social model in daily life has become largely confined to attempts at attitudinal change, through, for example, Disability Equality Training (DET). This was not the intention of its originators. Finkelstein considered: 'As long as we are trying to change the mental world, not much effort is needed in the real world ... Let us concentrate on changing the real world.'[48]

For UPIAS, Oliver and Barnes, the core feature of the social model was its focus on action. This seems to have been lost in interpretation. Oliver and Barnes stated in 2012: 'Almost to the point of boredom, we have constantly stated that the social model is a tool to be used to produce changes in society and is not and was never intended to be a social theory.'[49]

As a source of dispute and division, the social model defeats its purpose entirely. Dispute and division arise from attempts to conceptualise it as a perfect theory of disability, particularly when juxtaposed with the idea of a 'medical model'. Definition of impairment remains a sticking point, but laying this to one side, the general analysis presented by the social model – that people with impairments are disabled by socio-economic structures that enforce individualism – is widely applicable.

According to this analysis, priority issues for collective action will change over time because the way in which exclusion and oppression operate change subject to political-economic circumstances. In using the social model as a tool for social change, it is vital to understand this historicity.

A widespread criticism of the social model has been its link to the centrality of demands for equal access to employment within the DPM.[50] From this vantage point, the demand for a guaranteed income for disabled people was historically criticised as contributing to disabled people's oppression.

I would argue that this focus was a product of circumstances affecting the people with physical impairments who were self-organising at that time. For them, inclusion in the mainstream workplace represented financial independence and liberation from segregation. As Graby explains:

As the exclusion of disabled people from the labour market was identified as the origins of disabled people's oppression and social exclusion, so (re-)integration into the labour market was seen by early [Disabled People's Organisations] as the route to liberation and social inclusion. Therefore, a key activist focus of groups like UPIAS was on the removal of barriers to paid work.[51]

However, Finkelstein, one of the core members of UPIAS, was clear that 'for the severely incapacitated to have full employment rights, the maximum-profit motive of employers must be transcended'.[52]

Disabled people organising against institutionalisation in the 1970s had hopes that technological advances would lead to a more inclusive labour market. UPIAS argued against continuing segregation and institutionalisation on the grounds that 'society has produced that capability of providing' human, financial and technological help.[53] As things have played out, the opposite has actually been true, with those advances rendering the workplace less accessible. At the same time, disabled people are under attack from the individual model, which is being used to justify the removal of essential support and income. In this way, independent living and inclusion are being taken backwards. It is entirely in keeping with a social model approach that we should fight to prevent retrogressions, including benefit cuts.

The social model should be seen as a living tool for action, equipping us to respond effectively to historical socio-economic circumstances as they arise; it should be for grassroots disabled campaigners to own, apply and even adapt within our activism. In practice within the DPM, it has too often been received as a rigid dogma either to be strictly adhered to or rebelled against. Perhaps this is representative of a lack of confidence among disabled people, accustomed as we frequently are to having our lives and our very identities determined for us by others and to internalised self-doubt. As Finkelstein commented in 1974: 'The worst thing that can happen is when we, ourselves, come sometimes to accept this curtailment of potentiality with an accompanying loss of confidence and vitality.'[54]

The RITB campaign is a case in point. Its website states: 'We want a robust "Social Model of Madness, Distress & Confusion", placing mental health within the context of social justice and the wider class struggle.' This is a superfluous demand. The campaign itself is one of the strongest examples of the social model in action within the disability activist scene in Britain today. Having developed the concept of 'unrecovery', it promotes this through active campaigns against oppressive features of the mental health system. It is thus actively placing mental health within the context of social justice and wider class struggle. The demand for a complex theory specific to mental distress and the social model feels like a request for legitimation. However, RITB's work speaks for itself – as well as for the many of us for whom its message resonates so powerfully.

Individualism is fundamental to the politics of neoliberalism that are actively attacking disabled people in this current period. We arguably need the social model now more than ever to counter the onslaught. In establishing DPAC, its co-founders saw 'the social model of disability as a cornerstone in building a new, diverse anti-capitalist movement'.[55] To date, that ambition has been achieved only in so far as DPAC and DDPOs involved in ROFA have contributed to the fight against austerity and welfare reform. A reinvigorated social model has the potential to do more and to play an important role in the fight to transcend capitalism and build a new society organised on the principle of 'from each according to their ability, to each according to their needs'.[56]

The ongoing war against disabled people

In December 2019, the most right-wing government in modern British history was re-elected with a significantly increased majority. This was disastrous news for disabled people. Under Boris Johnson, the Conservatives now had the parliamentary power not simply to carry on in the same direction with the continuation of policies that are growing inequality, poverty and immiseration, but to ramp up their attacks and implement welfare reform measures they were previously beaten back from achieving.

An early indication of what the election result meant for disabled people was the decision announced in the New Year's honours list to award Iain Duncan Smith a knighthood. Duncan Smith had not held a ministerial appointment since his period as Secretary of State for Work and Pensions from 2010 to 2016. The honour effectively endorses the dismantling of the social security safety net over which he presided. It also suggests full government commitment to rolling out Duncan Smith's big idea, Universal Credit, in spite of the well-evidenced harms it is causing.

There are other warning signs that the Johnson government will take a particularly hard line and punitive approach towards social security policy that will intensify welfare reform. Johnson's first appointment to the post of Work and Pensions Secretary was Thérèse Coffey. This suggested a change of direction from the concession making for which Coffey's predecessor, Amber Rudd, had attempted to make her period in office known.

Coffey is a member of the Free Enterprise Group, 'a leading association of free-market orientated Conservative Members of Parliament'. Policy papers put together by this group include proposals to reduce Jobseeker's Allowance by 10 per cent if a claimant remains out of work after six months, with another 10 per cent withdrawn if they remain out of work after a further six months, and that small businesses be exempt from 'various regulations including unfair dismissal'. Such measures would have a disproportionate impact on disabled people. The group also supports the discredited ideas of workfare (work for benefits schemes), which we can assume will resurface in one form or another.

Disabled people should be under no illusion about who Boris Johnson is, however anti-establishment and affable he tries to portray himself. Both Johnson and his close adviser Dominic Cummings have expressed views that have been described as 'textbook examples of eugenic opinion'.[57] Speaking to city bankers during his time as Mayor of London, Johnson said:

> Whatever you think of the value of IQ tests it is surely relevant to a conversation about equality that as many as 16 per cent of our species have an IQ below 85 while about 2 per cent have an IQ above 130 ... the harder you shake the pack the easier it will be for some cornflakes to get to the top. And for one reason or another – boardroom greed or, as I am assured, the natural and God-given talent of boardroom inhabitants – the income gap between the top cornflakes and the bottom cornflakes is getting wider than ever.[58]

Inequality is a state that Johnson and Cummings both regard as natural and even desirable for the functioning of society. Progressive disability policymaking will not be on their agenda. What we must be prepared for are regressive measures deliberately aimed at re-segregating and isolating disabled people in the better interests of society according to a eugenicist view – in reality, in the interests of profit making.

The situation immediately following the 2019 General Election was a daunting one for disabled campaigners. There was a general shared feeling of exhaustion after nearly 10 years of constant fighting as well as demoralisation that a modern government can deliberately attack its disabled citizens and not just get away with it but effectively, through the Tories' increased majority, be rewarded for it. The urgent dangers to be confronted were the continued roll-out of Universal Credit and plans to merge ESA and Personal Independence Payment (PIP) benefit assessments alongside ever worsening cuts to social care support.

Iain Duncan Smith's knighthood sparked widespread outrage, showing that the spirit of resistance was far from dead. A petition objecting to the award for a man 'responsible for some of the cruellest, most extreme welfare reforms this country has ever seen' had nearly 250,000 signatures within a week. A letter to the *Guardian* from a disgusted retired social security commissioner and Upper Tribunal judge who 'spent a lifetime hearing thousands of appeals of decisions made by the Department for Work and Pensions' went viral and at least one former MBE recipient announced that they were giving back their honour.[59]

Many disabled activists recognise that even had Labour been elected in 2019, the fight would not have stopped. There would have been important ameliorations in the daily suffering experienced by disabled people but these would have been delivered within a policy framework underpinned by a failure to meaningfully grasp the nature of disabled people's oppression. The 2019 Labour manifesto commitment to establish a 'national care service' was evidence of a deeply paternalistic attitude towards disability that is incompatible with the concept of disability equality. Questions concerning disability and employment would inevitably have emerged as the government continued the path trodden by its predecessors – of attempting to fit disabled people into the capitalist workplace.

The war against disabled people cannot be attributed to individual ministers or Tory governments. Its existence is bound up with the relationship between capitalism and disability. Those of us who want a fairer world must fight for improvements in the living conditions of disabled people as part of – not in isolation from – the rest of the working class. But our resistance must also be consciously situated within the struggle to transcend capitalism itself. Only then can we guarantee freedom from oppression and a society where diversity is truly valued.

Notes

INTRODUCTION

1 Marx, K. (1852). 'Der 18te Brumaire des Louis Napoleon' ['The Eighteenth Brumaire of Louis Bonaparte'], *Die Revolution*.
2 Oliver 2017.
3 Morris 2015.
4 Oliver and Barnes 2006.
5 Baynton 2013, p. 52.
6 Morris 2018, p. 8.
7 As outlined in Article 19 of the United Nations Convention on the Rights of Persons with Disabilities (UN CRPD).
8 Theresia Degener speaking at the UN Disability Committee's public examination of the UK government in August 2017.
9 Oliver and Barnes 2012, p. 132.

PART I 'HIDDEN IN PLAIN SIGHT'

1 Baynton 2013, p. 52.
2 Parckar, G. (2008). *Disability Poverty in the UK*. London: Leonard Cheshire. Referenced in Smith, L. (2008). 'Call for action to cut poverty among disabled people', *Guardian*, 8 January.
3 Barleon, B. (2013). 'CCGs could play a key role in ending the health inequalities faced by people with a learning disability in the NHS', *Guardian*, 18 April.
4 Pring 2011, p. 345.
5 Quarmby 2011, p. 218.

1 WHO ARE DISABLED PEOPLE?

1 Slorach 2016, p. 9.
2 DWP (2018). 'Family Resources Survey 2016/17', Department for Work and Pensions (DWP), 22 March.

3 'Colin Barnes: the social model', YouTube, 2 January 2015, www. youtube.com/watch?v=mXuiP-n1h8s. The video was made for the Disabled People Against Cuts (DPAC) social model seminar in 2013.

4 London Councils and GLA (2017). '"Self-sufficient local government: 100% business rates retention": a joint consultation response'. London: London Councils and Greater London Authority (GLA), p. 11.

5 Moss, R. (2018). 'Number of children and young adults reporting mental health problems has skyrocketed in 20 years', *Huffington Post*, 11 September.

6 Blewett, S. (2018). 'Hospital admissions for self-harming girls double in 20 years, figures show', *Independent*, 6 August; Tyrell et al. 2018.

7 UK Coalition of Deaf and Disabled People's Organisations (2018). *Concluding Observations on the Initial Report of the United Kingdom of Great Britain and Northern Ireland: alternative report from civil society*, www.inclusionlondon.org.uk/wp-content/uploads/2018/10/DDPO-UNCRPD-Alternative-Report-from-Civil-Society-Oct-2018.doc.

8 Ferguson 2017, p. 43.

9 The disability movement has always seen the Disability Discrimination Act as a disappointment. Mike Oliver said in an interview shortly before he died: 'I don't regard the DDA as an important piece of legislation.' Oliver, M. (2018). 'Kicking down doors: from borstal boy to university professor', YouTube, 17 December, www.youtube.com/watch?v=NMfvoh-j9qw.

10 GMB Union (2018). 'At least 166,000 trapped in social care debt'. Press release, 4 June.

11 This was Damien Green's response to findings by the United Nations Disability Committee concerning the adverse impacts of welfare reform. The government argues that seeing disabled people as benefit-dependent is devaluing. Butler, P. (2016). 'Damian Green dismisses "offensive" UN report on UK disability rights', *Guardian*, 8 November.

12 Aiden, H. S. and McCarthy, A. (2014). *Current Attitudes Towards Disabled People*. London: Scope.

13 Slorach 2016, p. 18.

14 Slorach 2016, pp. 17–18.

15 Walker, P. and Topping, A. (2013). 'Paralympics legacy fails to shift attitudes to disabled people', *Guardian*, 29 August.

16 Blackmore and Hodgkins 2012, pp. 2–3.

17 Ledger and Shufflebotham 2006.

18 Quarmby 2011, p. 86.

19 Silberman 2015.

20 Yeo 2005, p. 4

21 EHRC 2018a, p. 78.

22 Ryan 2019, p. 31.

23 John et al. 2019.
24 WHO and World Bank Group 2011, p. 3.
25 Longmore and Goldberger 2000, p. 919.
26 Graby 2016.
27 Shakespeare 2006, p. 198.

2 JUSTIFIABLE EXCLUSION

 1 Oliver and Barnes 2012, p. 121.
 2 Abberley 1987, p. 8.
 3 For example, see Slorach 2016, pp. 42–57.
 4 Oswin 1971, p. 216.
 5 EHRC 2011, p. 7.
 6 Pring 2011, p. 69.
 7 Bulman, M. (2018). 'Abuse taking place in 99% of care homes amid "chronic" underfunding, survey shows', *Independent*, 22 March.
 8 WHO (n.d.). 'Violence against adults and children with disabilities', World Health Organization (WHO), www.who.int/disabilities/violence/en/.
 9 Voice UK, Respond and Mencap (2001). *Behind Closed Doors: preventing sexual abuse against adults with a learning disability*. London: Mencap. Cited in Pring 2011, p. 170.
10 The tweet appeared on 9 April 2019.
11 Pring 2011, p. 292.
12 Ibid., pp. 295–6.
13 Oliver 1990, p. 62.
14 *All in a Row* by Alex Oates premiered at the Southwark Playhouse in London in 2019.
15 Quarmby 2011, p. 227.
16 Scarlet, M. (2013). 'Assisted dying: for and against', *Disability Horizons*, 5 August.
17 UPIAS 2018, pp. 6–7.
18 Quarmby 2011, p. 13.
19 Ibid., p. 55. Galton experienced mental distress and proposed a connection between genius and insanity based on his own experience; Roosevelt was physically disabled but avoided being seen using his wheelchair in public; Churchill also experienced mental distress and described his depression as the 'black dog'.
20 Oswin 1971, p. 17.
21 UPIAS 2018, p. 40.
22 Vellani 2015, p. 943.
23 Baynton 2013, p. 33.
24 Ibid., p. 37.
25 Ibid., p. 42.
26 Ibid., p. 51.

27 Foner 2011, p. 113.
28 Ibid., p. 23.
29 Longmore and Goldberger 2000, p. 903.
30 See, for example, Henriques-Gomez, L. (2019). 'Andrew Bolt's mocking of Greta Thunberg leaves autism advocates "disgusted"', *Guardian*, 2 August.
31 Longmore and Goldberger 2000, p. 904.
32 Quarmby 2011, p. 221.
33 Oliver 1990, p. 70.
34 Gallagher 1995.
35 Sutherland, A. (1981). *Disabled We Stand*. London: Souvenir Press. Cited in Abberley 1987, p. 13.
36 This is A. J. Withers' preferred gender pronoun.
37 Withers 2012, pp. 8–9.
38 Ibid., p. 10.
39 Russell and Malhotra 2002, p. 216.
40 Marx, K. (1859). *A Contribution to the Critique of Political Economy*.

3 FROM ASYLUMS TO INDEPENDENT LIVING

1 Russell and Malhotra 2002, p. 223.
2 Slorach 2016.
3 Ibid., p. 42.
4 Oliver 1990, p. 44.
5 Ibid., p. 47.
6 Stone 1984, p. 179.
7 Morris 2018, p. 68.
8 Foner 2011, p. 36.
9 Rosenthal 2013; Longmore and Goldberger 2000, p. 908.
10 Rosenthal 2013.
11 Burleigh 1994, p. 164.
12 Gallagher 1995, p. 279.
13 Ibid., p. 39.
14 Ibid., p. 39.
15 Harman 2009, p. 137.
16 Ibid., p. 137.
17 Oliver and Barnes 2012, p. 5.
18 Slorach 2016, p. 74.
19 Barnes, C. (1991). *Disabled People in Britain and Discrimination: a case for anti-discrimination legislation*. London: C. Hurst. Cited in Slorach 2016, p. 74.
20 Borsay, A. (2005). *Disability and Social Policy in Britain since 1750: a history of exclusion*. London: Palgrave Macmillan, p. 126. Cited in Slorach 2016, p. 74.

21 Slorach 2016, p. 83.

22 Ibid., pp. 85–6.

23 Ibid., p. 96.

24 Cited in Slorach 2020, p. 146.

25 Baynton 2013, p. 47.

26 Slorach 2016, p. 92.

27 Quarmby 2011, p. 63.

28 Gallagher 1995, pp. 52–3.

29 Rosenthal 2016.

30 Slorach 2016, p. 103.

31 According to Russell 1998, pp. 26–7, one account puts the figure at over 1 million.

32 Gallagher 1995, p. 207.

33 Quarmby 2011, p. 67.

34 Keller 2005 [1938].

35 Slorach 2016, pp. 102–6.

36 Cited in Quarmby 2011, p. 69.

37 The black triangle conflated disability with being 'work-shy' and 'antisocial'.

38 See the case of Mazurka Rose detailed by Wolfgang Wippermann in Burleigh 1996, p. 119.

39 Slorach 2016, p. 106.

40 Beveridge, W. (1942). *Social Insurance and Allied Services*. Cm 6404. London: HMSO, p. 17.

41 Hampton 2016, p. 1.

42 Beresford et al. 2018, p. 83.

43 Morris 2018, pp. 68–9.

44 Beresford et al. 2018, p. 83.

45 Oswin 1971, p. 38.

46 Quarmby 2011, pp. 73–4.

47 Oswin 1971, p. 10.

48 Ibid., p. 150.

49 Oswin 2000, p. 143.

50 Ibid., pp. 143–4.

51 Ibid., p. 139.

52 Morris 1969, p. xiv.

53 Ibid., p. 314.

54 Ibid., p. xxv.

55 Slorach 2016, p. 174.

56 Morris 1969, p. 315.

57 Pring 2011. .

58 Quarmby 2011, p. 95.

59 Davies, J. (2013). 'Four things you probably didn't know about disability hate crime', Mencap.org.uk, 9 October.

60   Scope NDPP survey, February–March 2011.

61   Quarmby 2011, p. 207.

62   Ibid., p. 191.

63   Dodd, V. (2018). 'Police custody deaths hit 10-year high, with experts citing austerity', *Guardian*, 25 July.

64   Slorach 2016, pp. 27–9.

65   Hunt 2019, p. 4.

66   UPIAS 1975, pp. 3–4.

67   Oliver and Barnes 2012, p. 155.

68   Ibid., p. 156.

69   Shakespeare 2006, p. 153.

70   Quarmby 2011, p. 156.

71   Finkelstein 2001.

72   Finkelstein 2007.

73   Russell 1998, pp. 109–24.

74   Slorach 2016, p. 9.

75   Finkelstein 2007.

76   Clifford and Vogelmann 2018.

77   Oliver and Barnes 2012, p. 168.

78   Oliver and Barnes 2006.

79   Finkelstein 2007.

80   Shakespeare 2006.

81   Finkelstein 2007.

82   Oliver and Barnes 2012, pp. 156–7.

83   Oliver 2013, p. 1025.

84   Williams-Findlay 2011; see also Jolly 2012.

85   Oliver 2013, p. 1024.

86   Ibid., p. 1026.

87   Oliver and Barnes 2006, p. 5.

88   Ibid.

89   Morris 2011, p. 12.

90   Henwood and Hudson 2007; see Clifford 2013 on the use of the Henwood and Hudson report to justify closing the ILF.

91   Morris 2011, p. 10.

92   Oliver 1990, p. 128.

93   Oliver and Barnes 2006.

94   Blackmore and Hodgkins 2012, p. 22.

95   Oliver and Barnes 2012, p. 165.

96   Blackmore and Hodgkins 2012, p. 27.

97   Ibid., pp. 25–6.

98   Ibid., p. 1.

99   Oliver and Barnes 2012, pp. 169–70; Blackmore and Hodgkins 2012, p. 27.

100 Oliver and Barnes 2012, p. 169.
101 Finkelstein 2007, pp. 12–13.
102 Oliver and Barnes 2012, p. 157.
103 Finkelstein 2007.

PART II TARGETING DISABLED PEOPLE

1 Morris 2015.
2 Committee on the Rights of Persons with Disabilities (CRPD) (2016). 'Inquiry concerning the United Kingdom of Great Britain and Northern Ireland carried out by the Committee under Article 6 of the Optional Protocol to the Convention'. Geneva: Office of the High Commissioner on Human Rights.
3 The investigation focused on the following Articles of the United Nations Convention on the Rights of Persons with Disabilities (UN CRPD): Article 19 – the right to independent living and being included in the community; Article 27 – the right to work and employment; and Article 28 – the right to an adequate standard of living and social protection.
4 EHRC 2018a, p. 186.
5 Butler, P. (2018). 'Welfare spending for UK's poorest shrinks by £37bn', *Guardian*, 23 September.
6 Duffy 2013.
7 Harrop, A. (2019). *Inequality by Stealth: tax allowances and social security in 2019/20*. London: Fabian Society.
8 Reed and Portes 2018, p. 14.
9 Ibid., p. 10.

4 WELFARE 'REFORM'

1 Baumberg Geiger 2018, p. 69.
2 Children's Society, Disability Rights UK and Citizens Advice (2012). *Holes in the Safety Net: the impact of Universal Credit on disabled people and their families*. London: The Children's Society, p. 3.
3 O'Hara 2014, p. 182.
4 Howes, S. and Jones, K.-M. (2019). *Computer Says No! Stage one: information provision*. London: Child Poverty Action Group.
5 SNP (n.d.). 'What actions are the SNP taking in Government to mitigate Westminster's welfare reforms?', www.snp.org/policies/pb-what-actions-are-the-snp-taking-in-government-to-mitigate-westminster-s-welfare-reforms/.

6   DWP and DH 2017, p. 6.

7   DWP and DH 2016, p. 6.

8   Ibid., p. 24.

9   Wood, C. (2013). 'The hardest hit of the hardest hit', Scope blog, 26 March.

10   Freud 2007.

11   Ibid., foreword.

12   Ibid., p. 5.

13   Pring, J. (2015). 'WCA death scandal: Grayling ordered assessment roll-out, despite coroner's warning', *Disability News Service*, 9 November.

14   Jones, G. and Sparrow, A. (2005). 'Blair presses for million on incapacity benefit to go back to work', *Telegraph*, 2 February.

15   DWP and DH 2017, p. 8.

16   Wynne-Jones, R. (2013). 'Whistleblower tells the inside story of Atos', *Mirror*, 21 August.

17   Gentleman, A. (2012). 'Atos assessors told to keep disability benefit approvals low, film suggests', *Guardian*, 27 July.

18   Howard 2013.

19   Pring, J. (2016). 'DWP issued guidance that made suicides more likely, then "lied" to cover its tracks', *Disability News Service*, 29 September.

20   For excerpts from the research interviews, see ROFA 2018.

21   Baumberg Geiger 2018.

22   Dwyer et al., 2018.

23   Pollard 2019, p. 7.

24   Ibid., p. 9.

25   DWP (2015). *Welfare Reform and Work Bill: impact assessment to remove the ESA Work-Related Activity Component and the UC Limited Capability for Work Element for new claims.* London: Department for Work and Pensions (DWP), p. 1.

26   Pickles, C., Holmes, E., Titley, H. and Dobson, B. (2016). *Working Welfare: a radically new approach to sickness and disability benefits.* London: Reform, p. 13.

27   DBC (2015). 'Almost 70% of disabled people say cuts to ESA will cause their health to suffer and half may return to work later'. Disability Benefits Consortium (DBC) press release, 27 October.

28   Pring, J. (2017). 'Exposed: Mordaunt's "false promises" on WRAG cut mitigation', *Disability News Service*, 6 April.

29   Wynne-Jones, R. (2016). 'US firm doing Tories' dirty work on benefits is hit by whistleblower's shocking allegations', *Mirror*, 14 January.

30   Stewart 2016. On Unum's influence, see also Jolly 2012; Rutherford 2007.

31 Pring, J. (2017). 'Expert chosen by DWP appears to suggest scrapping "fitness for work" test', *Disability News Service*, 21 December.

32 *MM & DM, R (on the application of) v Secretary of State for Work and Pensions* [2013] EWCA Civ 1565 (4 December 2013).

33 PAC (2016). *Contracted Out Health and Disability Assessments*. HC 727. London: Public Accounts Committee (PAC).

34 Butler, P. (2017). 'Benefits assessor sanctioned for mocking disabled claimant', *Guardian*, 21 September.

35 Pring, J. (2017). 'Disgraced PIP assessor escapes being struck off', *Disability News Service*, 21 September.

36 Bloom, D. (2018). 'Tory minister says it's "shameful" to claim benefit cuts have driven people to suicide', *Mirror*, 30 January.

37 Ibid.

38 *R (Sumpter) v Secretary of State for Work and Pensions* [2015] EWCA Civ 1033.

39 Withnall, A. (2016). 'Budget 2016: one simple chart that shows who benefits most – and who loses out', *Independent*, 17 March.

40 *RF v Secretary of State for Work and Pensions* [2017] EWHC 3375 (Admin) Mostyn J (21 December 2017).

41 WPC (2018). *PIP and ESA Assessments*. HC 829. London: Work and Pensions Committee (WPC), p. 34.

42 Alston 2018, p. 7.

43 UC Diary (2019). 'The truth about Universal Credit', UCDiary.home.blog, 29 January.

44 NAO (2018). *Rolling Out Universal Credit*. HC 1123. London: National Audit Office (NAO), p. 10.

45 Pring, J. (2018). 'Campaigner's six-year battle to secure the truth about universal credit', *Disability News Service*, 22 November.

46 WPC 2018, p. 3.

47 Public Health England (2015). *Disability and Domestic Abuse: risk, impacts and response*. London: Public Health England, p. 9.

48 Smith Institute (2017). *Safe as Houses: the impact of universal credit on tenants and their rent payment behaviour in the London boroughs of Southwark and Croydon, and Peabody*. London: The Smith Institute.

49 Parliamentary Question 169883, 3 September 2018.

50 *R (TP and AR) v Secretary of State for Work and Pensions (Universal Credit)* [2018] EWHC 1474 (Admin).

51 NAO (2018). *Rolling Out Universal Credit*. HC 1123. London: National Audit Office, p. 31.

52 DPAC 2019.

53 NAO (2018). *Rolling Out Universal Credit*. HC 1123. London: National Audit Office, p. 10.

54 Gentleman, A. (2013). '"Shocking" bedroom tax should be axed, says UN investigator', *Guardian*, 11 September.

55 UK Parliament (2017). 'Housing Benefit: social rented housing: written question – 109181', 23 October.

56 Adam, S., Joyce, R. and Pope, T. (2019). *The Impacts of Localised Council Tax Support Schemes*. London: Institute for Fiscal Studies.

57 Perraudin, F. (2019). 'Council tax debts in England soar 40% in six years', *Guardian*, 13 April.

58 Chu, B. (2016). 'Taxpayer money paid to private landlords doubles over 10 years, reaching almost £10bn', *Independent*, 19 August.

59 Pollard 2019, p. 5.

5 INDEPENDENT LIVING CUTS

1 Morris, J. (2018). 'Charging for support: a tax on disability and old age', jennymorris.blogspot.com, 30 April.

2 *Davey, R (On the Application Of) v Oxfordshire County Council* [2017] EWHC 354 (Admin) (27 February).

3 Bowcott, O. (2018). 'Judge calls for Mental Health Act reform over rising detentions', *Guardian*, 5 July.

4 Matthews-King, A. (2018). 'Mental Health Act "needs major reform" as black patients four times as likely as whites to be sectioned', *Independent*, 5 December.

5 Dodd, V. (2018). 'Police custody deaths hit 10-year high, with experts citing austerity', *Guardian*, 25 July.

6 Mental Health Foundation (n.d.). 'Mental health in the workplace', mentalhealth.org.uk, www.mentalhealth.org.uk/our-work/mental-health-workplace.

7 Atkinson 2019, p. 165.

8 Department of Health and Social Care (2018). *Modernising the Mental Health Act: increasing choice, reducing compulsion. Final report of the Independent Review of the Mental Health Act 1983*. London: Department of Health and Social Care.

9 Salman, S. (2019). 'You can't rehabilitate someone into society when they're locked away', *Guardian*, 16 January.

10 Campbell, D. (2018). 'Physical restraint used on 50% more NHS patients with learning disabilities', *Guardian*, 2 October.

11 Baynes, C. and Agerholm, H. (2018). 'Grenfell Tower inquiry: disabled victim housed on 18th floor denied "human right to escape", says sister', *Independent*, 30 May.

12 Ryan 2019, p. 107.

13 Ofsted (2018) *The Annual Report of Her Majesty's Chief Inspector of Education, Children's Services and Skills 2017/18*. London: Ofsted.

14 Cited in Rieser, R. (2018). 'Where are we now with inclusive education?', Alliance for Inclusive Education, 29 October.

15 Rose, B. (2019). 'Disabled students' allowances: over half of eligible students miss out', BBC Ouch, 14 August.

16 Wheatley, H. (2017). 'New research: more than half of self-employed not earning a decent living', New Economics Foundation, 15 August.

17 WPC (2014). *Improving Access to Work for Disabled People*. HC 481. London: Work and Pensions Committee, p. 3.

18 Hale 2017.

19 *Barriers to Work* report launch organised by StopChanges2AtW campaign and hosted by Debbie Abrahams MP, Portcullis House, London, 24 October 2017.

20 The '30-hour rule' refers to the fact that AtW were telling many deaf and deafblind customers that if they have 30 or more hours interpreting a week they must recruit their own full-time interpreter.

21 Merrick, R. (2017). 'Legal aid cuts trigger 99.5% collapse in numbers receiving state help in benefits cases', *Independent*, 31 October.

22 Ryan 2019, p. 199.

23 See, for example, Rob Marris's 'Assisted Dying' Bill, which was defeated in the Commons in September 2015, and the legal challenge that Noel Conway lost in the Supreme Court in November 2018.

24 Preobrazhensky, E. A. (1912). 'The right to suicide', No. 57, 17 June.

PART III 'HUMAN CATASTROPHE'

1 Bell, S. (2017). 'UK Government has caused a "human catastrophe", says UN committee on disabled rights', *Commonspace*, 29 August.

2 Equality and Human Rights Commission ([EHRC) (2018). 'Britain in danger of becoming a two-speed society'. Press release, 25 October.

6 THE HUMAN COST

1 Ryan 2019, p. 51.

2 This is David Frayne's summation of findings from the Welfare Conditionality Project, which was carried out from 2013 to 2018 by researchers at the University of York. See Frayne 2019, p. 7.

3 EHRC (2017). *Being Disabled in Britain: a journey less equal*. Manchester: Equality and Human Rights Commission (EHRC).

4 Trussell Trust (2018). *The Next Stage of Universal Credit: moving onto the new benefit system and foodbank use*. Salisbury: The Trussell Trust.

5 Ryan 2019, pp. 140–1.

6   Hardy, G. (2018). *Doorway to Debt: protecting consumers in the home credit market*. London: Citizens Advice.

7   Marsh, S. and Greenfield, P. (2018). 'Deaths of mentally ill rough sleepers in London rise sharply', *Guardian*, 19 June.

8   Shelter (2017). *Shut Out: households at put at risk of homelessness by the housing benefit freeze*. London: Shelter.

9   Vale, J. (2017). 'Almost 80% of people on disability benefits "have seen health worsen since introduction of Tories' new system"', *Independent*, 13 September.

10   ILSG (2018). *Charging for Social Care: a tax on the need for support?* London: Independent Living Strategy Group (ILSG).

11   Duffy 2018.

12   Portes and Reed 2018, p. 15.

13   See www.ohchr.org/Documents/Issues/EPoverty/UnitedKingdom/2018/IndividualSubmissions/Maggie.docx.

14   Ibid.

15   Watkins, J., Wulaningsih, W., Da Zhou, C. et al. 2017). 'Effects of health and social care spending constraints on mortality in England: a time trend analysis', *BMJ Open*, vol. 7, p. e017722.

16   Ryan 2019, p. 52.

17   Barr et al. 2015.

18   Reeves et al., 2016, p. 1.

19   Ibid., p. 8.

20   Jones, K. S. (2017). 'PIP assessments are dehumanising, degrading, very distressing and potentially harmful', *Politics and Insight*, 28 June.

21   Maclean et al. 2017, p. 1.

22   Carr, S. (2018). 'Disabled Luton woman "hounded" for benefits claims', *Luton Today*, 18 May.

23   Mehta et al. 2018.

24   Ibid., p. 12.

25   Committee on the Rights of Persons with Disabilities (CRPD) (2016). 'Inquiry concerning the United Kingdom of Great Britain and Northern Ireland carried out by the Committee under Article 6 of the Optional Protocol to the Convention'. Geneva: Office of the High Commissioner on Human Rights, p. 8.

26   Merrick, R. (2016). 'Former DWP minister Stephen Crabb admits disability benefit test is "traumatic"', *Independent*, 8 November.

27   Speed, B. (2017). 'Iain Duncan Smith says work capability assessments don't work and are "too harsh"', *iNews*, 29 June.

28   Thorlby, R., Starling, A., Broadbent, C. and Watt, T. (2018). *What's the Problem with Social Care, and Why Do We Need to do Better?* London: Health Foundation, Institute for Fiscal Studies, The King's Fund and Nuffield Trust.

29 Clifford 2016, p. 14.

30 Belgrave, K. (2014). 'Disabled and without a carer for the night? Go to #Asda! #SaveILF #jobcentre #jsa', katebelgrave.com, 17 June.

31 Clifford 2016, p. 28.

32 Wynne-Jones, R. (2014). 'Patients occupy clinic to save it from David Cameron's savage NHS cuts', *Mirror*, 16 April.

33 Healthwatch Camden (2017). 'Audio diary project: recording lived experiences of changes to mental health services at the Highgate Day Centre'.

34 Foot, T. (2017). 'Health chiefs apologise after "unacceptable" impact of day centre cuts is revealed', *Camden New Journal*, 3 August.

35 Alston 2018, p. 17.

36 WPC 2018, p. 19.

37 DBC (2015). 'Almost 70% of disabled people say cuts to ESA will cause their health to suffer and half may return to work later'. Disability Benefits Consortium (DBC) press release, 27 October.

38 Baumberg Geiger 2017, p. 123.

39 Gandy et al. 2016, p. 55.

40 Maclean et al. 2017, p. 1.

41 Inclusion London (2017). *Inclusion London's Response to Improving Lives: work, health and disability*. London: Inclusion London, p. 2.

42 MS Society (2019). 'The cost of the PIP 20 metre rule', MS Society.

43 Association of Directors of Children's Services (ADCS) (2018). 'New research highlights increasing safeguarding pressures'. Press release, 7 November.

44 RT (2017). 'Autistic man serving life for murder despite never touching weapon has appeal rejected', RT.com, 14 August.

45 Alston 2018, p. 3.

46 WPC 2018, p. 3.

47 Ryan 2019, p. 191.

48 Alston 2018, p. 15.

7 RE-SEGREGATING SOCIETY

1 Care and Support Alliance (2018). *Voices from the Social Care Crisis: an opportunity to end a broken system, once and for all*. London: Care and Support Alliance.

2 Vale, J. (2017). 'Almost 80% of people on disability benefits "have seen health worsen since introduction of Tories' new system"', *Independent*, 13 September.

3 Johnson, E. and Spring, E. (2018). *The Activity Trap: benefits or being fit?* London: FlexMR for Dwarf Sports Association UK.

4 Petitions Committee 2019, p. 16.

5 Ibid., p. 17.

6 McKinstry, L. (2012). 'The Paralympics show up a corrupt benefits system', *Express*, 6 September.

7 Crow 2014.

8 Briant et al. 2011, p. 5.

9 O'Malley, K. (2019). '90% of people think they're helping society by challenging people who don't "look disabled", says study', *Independent*, 16 April.

10 Burch 2016, p. 24.

11 Edmiston 2018, p. 47.

12 'Condems' was a derogatory term used to refer to the Conservative and Liberal Democrat Coalition government that was in power from 2010 to 2015.

13 Crowther, N. (2018). 'It's time to be pro-investment, not anti-austerity where disability rights is concerned', *Making Rights Make Sense*, 19 December.

14 Beresford 2016b, p. 424.

15 DPAC (2014). 'A plea to the left – STOP using the "v" word', DPAC. uk.net, 3 November.

16 Ryan 2019, p. 191.

8 POLITICAL FALLOUT

1 Booth, R. (2019). 'UN poverty expert hits back over UK ministers' "denial of facts"', *Guardian*, 24 May.

2 *The Andrew Marr Show*, BBC One, 20 March 2016.

3 Ibid.

4 O'Hara 2014, p. 14.

5 WPC (2018). *PIP and ESA Assessments*. HC 829. London: Work and Pensions Committee (WPC), p. 9.

6 Baumberg Geiger 2018, p. 11.

7 Ibid., p. 11.

8 O'Hara 2014, p. 15.

9 Ibid., p. 14.

10 Frayne 2019, p. 19.

11 Ryan, F. (2019). 'The Lib Dems are deeply stained by austerity. Don't trust them', *Guardian*, 23 July.

12 House of Commons (HC) Debate, 20 July 2015.

13 Drench, M. (2019). 'BBC Question Time's Francesca Martinez praised for show's "best EVER moment"', *Mirror*, 14 June.

14 HC Debate, 16 March 2016.

15 Straw, W. (2015). 'The clue's in the name: the Party of Work', in Keeble, S. and Straw, W. (eds) (2015). *Never Again: lessons from Labour's key seats*. London: Fabian Society.

16 Scrapping of Council Tax Benefit and Disability Living Allowance and the introduction of the bedroom tax all increased the likelihood of those affected to vote Leave, according to Fetzer, T. (2019). 'Did austerity cause Brexit?', *American Economic Review*, vol. 109, no. 11, pp. 3849–86.

17 Robinson, S. (2019). 'Austerity, Brexit chaos and political failure – a warning of how the right can win', *Socialist Worker*, 7 October.

PART IV UNDERSTANDING THE WELFARE WAR

1 'The age of austerity' speech by David Cameron, 26 April 2009.

2 Morris 2011.

3 The full text is available at www.gov.uk/government/speeches/lord-mayors-banquet-2013-prime-ministers-speech.

4 O'Hara 2014, p. 10.

5 Jones 2014, p. xix.

9 A STORY OF IDEOLOGY AND INCOMPETENCE

1 Williams-Findlay 2011.

2 Morris 2018, p. 8.

3 Harman 2009, p. 139.

4 Marx, K. (2004 [1867]). *Capital: a critique of political economy*, Volume One. London: Penguin, p. 797.

5 Harman 2009, p. 137.

6 Marx, K. (2004 [1867]). *Capital: a critique of political economy*, Volume One. London: Penguin, p. 784.

7 Cameron, D. (2011). 'PM's speech on the fightback after the riots', 15 August, www.gov.uk/government/speeches/pms-speech-on-the-fightback-after-the-riots.

8 Harman 2009, p. 137.

9 Ibid., p. 138.

10 Cited in Piggott and Grover 2009, p. 161.

11 Ibid., p. 161.

12 Ibid., p. 162.

13 OECD 2003. Cited in Stewart 2019.

14 Stewart 2019.

15 Ibid.

16 Newkirk II, V. R. (2018). 'The real lessons from Bill Clinton's welfare reform', *The Atlantic*, 5 February.

17 Trump appears to be taking tips from the UK when it comes to surveillance of the disabled with a view to reducing benefits. See

Barbarin, I. (2019). 'How a Trump proposal could reduce "happy" disabled people', *Forbes*, 11 April.

18 McMillan, T. (2019). 'How one company is making millions off Trump's war on the poor', *Mother Jones*, January/February.

19 Knight, B. (2013). '"Hartz reforms": how a benefits shakeup changed Germany', *Guardian*, 1 January.

20 See Hannington 1940.

21 Ibid., pp. 46–7.

22 The particular change here was the introduction of a family means test that came into force in 1931 for workers who remained on unemployment benefits for more than 26 weeks. Unemployed workers whose family income exceeded a certain threshold had their benefits stopped. The immediate result was that 377,000 claimants ceased to be entitled to statutory benefit. Hannington comments: 'one can claim that it was actually the most savage and dangerous part of the economic measures' (ibid., p. 37).

23 Ibid., p. 46.

24 Ibid.

25 Edmiston 2018.

26 Stewart 2019.

27 Mulholland, H. and Watt, N. (2010). 'Spending review 2010: George Osborne announces extra £7bn of welfare cuts', *Guardian*, 20 October.

28 Morris 2018, p. 128.

29 Jones 2011, p. 92.

30 DWP (2006). *A New Deal for Welfare: empowering people to work*. Cm 6730. London: Department for Work and Pensions (DWP).

31 Berthoud 2011, p. 23.

32 Baumberg Geiger 2014, p. 299.

33 Morris 2018, p. 44.

34 Russell and Malhotra 2002, p. 220.

35 Freud 2007, p. 8.

36 Rutherford 2007.

37 Youle, E. (2018). 'Exclusive: government's £1.4 billion Universal Credit and Welfare Reform Outsourcing Bill revealed', *Huffington Post*, 19 December.

38 WPC (2018). *PIP and ESA Assessments*. HC 829. London: Work and Pensions Committee (WPC), p. 4.

39 Elward, L. (2016). 'Corporate welfare crime: two case studies in state–corporate harm'. MA dissertation, University of Liverpool. Cited in Stewart 2019, p. 223.

40 Cited in Rutherford 2007, p. 42.

41 Shakespeare et al. 2017, p. 34.

42 Rutherford 2007, p. 48.

43 Morris 2018, p. 152.

44 DWP and DH 2017, p. 33.

45 Stewart 2016, p. 30.

46 Under pressure, the government reduced the maximum sanction length to six months. This came into effect in November 2019. According to sanctions researcher Dr David Webster, this will affect only a very small number of people because the reduction applies only to 'higher-level' JSA or UC sanctions. By contrast, the number of people having their benefits removed for more than six months under 'low-level' sanctions, and who will not be helped by this reform, is much larger.

47 Harman 2009, p. 135.

48 Full Fact (2019). 'Employment: what's happened to wages since 2010', fullfact.org, 10 June.

49 HSE (2018). 'Work-related stress, depression or anxiety statistics in Great Britain, 2018'. Bootle: Health and Safety Executive (HSE), p. 3.

50 Saner, E. (2018). 'Employers are monitoring computers, toilet breaks – even emotions. Is your boss watching you?', *Guardian*, 14 May.

51 Redman 2019, p. 11, referencing Briken, K. and Taylor, P. (2018). 'Fulfilling the "British way": beyond constrained choice – Amazon workers' lived experiences of workfare', *Industrial Relations*, vol. 49, pp. 438–58.

52 Edmiston 2018, p. 52.

53 Giles, C. (2018). 'Britain's productivity crisis in eight charts', *Financial Times*, 13 August.

54 Redman 2019, p. 13.

55 Ibid., p. 13.

56 Ibid., p. 13.

57 Walker, J. (2019). 'Minister for the disabled admits people are being wrongly stripped of benefits', *Chronicle Live*, 24 April.

58 Bulman, M. (2019). 'DWP staff cut by 21% since Universal Credit rollout began, figures show', *Independent*, 7 July.

59 Choonara, J. (2019). 'Economic warnings', *Socialist Review*, vol. 450.

60 Ravetz 2006, p. 25.

61 DWP (2019). 'Amber Rudd sets out fresh approach to Universal Credit'. Department for Work and Pensions (DWP) press release, 11 January.

62 Crowther, N. (2017). 'Advancing disability rights under a Conservative government – bring on the negotiators', *Making Rights Make Sense*, 10 May.

10 COLLABORATORS

1 Pring, J. (2017). 'Oliver comes out of retirement to deliver stinging rebuke to "parasite" charities', *Disability News Service*, 30 November.

2 Oliver told *Disability News Service* in 2017 that the charities are 'parasitic on the lives of disabled people, and their attempts to

reposition themselves as defenders of disability rights are an attempt to disguise this' (ibid.).

3 Jolly, D. (2016). 'Scope #endthebullshit', DPAC.uk.net, 29 April.

4 DPAC (2013). 'Mental Health Resistance Network: victory on case against WCA!', DPAC.uk.net, 22 May.

5 Beresford, P. (2012). 'Why did large charities embrace the government's work schemes?', *Guardian*, 12 March.

6 Ibid.

7 Ibid.

8 Jolly, D. (2016). 'Scope #endthebullshit', DPAC.uk.net, 29 April.

9 *RF v Secretary of State for Work and Pensions* [2017] EWHC 3375 (Admin) Mostyn J (21 December 2017).

10 Pring, J. (2017). 'Boycott call after DWP wrongly claims DPOs helped devise punitive work scheme', *Disability News Service*, 4 May.

11 Oral evidence session for the inquiry 'Three Years On: Assessing the Impact of the Welfare Reform and Work Act 2016 on Children and Disabled Adults' conducted by the All Party Parliamentary Group on Health in All Policies, 22 July 2019.

12 UPIAS 2018, p. 31.

13 DRUK (2016). *The "Affordable Papers": contributions to an economy that includes disabled people.* London: Disability Rights UK (DRUK), p. 15.

14 Winchester, L. (2019). 'Universal Credit, PIP and ESA assessments MERGING – how it will work EXPLAINED', *Express*, 19 March.

15 Burleigh 1996, p. 108.

16 Jolly, D. (2016). 'Scope #endthebullshit', DPAC.uk.net, 29 April.

PART V FIGHTING BACK

1 DPAC et al. 2014, p. 45.

2 Oliver 2009, p. 137. Cited in Beresford 2016a, p. 210.

3 Rosenthal 2016.

4 Blackmore and Hodgkins 2012.

5 Russell 1998, p. 226.

11 FOREFRONT OF THE FIGHTBACK

1 HC Debate, 20 June 2012.

2 DPAC et al. 2014, p. 45.

3 Ibid., p. 10.

4 Kelsey-Fry, J. (2016). 'Disabled people lead the fight against austerity', *New Internationalist*, 1 November.

5 Graby 2016.

6 Jolly, D. (2012). 'A question of intent: DPAC's response to comments from Disability Rights UK on DPAC's "tactics"', DPAC.uk.net, 15 December.

7 DPAC et al. 2014, p. 7.

8 Williams-Findlay 2019, p. 139.

9 Ibid., pp. 138–9.

10 DPAC et al. 2014, p. 45.

11 Ref to insert at proof stage

12 Oliver and Barnes 2012, p. 157.

13 Graby 2016.

14 Ibid.

15 Williams-Findlay 2011.

16 Ibid.

17 Kelsey-Fry, J. (2016). 'Disabled people lead the fight against austerity', *New Internationalist*, 1 November.

18 Jolly, D. (2012). 'A question of intent: DPAC's response to comments from Disability Rights UK on DPAC's "tactics"', DPAC.uk.net, 15 December.

19 Sayce, L. (2011). *Getting In, Staying In and Getting On: disability employment support fit for the future.* Norwich: The Stationery Office.

20 Henderson, E. (2018). 'Three in four left jobless by betrayal of disabled', *Express*, 18 February.

21 Sayce, L. (2011). *Getting In, Staying In and Getting On: disability employment support fit for the future.* Norwich: The Stationery Office.

22 Ryan 2019, p. 193.

23 BBC News, *Look North*, 5 May 2015.

24 University of Nottingham Students' University (n.d.). 'Template for officer reports for officer accountability session', www.su.nottingham. ac.uk/pageassets/make-change/democracy-and-elections/student-democratic-meetings/scrutiny-panel/agendas-minutes-reports/ ESJ-Officers-Report-1.pdf.

25 Gentleman, A. (2015) 'After hated Atos quits, will Maximus make work assessments less arduous?', *Guardian*, 18 January .

26 SNP (n.d.). 'What plans do the SNP have to use new powers around social security?', www.snp.org/policies/pb-what-plans-do-the-snp-have-to-use-new-powers-around-social-security/.

27 Savage, M. (2019). 'Labour "will ban" outsourcing of public services to private firms', *Observer*, 24 March.

28 Dar, A. (2015). 'Work experience schemes'. Briefing Paper 06249, 25 June. London: UK Parliament, p. 5.

29 *Reilly (No. 2) & Anor, R (on the application of) v Secretary of State for Work and Pensions* [2014] EWHC 2182 (Admin) (4 July 2014).

30 Void, J. (2015). 'Workfare abandoned! Mandatory Work Activity and Community Work Placements both to be scrapped', *The Void*, 25 November.
31 Clark, W. (2013). 'Workfare: a policy on the brink', *Red Pepper*, 14 February.
32 d'Ancona 2014, p. 97.
33 MOJ (2019) 'Tribunal statistics quarterly, July to September 2019 (provisional)'. London: Ministry of Justice (MOJ).
34 OBR 2019, p. 4.

12 CONCLUDING THOUGHTS

1 Oliver and Barnes 2012, p. 132.
2 Marx, K. (1845–46). *A Critique of the German Ideology*.
3 Ryan 2019, p. 197.
4 Cited in Bambery 2006, p. 45.
5 UPIAS 2018, p. 40.
6 Williams-Findlay, B. (2018). 'The Disabled People's Movement in the age of austerity: rights resistance and reclamation'. Unpublished paper.
7 Crowther, N. (2018). 'It's time to be pro-investment, not anti-austerity where disability rights is concerned', *Making Rights Make Sense*, 19 December.
8 Morris 2011.
9 Oliver 2016.
10 Oliver and Barnes 2006.
11 Morris 2018, p. 233.
12 UPIAS 2018, p. 33.
13 Graby 2016.
14 Oliver and Barnes 2006.
15 Oliver, M. (2018). 'Kicking down doors: from borstal boy to university professor', YouTube, 17 December, www.youtube.com/watch?v=NMfvoh-j9qw.
16 UPIAS 2018, p. 34.
17 See Oliver and Barnes 2012, Chapter 9.
18 Mehta et al. 2018.
19 Russell 1998, p. 132.
20 Withers 2012, p. 9. Withers draws a distinction between the social model and disability rights models and attributes this progression to both.
21 Shakespeare 2006, p. 29.
22 Ibid., p. 31.
23 Oliver, M. and Campbell, J. (1996). *Disability Politics: understanding our past, changing our future*. London: Routledge. Referenced in Beresford 2016a, p. 209.

24 Oliver 2013, p. 1024.

25 Shakespeare 2006, p. 53.

26 Cited in Oliver and Barnes 2012, p. 165.

27 Engels, F. (1886). 'Letter to F. A. Sorge', 29 November.

28 Williams-Findlay 2019, p. 143.

29 Oliver 2009, p. 43.

30 Cited in Withers 2012, p. 5.

31 Oliver and Barnes 2012, pp. 139–40.

32 Frayne 2019, p. 13.

33 Beresford 2016a, pp. 213–16

34 Ibid., pp. 213–14.

35 Ibid., p. 215.

36 Oliver 2009, pp. 144–5.

37 DWP and ODI (2018). 'Concluding observations on the initial report of the United Kingdom of Great Britain and Northern Ireland: initial government response'. Policy Paper. London: Department for Work and Pensions (DWP) and Office for Disability Issues (ODI).

38 Morris 1991, p. 10.

39 Oliver 2016, p. 48.

40 Withers 2012, p. 91.

41 Oliver and Barnes 2012, p. 7.

42 Shakespeare 2006, p. 52.

43 UPIAS 2018, p. 31.

44 Withers 2012, p. 117.

45 Oliver 2016, p. 50.

46 Oliver 2013, p. 1024.

47 Oliver 2009, p. 49.

48 UPIAS 2018, pp. 27–8.

49 Oliver and Barnes 2012, p. 7.

50 For example, Withers 2012, pp. 86–7.

51 Graby 2016.

52 UPIAS 2018, p. 45.

53 Ibid., p. 38.

54 Ibid., p. 15.

55 Williams-Findlay 2011.

56 Marx, K. (1875). *Critique of the Gotha Programme*.

57 Slorach 2020, p. 133.

58 Cited in Slorach 2016, p. 93; Slorach 2020, p. 133.

59 Pidd, H. (2020). 'Why Iain Duncan Smith knighthood was "slap in the face"', *Guardian*, 3 January.

Select bibliography

Abberley, P. (1987). 'The concept of oppression and the development of a social theory of disability', *Disability, Handicap and Society*, vol. 2, no. 1, pp. 5–19.

Alston, P. (2018). 'Statement on visit to the United Kingdom, by Professor Philip Alston, United Nations Special Rapporteur on Extreme Poverty and Human Rights', Office of the High Commissioner for Human Rights [online], 16 November.

Atkinson, P. (2019). 'The IAPT assembly line' in Frayne, D. (ed.). *The Work Cure: critical essays on work and wellness*. Monmouth: PCCS Books.

Bambery, C. (2006). *A Rebel's Guide to Gramsci*. London: Bookmarks.

Barnes, H. and Sissons, P. (2013). 'Redefining "fit for work": welfare reform and the introduction of the Employment and Support Allowance' in Lindsay, C. and Houston, D. (eds). *Disability Benefits, Welfare Reform and Employment Policy*. Basingstoke: Palgrave Macmillan.

Barr, B., Taylor-Robinson, D. C., Stuckler, D., Loopstra, R., Reeves, A. and Whitehead, M. (2015). '"First, do no harm": are disability assessments associated with adverse trends in mental health? A longitudinal ecological study', *Journal of Epidemiology and Community Health*, vol. 70, no. 4, pp. 339–45.

Baumberg Geiger, B. (2014). 'Fit-for-work – or work fit for disabled people? The role of changing job demands and control in incapacity claims', *Journal of Social Policy*, vol. 43, pp. 289–310.

Baumberg Geiger, B. (2017). 'Benefits conditionality for disabled people: stylised facts from a review of international evidence and practice', *Journal of Poverty and Social Justice*, vol. 25, no. 2, pp. 107–28.

Baumberg Geiger, B. (2018). *A Better WCA Is Possible: disability assessment, public opinion and the benefits system*. London: Demos.

Baynton, D. C. (2013). 'Disability and the justification of inequality in American history' in Davis, L. J. (ed.). *The Disability Studies Reader*. 4th edn. New York: Routledge.

Beresford, P. (2012). 'From "vulnerable" to vanguard: challenging the Coalition' in Rutherford, J. and Davison, S. (eds). *Welfare Reform: the dread of things to come*. London: Lawrence and Wishart.

Beresford, P. (2016a). *All Our Welfare: towards participatory social policy*. Bristol: Policy Press.

Beresford, P. (2016b). 'Presenting welfare reform: poverty porn, telling sad stories or achieving change', *Disability and Society*, vol. 31, no. 3, pp. 421–5.

Beresford, P., Slasberg, C. and Clements, L. (2018). 'From dementia tax to a solution for social care', *Soundings: Grit, Oil and Grime*, issue 68, pp. 78–93.

Berthoud, R. (2011). 'Trends in the employment of disabled people in Britain'. ISER Working Paper Series 2011-03. Colchester: Institute for Social and Economic Research (ISER).

Blackmore, T. and Hodgkins, S. L. (2012). 'Discourses of disabled people's organisations: Foucault, Bourdieu and future perspectives' in Goodley, D., Hughes, B. and Davis, L. (eds). *Disability and Social Theory: new developments and directions*. London: Palgrave.

Bourhis. R. (2005). *Insult to Injury: insurance, fraud and the big business of bad faith*. San Francisco: Berrett-Koehler.

Briant, E., Watson, N. and Philo, G. (2011). *Bad News for Disabled People: how the newspapers are reporting disability*. Glasgow: Strathclyde Centre for Disability Research and Glasgow Media Unit.

Burch, L. (2016). '"All parasites should perish": online disablist hate speech and a welfare rhetoric on "Reddit"'. Master's degree dissertation, Liverpool Hope University.

Burleigh, M. (1994). 'Between enthusiasm, compliance and protest: the churches, eugenics and the Nazi 'Euthanasia' programme', *Journal of Contemporary European History*, vol. 3, no. 3, pp. 253–64.

Burleigh, M. (ed.) (1996). *Confronting the Nazi Past: new debates on modern German history*. London: Collins & Brown.

Campbell, S. J., Anon., Marsh, S., Franklin, K., Gaffney, D., Anon., Dixon, M., James, L., Barnett-Cormack, S., Fon-James, R., Willis, D. and Anon. (2012). *Responsible Reform: a report on the proposed changes to Disability Living Allowance*. Ekklesia [online].

Clifford, E. (2013). 'Why the Henwood and Hudson report failed in justifying the closure of the Independent Living Fund', Disabled People Against Cuts [online], 9 November.

Clifford, E. (2016). *One Year On: evaluating the closure of the Independent Living Fund*. London: Inclusion London.

Clifford, E. and Vogelmann, E. (2018). 'Co-operatives: an alternative solution to the UK independent living crisis?', Disabled People Against Cuts [online].

Crow, L. (2014). 'Scroungers and superhumans: images of disability from the summer of 2012: a visual inquiry', *Journal of Visual Culture*, 28 August.

d'Ancona, M. (2014). *In It Together: the inside story of the Coalition government*. London: Penguin.

DPAC (2019). *Hunger, Debt, Homelessness, Crime, Prostitution and Suicide: Mainstream media articles telling the effects of Universal Credit's hostile environment for benefit claimants.* Disabled People Against Cuts (DPAC) [online], May.

DPAC, Inclusion London and ROFA (2014). *From Cuts ... to Resistance: disabled people's experiences under "welfare reform" 2010–2014.* London: Disabled People Against Cuts (DPAC), Inclusion London and Reclaiming Our Futures Alliance (ROFA).

Duffy, S. (2013). *A Fair Society? How the cuts target disabled people.* Sheffield: Centre for Welfare Reform.

Duffy, S. (2018). 'Cumulative Impact Assessment (CIA): statement by the Centre for Welfare Reform', Centre for Welfare Reform [online].

DWP and DH (2016). *Improving Lives: the Work, Health and Disability green paper.* Cm 9342. London: Department for Work and Pensions (DWP) and Department of Health (DH).

DWP and DH (2017). *Improving Lives: the future of work, health and disability.* Cm 9526. London: Department for Work and Pensions (DWP) and Department of Health (DH).

Dwyer, P., Jones, K., McNeill, J., Scullion, L. and Stewart, A. (2018). *Final Findings: welfare conditionality project 2013–2018.* York: Welfare Conditionality Project.

Edmiston, D. (2018). *Welfare, Inequality and Social Citizenship: deprivation and affluence in austerity Britain.* Bristol: Policy Press.

EHRC (2011). *Hidden in Plain Sight: inquiry into disability-related harassment.* Manchester: Equality and Human Rights Commission (EHRC).

EHRC (2018a). *Is Britain Fairer? The state of equality and human rights in Britain.* Manchester: Equality and Human Rights Commission (EHRC).

EHRC (2018b). *Housing and Disabled People: Britain's hidden crisis.* Manchester: Equality and Human Rights Commission (EHRC).

Ferguson, I. (2017). *Politics of the Mind: Marxism and mental distress.* London: Bookmarks.

Finkesltein, V. (2001). 'A personal journey into disability politics' [online].

Finkelstein, V. (2007). 'The "social model of disability" and the Disability Movement' [online].

Foner, P. S. (ed.) (2011). *Helen Keller: her socialist years.* 2nd edn. New York: International Publishers.

Foster, D. J. and Wass, V. J. (2013). 'Disability in the labour market: an exploration of concepts of the ideal worker and organisational fit that disadvantage employees with impairments', *Sociology*, vol. 47, no. 4, pp. 705–21.

Frayne, D. (ed.) (2019). *The Work Cure: critical essays on work and wellness*. Monmouth: PCCS Books.

Freud, D. (2007). *Reducing Dependency, Increasing Opportunity: options for the future of welfare to work*. Leeds: Department for Work and Pensions.

Gallagher, H. G. (1995). *By Trust Betrayed: patients, physicians and the license to kill in the Third Reich*. Revised edn. Virginia: Vandamere Press.

Gandy, K., King, K., Streeter Hurle, P., Bustin, C. and Glazebrook, K. (2016). *Poverty and Decision-making: how behavioural science can improve opportunity in the UK*. London: The Behavioural Insights Team.

Graby, S. (2016). 'Unworkable conditions: work, benefits and disabled people's resistance to capitalism'. Paper presented at the Association for Social and Political Philosophy annual conference on 'Rebellion, Resistance, Revolution', 29 June.

Grover, C. and Piggott, L. (2006). 'Disabled people, the reserve army of labour and welfare reform', *Disability and Society*, vol. 20, no. 7, pp. 705–17.

Hale, C. (2017). *Barriers to Work: a survey of deaf and disabled people's experiences of the Access to Work programme in 2015/2016*. London: Inclusion London.

Hampton, J. (2016). *Disability and the Welfare State in Britain: changes in perception and policy 1948–1979*. Bristol: Policy Press.

Hannington, W. (1940). *Ten Lean Years*. London: Victor Gollancz.

Harman, C. (2009). *Zombie Capitalism: global crisis and the relevance of Marx*. London: Bookmarks.

Henwood, M. and Hudson, B. (2007). *Review of the Independent Living Funds*. London: Department for Work and Pensions.

Howard, A. (2013). '11 per cent was never intended to be the number of people in the Support Group: DWP BIG blunder', Disabled People Against Cuts [online], 23 February.

Hunt, J. (2019). *No Limits: the disabled people's movement: a radical history*. Manchester: TBR Imprint

John, E., Thomas, G. and Touchet, A. (2019). *The Disability Price Tag 2019*. London: Scope.

Jolly, D. (2012). 'A tale of two models: disabled people vs. Unum, Atos, government and disability charities', Disabled People Against Cuts [online], 8 April.

Jones, O. (2011). *Chavs: the demonization of the working class*. London and New York: Verso.

Jones, O. (2014). *The Establishment and How They Get Away With It*. London: Allen Lane.

Keller, H. (2005 [1938]). 'Letter to John H. Finley. 2 December' in Nielsen, K. E. (ed.). *Helen Keller: selected writings (the history of disability)*. New York: New York University Press.

Ledger, S. and Shufflebotham, L. (2006). 'Songs of resistance' in Mitchell, D. (ed.). *Exploring Experiences of Advocacy by People with Learning Disabilities: testimonies of resistance*. London: Jessica Kingsley.

Longmore, P. K. and Goldberger, D. (2000). 'The League of the Physically Handicapped and the Great Depression: a case study in the new disability history', *Journal of American History*, vol. 87, no. 3, pp. 888–922.

Maclean, G., Marks, A. and Cowan, S. (2017). *Mental Health and Unemployment in Scotland: understanding the impact of welfare reforms in Scotland for individuals with mental health conditions*. Edinburgh: Carnegie Trust.

Mehta, J., Taggart, D., Clifford, E. and Speed, E. (2018). *Where Your Mental Health Just Disappears Overnight: disabled people's experiences of the Employment and Support Allowance Work Related Activity Group*. London: University of Essex and Inclusion London.

Morris, J. (1991). *Pride against Prejudice: transforming attitudes to disability*. London: The Women's Press.

Morris, J. (2011). *Rethinking Disability Policy*. York: Joseph Rowntree Foundation.

Morris, J. (2015). 'Independent living and disabled people' [online].

Morris, P. (1969). *Put Away: a sociological study of institutions for the mentally retarded*. London: Routledge and Kegan Paul.

Morris, R. K. S. (2018). 'In/validating disability: changing labour markets and out of work disability benefits'. PhD thesis, University of Leeds.

OBR (2019). 'Welfare trends report', Office for Budget Responsibility (OBR) [online].

OECD (2003). *Transforming Disability into Ability: policies to promote work and income security for disabled people*. Paris: Organisation for Economic Co-operation and Development OECD.

O'Hara, M. (2014). *Austerity Bites: a journey to the sharp end of cuts in the UK*. Bristol: Policy Press.

Oliver, M. (1990). *The Politics of Disablement*. Critical Texts in Social Work and the Welfare State. London: Palgrave Macmillan.

Oliver, M. (2009). *Understanding Disability: from theory to practice*. 2nd edn. London: Palgrave Macmillan.

Oliver, M. (2013). 'The social model of disability: thirty years on', *Disability and Society*, vol. 28, no. 7, pp. 1024–6.

Oliver, M. (2016). 'Persuasion's failed as a way of changing attitudes', *Disability Now* [online], 15 July.

Oliver, M. (2017). 'Disability history, bleeding hearts and parasite people', University of Kent [online], 29 November.

Oliver, M. and Barnes, C. (2006). 'Disability politics and the disability movement in Britain: where did it all go wrong?' [online], August.

Oliver, M. and Barnes, C. (2012). *The New Politics of Disablement*. London: Palgrave Macmillan.

Oswin, M. (1971). *The Empty Hours: a study of the weekend life of handicapped children*. 2nd edn. Harmondsworth: Penguin Books.

Oswin, M. (2000). 'Revisiting the Empty Hours' in Brigham, L., Atkinson, D., Jackson, M., Rolph, S. and Walmsley, J. (2000). *Crossing Boundaries: change and continuity in the history of learning disability*. Kidderminster: British Institute for Learning Disabilities.

Petitions Committee (2019). *Online Abuse and the Experience of Disabled People*. HC 759. London: House of Commons Petitions Committee.

Piggott, L. and Grover, C. (2009). 'Retrenching Incapacity Benefit: Employment Support Allowance and paid work', *Social Policy and Society*, vol. 8, no. 2, pp. 159–70.

Pollard, T. (2019). *Pathways from Poverty: a case for institutional reform*. London: Demos.

Portes, J. and Reed, H. (2018). *The Cumulative Impact of Tax and Welfare Reforms*. Manchester: Equality and Human Rights Commission.

Pring, J. (2011). *Longcare Survivors: the biography of a care scandal*. York: Disability News Service.

Quarmby, K. (2011). *Scapegoat: why we are failing disabled people*. London: Portobello.

Ravetz, A. (2006). 'Green Paper: *A New Deal for Welfare: empowering people to work*. 2006. An independent assessment of the arguments for proposed Incapacity Benefit reform' [online].

Redman, J. (2019). 'The benefit sanction: a correctional device or a weapon of disgust?', *Sociological Research Online*.

Reed, H. and Portes, J. (2018). *The Cumulative Impact on Living Standards of Public Spending Changes*. Research Report 120. Manchester: Equality and Human Rights Commission.

Reeves, A., Clair, A., McKee, M. and Stuckler, D. (2016). 'Reductions in the United Kingdom's government Housing Benefit and symptoms of depression in low-income households', *American Journal of Epidemiology*, vol. 184, no. 6, pp. 421–9.

ROFA (2018). 'UK extreme poverty written submission from the Reclaiming Our Futures Alliance', Reclaiming Our Futures Alliance (ROFA) [online].

Rosenthal, K. (2013). 'Pioneers in the fight for disability rights: the League of the Physically Handicapped', *International Socialism Review* [online], issue 90.

Rosenthal, K. (2015). 'The politics of Helen Keller: disability and socialism', *International Socialism Review* [online], issue 96.

Rosenthal, K. (2016). 'Disability and the Russian Revolution', *International Socialism Review* [online], issue 102.

Russell, M. (1998). *Beyond Ramps: disability at the end of the social contract.* Monroe ME: Common Courage Press.

Russell, M. and Malhotra, R. (2002). 'Capitalism and disability', *Socialist Register*, vol. 38 ('A world of contradictions'), pp. 211–28.

Rutherford, J. (2007). 'New Labour, the market state, and the end of welfare', *Soundings: Politics and Markets*, issue 36, pp. 40–55.

Ryan, F. (2019). *Crippled: the austerity crisis and the threat to disability rights.* London and Brooklyn: Verso.

Sayce, L. (2011). *Getting In, Staying In and Getting On: disability employment support fit for the future.* Norwich: The Stationery Office (TSO).

Shakespeare, T. (2006). Disability Rights and Wrongs. Abingdon : Routledge.

Shakespeare, T., Watson, N. and Alghaib, O. A. (2017). 'Blaming the victim, all over again: Waddell and Aylward's biopsychosocial (BPS) model of disability', *Critical Social Policy*, vol. 37, no. 1, pp. 22–41.

Silberman S. (2015). *NeuroTribes: the legacy of autism and how to think smarter about people who think differently.* London: Allen and Unwin.

Slorach, R. (2016). *A Very Capitalist Condition: a history and politics of disability.* London: Bookmarks.

Slorach, R. (2020). 'From eugenics to scientific racism', *International Socialism Journal*, vol. 165, pp. 133–54.

Stewart, M. (2016). *Cash Not Care: the planned demolition of the UK welfare state.* London: New Generation Publishing.

Stewart, M. (2019). *Influences and Consequences: the conclusion to the Preventable Harm Project 2009–2019.* Sheffield: Centre for Welfare Reform.

Stone, D. A. (1984). *The Disabled State.* Philadelphia: Temple University Press.

Tyrell, E. G., Kendrick, D., Sayal, K. and Orton, E. (2018). 'Poisoning substances taken by young people: a population-based cohort study', *British Journal of General Practice*, vol. 68, no. 675, pp. 703–10.

UPIAS (1975). 'Fundamental principles', Union of the Physically Impaired Against Segregation (UPIAS) [online].

UPIAS (1976). 'Aims and policy statement (amended)', Union of the Physically Impaired Against Segregation (UPIAS) [online].

UPIAS (2018). *Are We Oppressed? Collected contributions from early UPIAS circulars.* 2nd edn. Manchester: TBR Imprint for Union of Physically Impaired Against Segregation (UPIAS).

Vellani, F. (2015). 'David Cameron, the politics of doublethink and contemporary discourses of disability in the United Kingdom', *Disability and Society*, vol. 30, no. 6, pp. 941–4.

Welfare Conditionality Project (2018). *Final Findings Report: Welfare Conditionality Project 2013–2018*. York: Welfare Conditionality Project.

WHO and World Bank Group (2011). *World Report on Disability*. Geneva: World Health Organization (WHO) and World Bank Group.

Williams-Findlay, B. (2011). 'Lifting the lid on Disabled People Against Cuts' [online]. Penultimate draft of an article that appeared in *Disability and Society*, vol. 26, no. 6, pp. 773–8.

Williams-Findlay, B. (2019). 'The Disabled People's Movement in the age of austerity: rights, resistance and reclamation' in Hart, E. L., Greener, J. and Moth, R. (eds). *Resist the Punitive State: grassroots struggles across welfare, housing, education and prisons*. London: Pluto Press.

Withers, A. J. (2012). *Disability Politics and Theory*. Halifax and Winnipeg: Fernwood Publishing.

WPC (2018). *Universal Credit: support for disabled people*. HC 1770. London: House of Commons Work and Pensions Committee (WPC).

Yeo, R. (2005). *Disability, Poverty, and the New Development Agenda*. Disability Knowledge and Research Programme.

Index